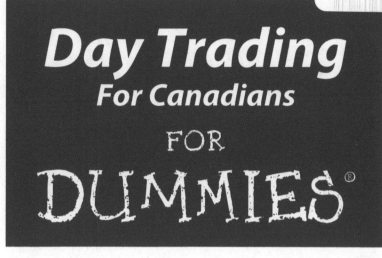

Day Trading
For Canadians
FOR DUMMIES®

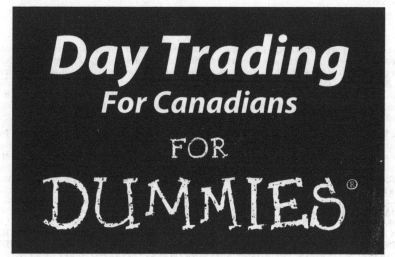

Day Trading For Canadians FOR DUMMIES®

by Ann C. Logue, MBA
and Bryan Borzykowski

John Wiley & Sons Canada, Ltd.

Day Trading For Canadians For Dummies®

Published by
John Wiley & Sons Canada, Ltd.
6045 Freemont Boulevard
Mississauga, Ontario, L5R 4J3
www.wiley.com

Published by John Wiley & Sons Canada. Ltd.

For general information on John Wiley & Sons Canada, Ltd., including all books published by Wiley Publishing, Inc., please call our warehouse, Tel 1-800-567-4797. For reseller information, including discounts and premium sales, please call our sales department, Tel 416-646-7992. For press review copies, author interviews, or other publicity information, please contact our marketing department, Tel 416-646-4584, Fax 416-236-4448.

For technical support, please visit www.wiley.com/techsupport.

Wiley also publishes its books in a variety of electronic formats. Some content that appears in print may not be available in electronic books.

Library and Archives Canada Cataloguing in Publication

Logue, Ann C.

Day trading for Canadians for dummies / Ann Logue, Bryan Borzykowski.

Includes index.

Issued also in electronic formats.

ISBN 978-0-470-94503-2

1. Day trading (Securities). 2. Electronic trading of

securities. 3. Day trading (Securities)–Canada.

4. Electronic trading of securities–Canada.

kowski, Bryan II. Title.

HG4515.95.L63 2011 332.63'228 C2010-906493-3

ISBN 978-0-470-94503-2 (print); 978-0-470-95198-9 (ePDF); 978-0-470-95199-6 (ePub); 978-0-470-95201-6 (eMobi)

7 6 5

About the Authors

Ann C. Logue, MBA, is the author of *Hedge Funds For Dummies* (Wiley, 2006). She has written for *Barron's, The New York Times, Newsweek Japan, Wealth Manager,* and the International Monetary Fund. She is a lecturer at the Liautaud Graduate School of Business at the University of Illinois at Chicago. Her current career follows 12 years of experience as an investment analyst. She has a B.A. from Northwestern University and an M.B.A. from the University of Chicago, and she holds the Chartered Financial Analyst (CFA) designation.

Bryan Borzykowski has been writing about personal finance and investing for a number of years, and has held editorial positions at several Canadian business magazines and Web sites. He writes regular features for *Canadian Business* magazine, *PROFIT, MoneySense,* the *Toronto Star, Moneyville.ca, Advisor.ca,* and has contributed to *Maclean's, Chatelaine, Yahoo! Finance,* and the *National Post,* among other publications. He has been nominated for several national magazine awards, including one for an article on day trading.

Dedication

Ann: Once again, to Rik and Andrew, for their love and support.

Bryan: To my wife, Lainie, and daughter Molly. I can't thank you enough for keeping this family moving forward. You two deserve as much, and probably more, credit for making this book — and everything else I write — happen.

Authors' Acknowledgments

Ann: So many wonderful people helped me with this book! I talked to many day traders, brokers, and others in the investment business, including Jack Alogna and Beth Cotner, Michael Browne of DTN Inc., Nihar Dalil, Greg Gocek and Robert Cohen of the CFA Society of Chicago, Mary Haffenberg and Curt Zuckert at the Chicago Mercantile Exchange, Anil Joshi of NuFact, Karen H. at Gamblers Anonymous, James Kupfer of Waterston Financial, James Lee of TradersLaboratory.com, Wayne Lee of NASDAQ, Khurram Naik and James Cagnina at Infinity Brokerage Services, Don Padou, Chris Tabaka, Elizabeth Tabaka, and Allen Ward. I also talked to several other traders who asked to remain anonymous; they know who they are, and I hope they also know how much I appreciate their help.

As for the mechanics of putting together the book, Corbin Collins and Stacy Kennedy of Wiley were great to work with through this tough schedule (*For Dummies* authors do not get to take time off!). Finally, my agent, Marilyn Allen, made it all happen.

Bryan: Day trading is a vast and complex topic. This book is a good starting point, but it takes years of reading and practice to really understand how it all works. Luckily, I was able to speak with people who have put in the time. First of all, I have to thank Ann, who wrote the original *Day Trading For Dummies*. She was spot on with her research and penned many of the concepts outlined in this book. But I couldn't have done my part without Bruce Seago, CMC Markets Canada's president and CEO and this book's technical editor. Thanks for taking my many calls and keeping all the facts straight. I also want to thank Jean-Francois Bernier, managing director and senior vice-president of Interactive Brokers Canada; day traders Wally Trenholm and Stephen Kelly; Jamie Golombek, managing director of tax and estate planning at CIBC; Benny Osher, CA with Toronto's Kopstick Osher; and several people from IIROC, the OSC, TMX Group, and other traders and publicists who helped answer seemingly random questions at all hours of the day and night. I also want to thank *Canadian Business* magazine's managing editor Duncan Hood, who worked with me on the original day trading story that ended up getting the *For Dummies* ball rolling.

A big thank you must go out to Robert Hickey, my editor at Wiley, who was always offering helpful advice and kept pushing me when I felt a little lost.

Thanks, and enjoy the book.

Publisher's Acknowledgments

We're proud of this book; please send us your comments at `http://dummies.custhelp.com`. For other comments, please contact our Customer Care Department within the U.S. at 877-762-2974, outside the U.S. at 317-572-3993 or fax 317-572-4002.

Some of the people who helped bring this book to market include the following:

Acquisitions and Editorial

Project Editor, U.S.: Corbin Collins

Acquisitions Editor, U.S.: Stacy Kennedy

Editor, Canada: Robert Hickey

Production Editor: Pauline Ricablanca

Editorial Assistant: Katie Wolsley

Copy Editor: Kelli Howey

Technical Editor: Bruce Seago

Cartoons: Rich Tennant (`www.the5thwave.com`)

Cover Photo: ©2011 iStockphoto LP

Composition Services

Project Coordinator: Kristie Rees

Layout and Graphics: Timothy C. Detrick, Samantha K. Cherolis

Proofreaders: Lindsay Amones, Leeann Harney

Indexer: Ty Koontz

John Wiley & Sons Canada, Ltd.

Deborah Barton, Vice President and Director of Operations

Karen Bryan, Vice-President, Publishing Services

Jennifer Smith, Publisher, Professional and Trade Division

Alison Maclean, Managing Editor

Publishing and Editorial for Consumer Dummies

Diane Graves Steele, Vice President and Publisher, Consumer Dummies

Kristin Ferguson-Wagstaffe, Product Development Director, Consumer Dummies

Ensley Eikenburg, Associate Publisher, Travel

Kelly Regan, Editorial Director, Travel

Composition Services

Debbie Stailey, Director of Composition Services

Contents at a Glance

Table of Contents

Introduction

So you want to make money from home, eh?

If you love the thrill of the markets and have the patience to sit and stare at a screen for hours waiting for the right moment to get in and get out of securities, then day trading might be a great career option. But it has risks, too. It requires the right psychological makeup. Good day traders are patient and decisive, confident but not arrogant. They most certainly are not gamblers, although day trading attracts gamblers who discover it's a great way to *lose* money from home. Any day can be your best day, but it can also put you out of business forever.

Day Trading For Canadians For Dummies is for people who are looking for a career change or who simply want to supplement investment return with new techniques. We give you what you need to know, from determining whether you are cut out for it, to laying out your home office, to researching and planning trades.

Maybe you'll decide day trading is not for you — if so, you'll be glad that you spent only the price of this book and not thousands on research and training. A lot of people make a lot of money selling services to neophyte day traders, claiming to be the best thing going. And maybe so — for some people. We give a wider perspective. If you decide to day trade, this book shouldn't be your only guide. Find a trading system that works for you.

About This Book

First, let us tell you what this book is not: It's not a textbook, and it's not a guide for professional investors. Several of those are on the market already, and they are fabulous — but often dry and assume underlying knowledge.

This book assumes you don't know much about day trading, but that you are a smart person who is thinking about doing it. It contains straightforward explanations of how day trading works, how to get started, what the pitfalls are, and what some of the alternatives are for your portfolio and for your career. If you really want to read some textbooks, we list a few in the Appendix.

Conventions Used in This Book

We'll start with the basics: we put important definitions in *italics*. We often **bold** the key words of lists to bring the important ideas to your attention. And we place all Web addresses in `monofont` to set them apart.

We cover investment research in this book, and make an effort to introduce you to some technical terms that will come up in the investment world. You don't need to know everything in this book to day trade; most successful day traders pick one system that works for them and stick to it. It's helpful to show the array of possibilities to help you make decisions about what might suit *you*. Sometimes we'll throw in references to deeper, academic investment theories. To alert you to these topics, we flag them with Technical Stuff icons (see the section "Icons Used in This Book").

During printing of this book, some of the Web addresses may have broken across two lines of text. If you come across such an address, rest assured that we haven't put in any extra characters (such as hyphens) to indicate the break. When using a broken Web address, type in exactly what you see on the page, pretending that the line break doesn't exist.

We include sidebars in the book that you don't really need to read in order to follow the chapter text. With that stated, though, we do encourage you to go back and read through this extra material when you have the time. Many of the sidebars contain practice examples that help you get an even better idea of how some of the investment concepts work.

Foolish Assumptions

The format of this book requires us to make some assumptions about you, the reader. We assume that you're someone who needs to know a lot about day trading in a short period of time. You may be considering a career change or looking for a productive hobby in retirement, and you want to know how to decide whether day trading is right for you. And if you determine that day trading *is* right for you, you want to know how to get started, right down to the setup for your computer monitors.

We assume that you're someone who has extra money to trade (whether it's yours or not) and who wants to try day trading techniques to goose up your portfolio returns.

We also assume that you have some understanding of the basics of investing — that you know what mutual funds and brokerage accounts are, for example. If you don't feel comfortable with that much, you may want to read *Investing For Canadians For Dummies* or *Mutual Fund Investing For Canadians For Dummies* and then come back here.

No matter your situation or motives, our goal is to give you enough information so that you can ask smart questions, do careful research, and handle your money so that you can meet *your* goals. And if you don't have enough money right now to make a living from day trading, we want you to discover plenty of information from this book so that you will have it at the ready someday. Some research and trading techniques used by day traders can help you make better buy and sell decisions for the securities that you hold now. You can find more strategies than you may expect.

How This Book Is Organized

Day Trading For Canadians For Dummies is sorted into four parts so that you can find what you need to know quickly.

Part I: Day Trading Fundamentals

The first part describes what day trading is, how it works, and what basic asset classes are used by day traders. It distinguishes among investing, trading, and gambling; knowing which is which can help you avoid costly mistakes. And it covers regulatory issues that will affect you as a day trader.

Part II: Day Trading Tools

Here, you'll find a guide to the practicalities: how to set up your office to improve your response times; choose the support services you need to research trades; get through the treacherous days with your sanity intact and your positions under control; pay taxes on your gains; and figure out how well you performed. This is the nitty-gritty, day-in-the-life stuff that separates day trading from video games. (Because, yes, in some ways they're similar.)

Part III: Day Trading Strategies

This part is all about the different strategies and research techniques that day traders use to determine where and when to buy and sell their positions. This includes selling short to profit from securities that are declining in price and using leverage to make bigger trades in hopes of bigger returns.

The information here can help you make better portfolio decisions, even if you decide not to become a day trader. And it's just a start. The markets teach traders new things every day, and the smart ones pay attention.

Part IV: The Part of Tens

In this . . . *For Dummies*–only part, you get to enjoy some top-ten lists. We present ten reasons to day trade, ten reasons to avoid day trading, ten common mistakes that day traders make, and ten alternative careers for people who love the excitement of trading but who don't want to work for themselves as day traders.

We also include an Appendix full of references so that you can get more information if you desire.

Icons Used in This Book

You'll see four icons scattered around the margins of the text. Each icon points out a certain type of information, most of which you should know or may find interesting about day trading. They go as follows:

This icon notes something you should keep in mind about day trading. It may refer to something we cover earlier in the book, or it may highlight something you need to remember for future investing decisions.

Tip information tells you how to invest a little better, a little smarter, a little more efficiently. The information can help you make better day trades or ask better questions of people who want to supply you with research, training, and trading systems.

We've included nothing in this book that can cause death or bodily harm, as far as we can figure out, but plenty of things in the world of day trading can cause you to lose big money or, worse, your sanity. These points help you avoid big problems.

We put the boring (but sometimes helpful) academic stuff here. We even throw in a few equations here and there. By reading this material, you get the detailed information behind the investment theories or, sometimes, some interesting trivia or background information.

Where to Go from Here

Well, open up the book and get going! Allow us to give you some ideas. You may want to start with Chapter 1 if you know nothing about day trading so you can get a good sense of what we're talking about. If you need to get set up to start trading, look at Chapters 6 and 7. If you want to know about some of the potential problems in day trading, turn to Chapters 5, 8, 10, and 19.

If you are thinking about day trading as a career, Chapter 2 describes what day traders do all day, and Chapter 20 can give you some good alternatives. For ideas about developing strategies, whether you're going to hold for a few minutes or several years, go to Part III. If you have a particular area of interest, use the index and table of contents to go to the topic you want. If you're not sure, you may as well turn the page and start at the beginning.

Part I

Day Trading Fundamentals

"She had a great first week day trading. We're hoping for another so she can buy the matching desk."

In this part . . .

Day trading seems like an exciting way to make money, but is it right for you? And how is it different from investing — or gambling? Well, you've come to the right place. This part describes what day trading is, how it works, and what basic asset classes are used by day traders. It also covers some of the basic regulatory issues that will affect you as a day trader.

Chapter 1

Wake Up to Day Trading

In This Chapter

- Figuring out just what day traders do anyway
- Setting up a trading business
- Concentrating on a few assets, a few dollars at a time
- Knowing what it takes to be a successful trader
- Dispelling some of the myths of trading

Make money from the comfort of your home! Be your own boss! Beat the market with your own smarts! Build real wealth! Tempting, isn't it? Day trading can be a great way to make money all on your own. It's also a great way to lose a ton of money, all on your own. Are you cut out to take the risk?

Day trading is a crazy business. Traders work in front of their computer screens, reacting to blips, each of which represent real dollars. They make quick decisions, because their ability to make money depends on successfully executing a large number of trades that generate small profits. Because they close out their positions in the stocks, options, and futures contracts they own at the end of the day, some of the risks are limited. Each day is a new day, and nothing can happen overnight to disturb an existing profit position.

But those limits on risk can limit profits. After all, a lot can happen in a year, increasing the likelihood that your trade idea will work out. But in a day? You have to be patient and work fast. Some days nothing seems good to buy. Other days it feels like every trade loses money. Do you have the fortitude to face the market every morning?

In this chapter, we give you an overview of day trading. We cover what exactly day traders do all day, go through the advantages and disadvantages of day trading, cover some of the personality traits of successful day traders, and give you some information on your likelihood of success.

You may find that day trading is a great career option that takes advantage of your street smarts and clear thinking — or that the risk outweighs the potential benefits. That's okay: The more you know before you make the decision to trade, the greater the chance of being successful. If it turns out that day trading isn't right for you, you can apply strategies and techniques that day traders use to improve the performance of your investment portfolio.

It's All in a Day's Work

The definition of day trading is that day traders hold their securities for only one day. They close out their positions at the end of every day and then start all over again the next day. By contrast, *swing traders* hold securities for days and sometimes even months, whereas *investors* sometimes hold for years.

The short-term nature of day trading reduces some risks, because no chance exists of something happening overnight to cause big losses. Meanwhile, many investors have gone to bed thinking their position is in great shape, then woken up to find that the company has announced terrible earnings or that its CEO is being indicted on fraud charges.

But there's a flip side (there's always a flip side, isn't there?): The day trader's choice of securities and positions has to work out in a day, or it's gone. There's no tomorrow for any specific position. Meanwhile, the swing trader or the investor has the luxury of time, as it sometimes takes a while for a position to work out the way your research shows it should. In the long run, markets are efficient, and prices reflect all information about a security. Unfortunately, it can take a few days of short runs for this efficiency to kick in.

Day traders are speculators working in zero-sum markets one day at a time. That makes the dynamics different from other types of financial activities you may have been involved in.

When you take up day trading, the rules that may have helped you pick good stocks or find great mutual funds over the years will no longer apply. This is a different game with different rules.

Speculating, not hedging

Professional traders fall into two categories: speculators and hedgers. Speculators look to make a profit from price changes. Hedgers are looking to protect against a price change. They're making their buy and sell choices as insurance, not as a way to make a profit, so they choose positions that offset their exposure in another market. For example, a food-processing company might look to hedge against the risks of the prices of key ingredients — like corn, cooking oil, or meat — going up by buying futures contracts on those ingredients. That way, if prices do go up, the company's profits on the contracts help fund the higher prices that it has to pay to make its products. If the prices stay the same or go down, it loses only the price of the contract, which may be a fair tradeoff to the company.

The farmer raising corn, soybeans, or cattle, on the other hand, would benefit if prices went up and would suffer if they went down. To protect against a price decline, the farmer would sell futures on those commodities. Then, his futures position would make money if the price went down, offsetting the decline on his products. And if the prices went up, he'd lose money on the contracts, but that would be offset by his gain on his harvest.

The commodity markets were intended to help agricultural producers manage risk and find buyers for their products. The stock and bond markets were intended to create an incentive for investors to finance companies. Speculation emerged in all of these markets almost immediately, but it was not their primary purpose.

Markets have both hedgers and speculators in them. Day traders are all speculators. They look to make money from the market as they see it now. They manage their risks by carefully allocating their money, using stop and limit orders (which close out positions as soon as predetermined price levels are reached) and closing out at the end of the night. Day traders don't manage risk with offsetting positions the way a hedger does. They use other techniques to limit losses, like careful money management and stop and limit orders (all of which you can read about in Chapter 2).

Knowing that different participants have different profit and loss expectations can help a day trader navigate the turmoil of each day's trading. And that's important, because in a zero-sum market you only make money if someone else loses.

Understanding zero-sum markets

A zero-sum game has exactly as many winners as losers. No net gain exists, which makes it really hard to eke out a profit. And here's the thing: Options and futures markets, which are popular with day traders, are zero-sum markets. If the person who holds an option makes a profit, then the person who *wrote* (which is option-speak for *sold*) that option loses the same amount. No net gain or net loss exists in the market as a whole.

Now, some of those buying and selling in zero-sum markets are hedgers who are content to take small losses in order to prevent big ones. Speculators may have the profit advantage in certain market conditions. But they can't count on having that advantage all the time.

So who wins and loses in a zero-sum market? Some days, it all depends on luck, but over the long run, the winners are the people who are the most disciplined. They have a trading plan, set limits and stick to them, and can trade based on the data on the screen — not based on emotions like hope, fear, and greed.

Unlike the options and futures markets, the stock market is not a zero-sum game. As long as the economy grows, company profits will grow, and that will lead to growing share prices. There really are more winners than losers over the long run. That doesn't mean there will be more winners than losers today, however. In the short run, the stock market should be treated like a zero-sum market.

If you understand how profits are divided in the markets that you choose to trade, you'll have a better understanding of the risks that you face as well as the risks that are being taken by the other participants. People do make money in zero-sum markets, but you don't want those winners to be making a profit off of you.

Some traders make money — lots of money — doing what they like. Trading is all about risk and reward. Those traders who are rewarded risked the 80 percent washout rate. Knowing that, do you want to take the plunge? If so, read on. And if not, read on anyway, as you might get some ideas that can help you manage your other investments.

Keeping the discipline: Closing out each night

Day traders start each day fresh and finish each day with a clean slate. That reduces some of the risk, and it forces discipline. You can't keep your losers longer than a day, and you have to take your profits at the end of the day before those winning positions turn into losers.

And that discipline is important. When you're day trading, you face a market that doesn't know or care who you are, what you're doing, or what your personal or financial goals are. No kindly boss who might cut you a little slack today, no friendly coworker to help through a jam, no great client dropping you a little hint about her spending plans for the next fiscal year. Unless you have rules in place to guide your trading decisions, you will fall prey to hope, fear, doubt, and greed — the Four Horsemen of trading ruin.

So how do you start? First, you develop a business plan and a trading plan that reflect your goals and your personality. Then, you set your working days and hours and you accept that you will close out every night. Both of these steps are covered in Chapter 2. As you think about the securities that you will trade (Chapter 3) and how you might trade them (Chapters 12 and 13), you'll also want to test your trading system (Chapter 11) to see how it might work in actual trading.

In other words, you do some preparation and have a plan. That's a basic strategy for any endeavour, whether it's running a marathon, building a new garage, or taking up day trading.

Committing to Trading as a Business

For many people, the attraction of day trading is that traders can very much control their own hours. Many markets, like foreign exchange, trade around the clock. And with easy Internet access, day trading seems like a way to make money while the baby is napping, on your lunch hour, or working just a few mornings a week in between golf games and woodworking.

That myth of day trading as an easy activity that can be done on the side makes a lot of traders very rich, because they make money when traders who are not fully committed lose their money.

Day trading is a business, and the best traders approach it as such. They have business plans for what they will trade, how they will in invest in their business, and how they will protect their trading profits. So, much of this book is about this business of trading: how to do a business plan (Chapter 2), how to set up your office (Chapter 6), tax considerations (Chapter 10), and performance evaluation (Chapter 11). If you catch a late-night infomercial about trading, the story will be about the ease and the excitement. But if you want that excitement to last, you have to make the commitment to doing trading as a business to which you dedicate your time and your energy.

Trading part-time: An okay idea if done right

Can you make money trading part-time? You can, and some people do. To do this, they approach trading as a part-time job, not as a little game to play when they have nothing else to going on. A part-time trader may commit to trading three days a week, or to closing out at noon instead of at the close of the market. A successful part-time trader still has a business plan, still sets limits, and still acts like any professional trader would, just for a smaller part of the day.

Part-time trading works best when the trader can set and maintain fixed business hours. Your brain knows when it needs to go to work and concentrate on the market, because the habit is ingrained.

The successful part-timer operates as a professional with fixed hours. Think of it this way: Bryan's wife's kindergarten teaching partner only works half days. She shows up when she's scheduled and, when she's there, she's doing as much work as any of the other educators. She commits her attention to her job when she's in the classroom; when she's not there she's teaching spin classes and is as focused on getting people into shape as she is getting children to learn. She doesn't pop into school to teach an extra lesson during a break from her spin class gig, nor does she sneak around setting up meetings with parents while she's helping people exercise. If she worked on one job while she was at the other, her work would suffer. And what parent wants their children to be taught by someone who won't dedicate themselves to the kids, even if it's just for a few hours a day?

If you want to be a part-time day trader, approach it the same way that a part-time teacher, part-time lawyer, or part-time accountant would approach work. Find hours that fit your schedule and commit to trading during them. Have a dedicated office space with high-speed Internet access and a computer that you use just for trading. If you have children at home, you may need to have child care during your trading hours. And if you have another job, set your trading hours away from your work time. Trading via cell phone during your morning commute is a really good way to lose a lot of money (not to mention your life if you try it while driving).

Trading as a hobby: A bad idea

Because of the excitement of day trading and the supposed ease of doing it, you may be thinking that it would make a great hobby. If it's a boring Saturday afternoon, you could just spend a few hours day trading in the forex market (foreign exchange), and that way you'd make more money than if you spent those few hours playing video games! Right?

Uh, no.

Trading without a plan and without committing the time and energy to do it right is a route to losses. Professional traders are betting that there will be plenty of suckers out there, because they create the situations that allow the pros to take profits in a zero-sum market.

The biggest mistake an amateur trader can make is to make a lot of money the first time trading. That first success was almost definitely due to luck, and that luck can turn against a trader on a dime. If you make money your first time out, take a step back and see if you can figure out why. Then test your strategy, using Chapter 11 as a guide, to see if it's a good one that you can use often.

Yes, we have two warnings in this section, and for good reason: Successful day traders commit to their business. Even then, most day traders fail in their first year. Brokerage firms, training services, and other traders have a vested interest in making trading seem like an easy activity that you can work into your life. But it's a job — a job that some people love, but a job nonetheless.

If you really love the excitement of the markets, there are ways to invest on a hobbyist's schedule. First, you can spend your time doing fundamental research to find long-term investments, which is described a little bit in Chapter 12. You can look into alternative investments to help diversify your portfolio; Chapter 3 can get you started on that. You can also trade with play money, either in demo accounts or in trading contests, to try out trading without committing real money. Chapter 20 has some ideas on that.

Working with a Small Number of Assets

Most day traders pick one or two markets and concentrate on those to the exclusion of all others. That way, they can learn how the markets trade, how news affects prices, and how the other participants react to new information. Also, concentrating on just one or two markets helps a trader maintain focus.

And what do day traders trade? Chapter 3 has information on all of the different markets and how they work, but here's a quick summary of the most popular assets with day traders right now:

- **Derivatives:** Futures, options, and CFDs (contracts for difference) allow traders to profit from price changes in such market indexes as the TSX/S&P Composite Index in Canada, or the Dow Jones Industrial Average in the U.S. They give traders exposure to the prices at a much lower cost than buying all of the stocks in the index individually. Of course, they tend to be more volatile than the indexes they track, because they are based on expectations.
- **Forex:** *Forex,* short for *foreign exchange,* involves trading in currencies all over the world to profit from changes in exchange rates. Forex is the largest and most liquid market, and it's open for trading all day, every day except Sunday. Traders like the huge number of opportunities. Because most price changes are small, they have to use *leverage* (borrowed money) to make a profit. The borrowings have to be repaid no matter what happens to the trade, which adds to the risk of forex. (Leverage isn't unique to forex — investors can borrow money to trade derivatives and stocks too.)

- **Common stock:** The entire business of day trading began in the stock market, and the stock market continues to be popular with day traders. They look for news on company performance and investor perception that affects stock prices, and they look to make money from those price changes. Day traders are a big factor in some industries, such as technology. The big drawback? Stock traders can get killed at tax time if they are not careful. (See Chapter 10 for more information.)

Managing your positions

A key to successful trading is knowing how much you're going to trade and when you're going to get out of your position. Sure, day traders are always going to close out at the end of the day — or they wouldn't be day traders — but they also need to cut their losses and take their profits as they occur during the day.

Traders rarely place all their money on one trade. That's a good way to lose it! Instead, they trade just some of it, keeping the rest to make other trades as new opportunities in the market present themselves. If any one trade fails, the trader still has money to place new trades. Some traders divide their money into fixed proportions, and others determine how much money to trade based on the expected risk and expected return of the security that they are trading. Careful money management helps a trader stay in the game longer, and the longer a trader stays in, the better the chance of making good money. Chapter 2 has more information on this.

To protect their funds, traders use *stop and limit orders*. These are placed with the brokerage firm and kick in whenever the security reaches a predetermined price level. If the security starts to fall in price more than the trader would like, *bam*! It's sold, and no more losses will occur on that trade. The trader doesn't agonize over the decision or second-guess herself. Instead, she just moves on to the next trade, putting her money to work on a trade that's likely to be better.

Day traders make a lot of trades, and a lot of those trades are going to be losers. The key is to have more winners than losers. By limiting the amount of losses, the trader makes it easier for the gains to be big enough to generate more than enough money to make up for them.

Focusing your attention

Day traders are often undone by stress and emotion. It's hard, looking at screens all day, working alone, to keep a steady eye on what's happening in the market. But traders have to do that. They have to concentrate on the market and stick to their trading system, staying as calm and rational as possible.

Those who do well have support systems in place. They are able to close their positions and spend the rest of the day on other activities. They do something to get rid of their excess energy and clear their minds, such as running or yoga or meditation. They understand that their ability to maintain a clear mind when the market is open is crucial.

Traders sometimes think of the market itself, or everyone else who is trading, as the enemy. The real enemies are emotions: doubt, fear, greed, and hope. Those four feelings keep traders from concentrating on the market and sticking to their systems.

One of the frustrations of trading is that some days, there will be more opportunities to trade than you have time or money to trade. Good trades are getting away from you. You simply don't have the resources to take advantage of every opportunity you see. That's why it's important to have a plan and to concentrate on what works for you.

Personality Traits of Successful Day Traders

Traders are a special breed. They can be blunt and crude, because they act fast against a market that has absolutely no consideration for them. For all their rough exterior, they maintain strict discipline about how they approach their trading day and what they do during market hours.

The discipline begins with a plan for how to start the day, including reviews of news events and trading patterns. It includes keeping track of trades made during the day, to help the trader figure out what works and why. And it depends on cutting losses as they occur, reaping all profits that appear, and refining a set of trading rules so that tomorrow will be even better. No, it's not as much fun as just jumping in and placing orders, but it's more likely to lead to success.

Not everyone can be a day trader, nor should everyone try it. In this section we cover some of the traits that make up the best of them.

Independence

For the most part, day traders work by themselves. Although some cities have offices for traders, known as *trading arcades,* the number of these places has been declining over the years because the cost of setting up at home has gone down dramatically. Computers and monitors are relatively inexpensive, high-speed Internet connectivity is easier to get, and many brokerage firms cater to the needs of traders who are working by themselves.

So that leaves the day trader at home, alone, stuck in a room with nothing but the computer screen for company. It can be boring, and it can make it hard to concentrate. Some people can't handle it.

But other traders thrive on being alone all day, because it brings out their best qualities. They know that their trading depends on them alone, not on anyone else. The trader has sole responsibility when something goes wrong, but he also gets to keep all the spoils. He can make his own decisions about what works and what doesn't, with no pesky boss or annoying corporate drone telling him what he needs to do today.

If the idea of being in charge of your own business and your own trading account is exciting, then day trading might be a good career option for you.

And what if you want to trade but don't want to be working by yourself? Consider going to work for a brokerage firm, a hedge fund, a mutual fund, or a commodities company. These businesses need traders to manage their own money, and they usually have large numbers of people working together on their trading desks to share ideas, cheer each other on, and give each other support when things go wrong.

No matter how independent you are, your trading will benefit if you have friends and family to offer you support and encouragement. That network will help you better manage the emotional aspects of trading. Besides, it's more fun to celebrate your success with someone else!

Quick-wittedness

Day trading is a game of minutes. An hour may as well be a decade when the markets are moving fast. And that means a day trader can't be deliberative or panicky. When it's time to buy or sell, it's time to buy or sell, and that's all there is to it.

Many investors prefer to spend hours doing a careful study of a security and markets before committing money. Some of these people are enormously successful. Warren Buffett, the CEO of Berkshire Hathaway, amassed $37 billion from his careful investing style, money that he is giving to charity. But Buffett and people like him are not traders.

Traders have to have enough trust in their system and enough experience in the markets that they can act quickly when they see a buy or sell opportunity. Many brokerage firms offer their clients demonstration accounts or backtesting services that allow traders to work with their system before committing actual dollars, helping them learn to recognize market patterns that signal potential profits.

A trader with a great system who isn't quick on the mouse button has another option: automating trades. Many brokerage firms offer software that will execute trades automatically whenever certain market conditions occur. For many traders, it's a perfect way to take the emotion out of a trading strategy. Others dislike automatic trading, because it takes some of the fun out of it. And let's face it, successful traders find the whole process to be a good time.

Decisiveness

Day traders have to move quickly, so they also have to be able to make decisions quickly. There's no waiting until tomorrow to see how the charts play out before committing capital. If the trader sees an opportunity, she has to go with it. Now.

But what if it's a bad decision? Well, of course some decisions are going to be bad. That's the risk of making any kind of an investment — and no risk, no return. Anyone playing around in the markets has to accept that.

But two good day trading practices help limit the effects of making a bad decision. The first is the use of stop and limit orders, which automatically close out losing positions. The second is closing out all positions at the end of every day, which lets traders start fresh the next day.

If you have some downside protection in place, then it's psychologically easier to go ahead and make the decisions you need to make in order to make a profit. And if you're one of those people who has a hard time making a decision, day trading probably isn't right for you.

What Day Trading Is Not

Much mythology exists about day trading: Day traders lose money. Day traders make money. Day traders are insane. Day traders are cold and rational. Day trading is easy. Day trading is a direct path to alcoholism and ruin.

We're going to bust a few day trading myths. Someone has to do it, right? We bring both good news and bad news in this section, so read it through to get some perspective on what, exactly, the day trader can expect from this new endeavour.

It's not investing . . .

Day traders never hold a position for more than a day. Swing traders hold positions for a few days, maybe even a few weeks, but rarely longer than that.

Investors hold their stakes for the long term, with some looking to hang on to their securities for decades and maybe even hand them down to their children.

Day trading is most definitely not investing. It's an important function to the capital markets because it forces the price changes that bring the supply and demand of the market into balance, but it doesn't create new sources of funding for companies and governments. It doesn't generate long-term growth.

Many day traders withdraw their trading capital on a regular basis to put into investments, helping them build a long-term portfolio for their retirement or for other ventures they might want to take on. A good chance exists the trader will have someone else manage this money, because investing and trading have different mindsets.

But it's not gambling . . .

One of the biggest knocks on day trading is that it's just another form of gambling. And as everyone knows, or should know: In gambling, the odds always favour the house.

In day trading, the odds are even in many markets. The options and futures markets, for example, are zero-sum markets with as many winners as losers, but those markets also include people looking to hedge risk and who thus have lower profit expectations than do day traders.

The stock market has the potential for more winning trades than losing trades, especially over the long run, so it's not a zero-sum market. The odds are ever-so-slightly in the trader's favour.

And in all markets, the prepared and disciplined trader can do better than the frantic, naïve trader. That's not the case when gambling, because no matter how prepared the gambler is, the casino has the upper hand.

People with gambling problems sometimes turn to day trading as a socially acceptable way to feed their addiction. If you know you have a gambling problem or suspect you are at risk, it's probably not a good idea to take up day trading. Day traders who are closet gamblers tend to make bad trades and have trouble setting limits and closing out at the end of the day. They turn the odds against them. Chapter 4 has some information on the line between day trading and gambling.

It's hardly guaranteed . . .

Given the participation of day traders in securities markets, researchers are always trying to figure out whether they make money. And the answers aren't good. Here we review some of the literature to show you the current state of day trading success rates. Note that they are low. Few people who take this up succeed, in part because few people who take this up are prepared. And even many of the prepared traders fail.

Much of the research covers performance in the late 1990s, when day trading became wildly popular. It grew along with the commercial Internet, and it fell out of favour when the Internet bubble burst.

Day trading is difficult, but it is not impossible. You can improve your chances of success by taking the time to prepare and by having enough money to fund your initial trading account. During the first year, you'll want to handle trading losses and still be able to pay your rent and buy your groceries. Knowing that the basics of your life are taken care of will give you more confidence, and that will help your performance.

"Do Day Traders Make Money? Evidence from Taiwan"

This paper, written in 2004 by Brad Barber, Yi-Tsung Lee, Yu-Jane Liu, and Terrance Odean (and available at `http://faculty.haas.berkeley.edu/odean/papers/Day%20Traders/Day%20Trade%20040330.pdf`) found that only 20 percent of day traders in Taiwan tracked between 1995 and 1999 made money in any six-month period, after considering transaction costs. Median profits, net of costs, were US$4,200 for any six-month period, although the best traders showed semi-annual profits of US$33,000. The study also found that those who placed the most trades made the most money, possibly because they are the most experienced traders in the group.

"Report of the Day Trading Project Group"

In 1999, the North American Securities Administrators Association, which represents state and provincial securities regulators in the United States, Canada, and Mexico, researched day trading so that its members could provide appropriate oversight. The report, which you can see at `www.nasaa.org/content/Files/NASAA_Day_Trading_Report.pdf`, did not include performance data. However, it cited several cases where brokerage firms were sanctioned by regulators for misrepresenting their clients' performance numbers, including one firm that had no clients with profits.

"Trading Profits of SOES Bandits"

Paul Schultz and Jeffrey Harris looked into the profits made by the so-called SOES bandits, day traders who took advantage of loopholes that existed in NASDAQ's Small Order Entry System in the 1990s. These people were the first day traders. Did they make money? The authors looked at a few weeks of trade data from two different firms. What they found was that about a third of all round-trip trades (buying and then later selling the same security) lost money before commissions. Only a quarter of the round-trip trades had a profit of $250 or more before commissions. The 69 traders in the study made anywhere from one to 312 round-trip trades per week. They had an average weekly profit after commission of $1,690; however, almost half of the traders, 34 of them, lost money in an average week.

You can see the abstract at `http://papers.ssrn.com/sol3/papers.cfm?abstract_id=137949`. The full article is available through many libraries.

But it's not exactly dangerous . . .

Yes, a lot of day traders lose money, and some lose everything that they start out with. Many others don't lose all of their trading capital; they just decide that there are better uses of their time and better ways to make money.

A responsible trader works with *risk capital,* which is money that she can afford to lose. She uses stop and limit orders to minimize her losses, and she always closes out at the end of the day. She understands the risks and rewards of trading, and that keeps her sane.

Many day trading strategies rely on *leverage,* which is the use of borrowed money to increase potential returns. That carries the risk of the trader losing more money than is in his account. However, the brokerage firm doesn't want that to happen, so it will probably close a leveraged account that's in danger of going under. That's good, because it limits your potential loss.

It's not easy . . .

Along with the relatively low rate of success, day trading is really stressful. It takes a lot of energy to concentrate on the markets, knowing that real money is at stake. The profit amounts on any one trade are likely to be small, which means the trader has to be persistent and keep placing trades until the end of the day.

Some traders can't handle the stress. Some get bored. Some get frustrated. And some can't believe that they can make a living doing something that they love.

But then, neither are a lot of other worthwhile activities

Day trading is tough, but many day traders can't imagine doing anything else. The simple fact is that a lot of occupations are difficult ways to make a living, and yet they are right for some people. Every career has its advantages and disadvantages, and day trading is no different.

When you finish this book, you should have a good sense of whether or not day trading is right for you. If you realize that it's the career you have been searching for, we hope it leaves you with good ideas for how to get set up and learn more so that you are successful.

And if you find that maybe day trading isn't right for you, we hope you get some ideas that can help you manage your long-term investments better. After all, the attention to price movements, timing, and risk that is critical to a day trader's success can help any investor improve their returns. What's not to like about that?

Putting day trading success rates in perspective

When Ann was researching this book, she talked to one very successful trader who told her two things. First, he was suspicious of all the books and training programs on day trading, because he didn't think that they really helped people learn to trade. Despite that, he liked that they existed, because trading had proven to be a great way for him to make a good living and support his family, and he thought it would be great if those people who are cut out for trading discovered the business.

Yes, most day traders fail — about 80 percent in the first year, as we note earlier. But so do a large percentage of people who start new businesses or enter other occupations. That's why we've combed through several different reports and databases to show how well people do in other fields. (Our sources are *Realty Times*; Barber, Lee, Liu, and Odean; American College of Sports Medicine; Canada Millennium Scholarship Foundation; Ohio State University; and the National Center for Education Statistics.)

Field	*First-Year Failure Rate (%)*
Real estate sales	86
Day trading	80
Training for a marathon	70
Restaurants	26
Teaching	13
Canadian college students	13
Canadian university students	8

If you understand the risks and keep them in perspective, you'll be better able to handle the slings and arrows of misfortune on the way to your goal.

When you finish this book, you should have a good sense of whether or not day trading is right for you. If you realize that it is the career you have been searching for, we hope it leaves you with good ideas for how to get set up and learn more so that you are successful.

And if you find that maybe day trading isn't right for you, we hope you get some ideas that can help you manage your long-term investments better. After all, the attention to price movements, timing, and risk that are critical to a day trader's success can help any investor improve their returns. What's not to like about that?

Putting day trading success rates in perspective

When Ann was researching this book, she talked to one very successful trader who told her two things. First, he was suspicious of all the books and training programs on day trading, because he didn't think that they really helped people learn to trade. Despite that, he liked that they existed, because trading had proven to be a great way for him to make a good living and support his family, and he thought it would be great if those people who are outside trading discovered the business.

Yes, most day traders fail — about 80 percent in the first year, as we note earlier. So do a large percentage of people who start new businesses or enter other occupations. That's why we've combed through several different reports and databases to show how well people do in other fields. (Our sources: the *Realty Times*, Barnett, Lee, Lilly and Odom, American College of Sports Medicine, Canada Millennium Scholarship Foundation, Ohio State University, and the National Center for Education Statistics.)

Field	*First-Year Failure Rate (%)*
Real estate sales	85
Day trading	80
Training for a marathon	70
Restaurants	26
Teaching	11
Canadian college students	13
Canadian university students	[illegible]

If you understand the risks and keep them in perspective, you'll be better able to handle the ups and downs of making a living on the way to your goal.

Chapter 2

Making a Day Trade of It

In This Chapter

- Organizing your business
- Planning trades to start your day
- Making short-term and long-term choices
- Raining clichés like cats and dogs
- Taking a peek into the life of a day trader

Day trading is sometimes presented as a profitable hobby. Anyone who buys a day trading DVD course via infomercial can make money easily in just a few hours a week, right? Well, no. Day trading is a job. It can be a full-time job or a part-time job, but it requires the same commitment to working regular hours and the same dedication to learning a craft and honing skills as any other job.

The best traders have plans for their business and for their trades. They know in advance how they want to trade and what they expect to do when they face the market. They may find themselves deviating from their plans at times, due to luck or circumstance or changing markets, but in those cases at least they understand why they are trying something else.

Failing to plan is planning to fail. And if you can't remember that right now, don't worry. We repeat it several times in this book.

Here's another reason for planning: Trading comes in many flavours, and many of those who call themselves day traders are actually doing other things with their money. If you know in advance what you want to do, you'll be less likely to panic or follow fads. You'll be in a better position to take advantage of opportunities in a way that suits your personality, trading skills, and goals. And that's why this entire chapter is devoted to planning.

Planning Your Trading Business

The day trader is an entrepreneur who has started a small business that trades in securities in hopes of making a return. You'll get your business off to a good start if you have a plan for what you want to do and how you're going to do it. That way, you know what your goals are and what you need to do to achieve them.

You can find a lot of sample business plans in books and on the Internet, but most of them are not appropriate for a trader. A typical business plan is designed not only to guide the business, but also to attract outside financing. Unless you're going to take in partners or borrow money from an outside source, your day trading business plan is for you only. No executive summary and no pages of projections needed.

So what do you need instead? How about a list of your goals and a plan for what you will trade, what your hours will be, what equipment you'll need, and how much to invest in the business?

Setting your goals

The first thing you need in your plan is a list of your goals, both short term and long term. Here is a sample list to get you started:

- Where do you want to be in the next three months, six months, nine months, a year, three years, five years, and ten years?
- How many days a year do you want to trade?
- What do you need to know to trade better?
- How much do you want to make?
- What will you do with your profits?
- How will you reward yourself when you hit your goals?

Be as specific as possible when you think about what you want to do with your trading business, and don't worry if your business goals overlap with your personal goals. When you're in business for yourself, the two often mix.

You might be tempted to say, "I want to make as much money as I possibly can," and forget the rest, but that's not a goal that's quantifiable. If you don't know that you've reached your goal, how can you go on to set new ones? And if you don't meet your goal, how will you know how to make changes?

Picking the markets

There are so many different securities and derivatives that you can day trade! Sure, you want to trade anything that makes money for you, but what on earth is that? Each market has its own nuances, so if you flit from futures to forex (foreign exchange), you might be courting disaster. That's another reason why you need a plan. If you know what markets you want to trade, you'll have a better sense of what research services you'll need, what ongoing training you might want to consider, and how to evaluate your performance.

Chapter 3 covers different asset classes and how day traders might use them in great detail. For now, Table 2-1 gives a little cheat sheet that covers those that are most popular with day traders. Think about your chosen markets in the same way: What do you want to trade, where will you trade it, what is the risk and return, and what are some of the characteristics that make this market attractive to you?

And what do zero sum, leverage, and upward bias mean? Well, *zero sum* means that for every winner, there is a loser. No net gain exists in the market. *Leverage* is the use of borrowed money, which increases potential return and also increases risk. *Upward bias* means that in the long run, the market is expected to increase in price, but that doesn't mean it will go up on any given day that you are trading.

Table 2-1 Popular Things for Day Traders to Trade

Item	*Main Exchange*	*Risk/Reward*	*Characteristics*
Stock index futures	MX, CME	Zero sum/leverage	Benefits from movements of broad markets
Treasury bond futures	CBT	Zero sum/leverage	Best way for day traders to play the bond market
Foreign exchange	OTC	Zero sum/leverage	Markets open all day, every day, except Sunday
Commodities	CBT, CME	Zero sum/leverage	An agricultural market liquid enough for day traders
Large-cap stocks	TSX, NYSE	Upward bias	Good stocks for day trading, large and volatile

Key: TSX = Toronto Stock Exchange, MX = Montreal Exchange, CME = Chicago Mercantile Exchange, CBT = Chicago Board of Trade, OTC = Over the counter, NYSE = New York Stock Exchange

The characteristics of the different markets and assets will affect both your business plan and your trading plan. The business plan should include information on what you will trade and why, as well as on what you hope to learn to trade in the future. The trading plan looks at what you want to trade each day and why, so that you can channel your efforts.

Many day traders work in a few different markets, depending on their temperament and trading conditions, but successful traders have narrowed down the few markets where they want to concentrate their efforts. Start slowly, working just one or two different securities, but consider adding new markets as your experience and trading capital grows.

Fixing hours, vacation, and sick leave

The markets are open more or less continuously. Although many exchanges have set trading hours, there are traders working after hours who are willing to sell if you want to buy. Some markets, such as foreign exchange, take only the briefest of breaks over the course of a week. This gives day traders incredible flexibility — no matter what hours and what days are best for you to trade, you can find something that works for you. If you are sharpest in the evenings, you might be better off trading Asian currencies, because those markets are active when you are. Of course, this can be a disadvantage, because no one is setting limits for you. Few markets are great places to trade every hour of every day.

If you want to, you can trade almost all the time. But you probably don't want to. To keep your sanity, maintain your perspective, and have a life outside of your trading, you should set regular hours and stick to them. In your business plan, determine when you're going to trade, how often you're going to take a vacation, how many sick days you'll give yourself, and how you'll know to take a day off. One of the joys of self-employment is that you can take time off when you need to, so give yourself that little perk in your business plan.

Trading is a stressful business. You need to take time off to clear your head, and you'll probably find that working while sick is a sure-fire route to losses. Build in some sick and vacation time — and read Chapter 8 for more information on how to manage the stress of the markets.

Getting yourself set up

Part of your business plan should cover where you work and what equipment you need. (Chapter 6 has some ideas on that subject.) What can you afford now, and what is on your wish list? Do you have enough computing equipment, the right Internet connection, and a working filing system? This is part of your plan for getting your business underway, so put some thought into your infrastructure.

And yes, this is important. You don't want to lose a day of trading because your computer has crashed, nor do you want to be stuck with an open position because your Internet service provider has a temporary outage. And you certainly don't want to lose your concentration because you're trying to work in the family room while other members of your household are playing video games.

Investing in your business

You won't have the time and money to do everything you want to do in your trading business, so part of your business plan should include a list of things that you want to add over time. A key part of that is continuous improvement: No matter how good a trader you are now, you can always be better. Furthermore, the markets are always changing. New products come to market, new trading regulations are passed, and new technologies appear. You will always need to absorb new things, and part of your business plan should consider that. Ask yourself

- What percentage of your time and trade gains will go into expanding your knowledge of trading?
- Do you want to do that by taking seminars or by allocating the time to simulation testing?
- What upgrades will you make to your trading equipment?
- How are you going to set yourself up to stay in trading for the long haul?

It takes money to make money — another cliché. It doesn't mean that you should spend money willy-nilly on any nifty gadget or fancy video seminar that comes your way. Instead, it means that an ongoing, thoughtful investment in your trading business will pay off in a greater likelihood of long-run success.

Evaluating and revising your plan

One component of your business plan should be a plan for revising it. Things are going to change. You may be more or less successful than you hope, market conditions may change on you, and you may simply find out more about how you trade best. That's why you should set a plan for updating your business plan to reflect where you are and where you want to be as you go along. At least once a year, and more often if you feel the need for a change, go through your business plan and revise it to reflect where you are now. What are your new goals? What are your new investment plans? What are you doing right, and what needs to change?

Business plans are living documents. Use your plan to run your trading business; as your business runs, use the results to update your plan. You can keep the old ones around to show you how much progress you have made, if you're so inclined.

A sample business plan

Not sure what should be in a business plan? Here's a sample to get you thinking about how to plan your trading business.

Where I Am Now

I am about to start a career as a day trader. I have $50,000 in capital that I can risk without affecting my livelihood. I will rely on my spouse's job to cover our family spending needs and our health insurance. This trading account will be used to meet our long-term goals: paying off the mortgage, sending the children to university, paying for our retirement, and ultimately buying a vacation house in the mountains.

This business plan covers what I need to get started.

My Business Goals

In three months, I will have spent $5,000 of my capital on a functional office and will have a tested trading strategy that works well in simulation.

In six months, I will be trading daily. I will have lost no more than $5,000 of my trading capital.

In nine months, I will be trading daily, and I will have more winning trades than losing trades.

In a year, I will have gained 10 percent on my account. I will withdraw $1,000 to pay toward our mortgage and another $1,000 toward an ergonomic chair and other office equipment upgrades. I will have mastered my first trading system and will be testing a second one in order to expand my trading opportunities.

In three years, my trading account will have $150,000 in it from my trading successes, after making investments in my business and paying an additional $10,000 in principal on the mortgage. I will be trading three different systems with satisfactory success.

In five years, I will have $300,000 in my trading account. I will have made enough money to have paid off our mortgage, after making regular payments on principal and interest every month, paying $10,000 in year three, and paying off the rest with the profits that I expect to earn between years three and five. I will be known as a successful trader.

In ten years, I will have a second house, and I will continue my record of trading success. I will take $100,000 out of my trading account to cover university tuition.

Markets Traded

My primary trading strategy will involve momentum trades on the S&P/TSX Composite Index Mini Futures, E-Mini NASDAQ, and E-Mini Russell 2000 futures contracts traded on the Chicago Mercantile Exchange. I will put no more than 10 percent of my capital into any one trade and I will close out positions each night.

I am interested in news-driven *swing trading* (holding for short periods of time but longer than a day) in large technology companies, so I will research and test strategies with those. I am also interested in trading Asian currencies, so I will make the time to learn more about those markets and determine whether I can trade them effectively during my preferred trading hours.

Trading Hours and Days

Because my primary strategy is equity driven, I will trade only while the equity markets are open, from 9:30 a.m. until 4:00 p.m. Monday through Friday. I will spend an hour before the markets open researching current trends and news events so that I know what people will be looking for that day. I will spend an hour after the market closes doing paperwork and reviewing the day's trades.

I will take off three full weeks for vacation: the week of my children's spring break, a week in August for a family vacation, and the last week of December. I will also take off any day that I am ill so that I can maintain my health and my concentration.

My Business Setup

I work from a home office. I use my startup funds to purchase two monitors working off of one computer, with a second clone computer on hand in case something goes wrong. I have cable Internet access as well as a DSL backup through my phone line. I have a wireless router, so that I can check my email and instant messages through a third computer, a laptop, instead of through my trading computer. I also have a smartphone so I can read the news, check e-mail, and stay on top of relevant current events when I'm not at a computer during the day.

I have an account with a full-service online brokerage firm that can offer me the necessary research services. I also subscribe to *The Globe and Mail,* the *National Post* and *The Wall Street Journal,* which I read each morning to help me gauge sentiment.

I track my trades on a paper form that I collect in ring binders. I collect my other paperwork in ring binders that I keep on the shelf in my office.

Investing in My Business

To stay successful in the long run, I need to keep my skills sharp. To do this, I will read one book on trading psychology or a successful trader's memoir each month. I will also work on simulation trading for swing trading in technology stocks, as I plan to add that to my trading system.

As my trade profits grow, I will invest some of them in trying new trading techniques, knowing that I may have short-term losses until I understand a market better. I will spend one day at the end of each quarter on backtesting and simulation of new strategies.

My wish list includes a more comfortable chair for my office.

Evaluating my Business Plan

Before each vacation, I will read over this business plan. I will use the time away from the markets to think about what changes I need to make and will revise the plan upon my return.

Planning Your Trades

A good trader has a plan. She knows what she wants to trade and how to trade it. She knows what her limits are before she places the order. She's not afraid to take a loss now in order to prevent a bigger loss in the future, and she's willing to sit out the market if nothing is happening that day. Her plan gives her the discipline to protect her capital so that she has money in her account to profit when the opportunities present themselves.

In this section, we cover the components of trade planning. When you start trading, you'll probably write notes to set up a trading plan for each day that covers what you expect for the day, what trades you hope to make, and what your profit goals and loss limit are. As you develop experience, trade planning may become innate. You develop the discipline to trade according to plan, without needing to write it all down — although you might find it useful to tape a list of the day's expected announcements to your monitor.

Like a business plan, a trading plan is flexible. The markets don't know what you've planned, and you'll probably end up deviating on more than one occasion. The key thing is knowing *why* you deviated: Was it because of the information that you saw when you were looking at your screen, or was it because you became panicky?

What do you want to trade?

The first step in your trading plan should also be addressed in your business plan: What is it that you want to trade? Many traders work in more than one market, and each market is a little different. Some trade different products simultaneously, whereas others choose one for the day and work only on that.

You need to figure out which markets give you the best chance of getting a profit that day. It's going to be different. Some days, no trades will be good for you in one market. If you're too antsy for that, then find another market to keep you busy so that you don't trade just to stay awake. (Of course, many traders report that the big money opportunities are in the slower, less glamorous markets.)

As a day trader, you are self-employed. You don't answer to a boss and don't have to trade today if you don't want to. So if you have a headache, or if no good trades are available to you, or if recent losses have gotten you down, take the day off and do something fun.

How do you want to trade it?

Figuring out how to trade an asset involves a lot of considerations: What is your mood today? What will other traders be reacting to today? How much risk do you want to take? How much money do you want to commit? This is the nitty-gritty stage of trade planning that can help you manage your market day better.

Starting the day with a morning review

Before you start trading, take some time to determine where your head is relative to the market. Is today a day that you can concentrate? Are there things happening in your life that might distract you, are you coming down with the flu, or were you out too late last night? Or are you raring to go, ready to take on whatever the day brings? Your mindset should influence how aggressively you want to trade and how much risk you want to take. You have to pay attention to do well in the markets, but you also have to know when to hang back during the day's activities. For example, many traders find that their strategies work best at certain times of the day, such as at the open or before major news announcements.

Think about what people will be reacting to. Go through the newspapers and check the online newswires to gather information. Then figure out the answers to these questions:

- Are there big news announcements scheduled for today? At what time? Do you want to trade ahead of the news or want to wait and see what the market does?
- Did something happen overnight? Will that affect trading on the open, or is it already in the markets? Do you want to trade on the open or wait?
- What are the other people who trade the same future, commodity, stock, or currency that you do worried about today? How are they likely to respond? Do you want to go with the market or strike a contrary position?

For a handy list of expected news announcements on any given trading day, check out www.tradethenews.com/weekly-calendar.php. For Canadian company news, visit CNW Group at www.newswire.ca and review the day's press releases.

Drawing up a sample order

After you have a sense of how you're going to tackle the day, you want to determine how much you're going to trade. The key considerations are the following:

- Do you want to be long or short? That is, do you want to bet that the asset you're trading is going up in price or down?
- Do you want to borrow money? If so, how much? Borrowing — also known as *margin* or *leverage* — increases your potential return as well as your risk. (Margin, leverage, and short selling are discussed in Chapter 14.)

  Some contracts, such as futures, have built-in leverage. As soon as you decide to trade them, you are borrowing money.

- How much money do you want to trade — in dollars, and as a percentage of your total account size? (Money management is discussed in detail in Chapter 9.)

After you have those items detailed, you're in good shape to get started for the day.

Figuring out when to buy and when to sell

After you get insight into what the day might be like and how much money you want to allocate to the markets, your next step is to figure out when you will buy and when you will sell. Ah, but if that were easy, do you think we'd be writing a book on day trading? No. If knowing when to buy and sell were easy, Ann would be too busy taking private surfing lessons in front of her beachfront mansion on Maui to be writing a book; Bryan would be kicking back with a guitar at his cottage in Winnipeg Beach. (Yes, there are beaches near Winnipeg.)

The very best traders aren't selling trading advice; they're already retired. Everyone else is figuring it out as they go along, with varying degrees of success.

Many traders rely on *technical analysis,* which involves looking at patterns in charts of the price and volume changes. We discuss technical analysis in Chapter 12. Other traders look at news and price information as the market changes, rather than looking at price patterns, and that's discussed in Chapter 13. Still others care only about very short-term price discrepancies, covered in Chapter 14. But the most important thing, no matter what approach you prefer, is that you *backtest* and simulate your trading before you commit real dollars. That way, you have a better sense of how you'll react in real market conditions. We cover that key step in Chapter 11.

Setting profit goals

When you trade, you want to have a realistic idea how much money you can make. What's a fair profit? Do you want to ride a winning position until the end of the day or do you want to get out quickly when you've made enough money to compensate for your risk? No one answer to this question exists, because so much depends on market conditions and your trading style. In this section we give some guidelines that can help you determine what's best for you.

But first, we take a detour and define all the different terms for profits that you might come across.

The language of money

Profits are discussed differently in different markets, and you may as well have the right lingo when you write your plan:

- **Pennies:** Stocks trade in decimal form, so each price movement is worth at least a penny — one cent. It's an obvious way to measure a profit.
- **Pips:** A *pip* is the smallest unit of currency that can be traded. In foreign exchange markets (forex), a pip is generally equal to one one-hundredth of a cent. If the value of the euro moves from $1.2934 to $1.2935, it has moved a pip.

Do not confuse a pip in the forex market with an investment scheme known as *PIP,* sometimes called People in Profit or Pure Investor. (The fraud also operates as *HYIP,* for High Yield Investment Program.) PIP has been promoted as a trading system with a guaranteed daily return, but it's really a pyramid scheme that takes money from participants and returns little or nothing. You can get more information from the U.S.

Securities and Exchange Commission's Web site, www.sec.gov/divisions/enforce/primebank.shtml.

- **Points:** A *point* is a single percentage. A penny is a point, as is a 1 percent change in a bond price. A related number, a *basis point,* is a percent of a percent, or .0001.
- **Teenies:** Many securities, especially bonds and derivatives on them, trade in increments of ⅛ of a dollar. Half of an eighth is a sixteenth, also known as a *teeny*.
- **Ticks:** A *tick* is the smallest trading increment in a futures contract. It varies from product to product. How much it works out to be depends on the contract structure. For the S&P/TSX Composite Index Mini Futures (SCF), one tick value equals five index points, and each index point represents $5. That means the tick value is equal to $25. The value of an SCF futures contract is calculated by multiplying the current level of the contract by the tick value. On the Chicago Mercantile Exchange's E-Mini S&P 500 contract a tick is equal to US$12.50, calculated as a 0.25 change in the underlying S&P 500 index multiplied by a US$50 multiplier. A tick on a Chicago Board of Trade E-Mini soybean contract is US$1.25, calculated as ⅛ cent on a bushel of soybeans in a contract covering 1,000 bushels. You can get information on the tick size of contracts that interest you on the Web site of the offering exchange (they're listed in Chapter 3).

No one ever lost money taking a profit, as the cliché goes. (The trading business is rife with clichés, if you haven't noticed.) The newer you are to day trading, the more sense it makes to be conservative. Close your positions and end your day when you reach a target profit — and then make note of what happens afterward. Can you afford to hold on to your positions longer in order to make a greater profit?

Thinking about profits

Your profit goals can be sliced and diced a few different ways. The first is the *gain per trade,* on both a percentage basis and an absolute basis. The second is the *gain per day,* also on both a percentage basis and an absolute basis. What do you have to do to reach these goals? How many successful trades will you have to make? Do you have the capital to do that? And what is right for the trade you're making right now, regardless of what your longer-term goals are?

Setting limits on your trades

It's a good idea to set a *loss limit* along with a profit goal.

For example, many futures traders have a rule to risk two ticks in pursuit of three ticks. That means they'll sell a position as soon as it loses two ticks in value, and they'll also sell a position as soon as it gains three ticks in value.

And for anything in between? Well, they close out their positions at the end of the day, so whatever happens happens.

Even traders who do not have a rule like that often set a limit on how much they will lose per trade. Other traders use computer programs to guide their buys and their sells, so they need to sell their positions automatically. Brokers make this easy by giving customers the choice of a stop order or a limit order to protect their positions.

You want to limit your loss per trade *as well as* your loss per day. If today is not a good one, close up shop, take a break, and come back fresh tomorrow.

Stop orders

A *stop order,* also known as a *stop loss order,* is an order to sell a security at the market price as soon as it hits a predetermined level. If you want to make sure you sell a block of stock when it falls below $30 per share, for example, you could enter a stop order at $30 (telling your broker "Sell Stop 30"). As soon as the stock hits $30 the broker sells it, even if the price goes to $29 or $31 before all the stock is sold.

Limit orders

A *limit order* is an order to buy or sell a security at a specific price or better: lower than the current price for the buy order, higher than the specific price for a sell order. If you want to make sure you sell a block of stock when it reaches $30 per share, for example, you could enter a limit order at $30 (telling your broker "Sell Limit 30"). As soon as the stock hits $30, the broker sells it, as long as the price stays at $30 or higher. If the price goes even a penny below $30, the limit is no longer enforced. After all, no buyers are going to want to pay an above-market price just so you can get your order filled all the way!

Stop limit orders

A *stop limit* order is a combination of a stop order and a limit order. It tells the broker to buy or sell at a specific price or better, but only after the price reaches a given stop price. If you want to make sure you sell a block of stock when it falls below $30 per share, but you do not want to sell it if it starts to go back up, for example, you could enter a stop order at $29 — the price is usually set lower than your stop price — with a limit of $31 (telling your broker "Sell 29 Limit 31"). As soon as the stock hits $29, the broker sells it as long as the price stays under $31. If the price goes above $31, the order is no longer enforced. The price range where this order will be executed is very small. Stop limit orders aren't typically used as a trading strategy, but it can come in handy if there's a sudden drop in the market like we saw with the "flash crash" on May 6, 2010. On that day the market fell, for reasons not fully understood, by 600 points and then minutes later shot back up. A stop limit order would have prevented your stocks from selling.

Are you confused? Well, the differences may be confusing, but understanding them is important to helping you manage your risks. That's why Table 2-2 is a handy breakout of the different types of orders.

Table 2-2 Different Types of Orders

Buy Orders			
	Stop Order	**Limit Order**	**Stop Limit Order**
Order instructions	Buy Stop 30	Buy Limit 30	Buy Stop 30 Limit 31
Market Price ($)	**Action after the stock hits $30**		
28.50	Buy	Buy	Buy
29.00	Buy	Buy	Buy
29.50	Buy	Buy	Buy
30.00	Buy	Buy	Buy
30.50	Buy	Nothing	Buy
31.00	Buy	Nothing	Nothing
31.50	Buy	Nothing	Nothing

Sell Orders			
	Stop Order	**Limit Order**	**Stop Limit Order**
Order Instructions	Sell Stop 30	Sell Limit 30	Sell Stop 30 Limit 29
Market Price ($)	**Action after the stock hits $30**		
28.50	Sell	Nothing	Nothing
29.00	Sell	Nothing	Sell
29.50	Sell	Nothing	Sell
30.00	Sell	Sell	Sell
30.50	Sell	Sell	Sell
31.00	Sell	Sell	Sell
31.50	Sell	Sell	Sell

A sample trading plan

A trading plan may be good for only a short time, but having an idea of what to expect in the market and how you will react goes a long way toward keeping trading discipline, which improves your likelihood of long-run profits. What does such a plan look like? Well, here's a sample to get you started.

What I'm Trading Today

Today, I'll be trading the S&P/TSX Composite Index Mini Futures. They closed down yesterday, but I'm expecting an uptick in the market today as companies report good earnings, so I'm going to trade on the long side. My plan is to start the day buying two contracts with stop orders to sell if they decline more than three ticks each. These contracts will remain open until the end of the day unless the stop is reached. I will add a third contract if the market shows momentum in the morning and a fourth contract if it shows momentum in the afternoon. These two additional contracts can be long or short, depending on the market direction, although it's unlikely that the purchasing manager or home sales surveys will have a large effect on the market's direction. (Naturally, I will not take out a short contract during the day if my two initial long contracts are still open.) I will close all positions at the end of the day, if not sooner.

Because the margin on each contract is $3,500, my maximum exposure today will be approximately 28 percent of my total account, with no contract accounting for more than 7 percent of my account.

Today's Expected News Announcements

Before the open: earnings announcements from RIM (expect $0.62), PG (expect $0.74)

10:00 a.m. Ivey Purchasing Managers Index — survey of purchasing managers — market expects 51.0

10:00 a.m. Pending Home Sales — market expects up 0.2 percent

After the close: earnings announcements from AC.B (expect $0.20), AGU (expect $1.29)

5:00 p.m. Auto Sales — market expects up 10%

5:00 p.m. Merchandise exports — market expects down 2 percent

My Profit and Loss Goals for the Day

My profit goal is five ticks or $125 per contract traded, for a target of $500 if I acquire my planned maximum of four contracts, but I plan to ride my profits until the end of the day. If all four contracts decline in value, I will close when they fall three ticks apiece, for a maximum loss of $75 per contract or $300 for the day.

What if the trade goes wrong?

No matter how in tune you feel with the market, no matter how good your track record, and no matter how disciplined you are with setting stops, stuff is going to happen. Just as you can make more money than you plan to, you can also *lose* a lot more. If you're going to day trade, you have to accept that you'll have some really bad days.

So what do you do? You suck it up, take the loss, and get on with your life.

Yes, the market may have blown past your stops. That happens sometimes, and it's hard to watch real dollars disappear into someone else's account, someone you will never know. Still, close your position and just remember that tomorrow is another day with another chance to do better.

Don't hold in hopes of making up a loss. The market doesn't know what you own, and it won't reward your loyalty and best hopes.

After you take the loss and clear your head, see if you can learn something for next time. Sometimes a loss can teach you valuable lessons that make you a smarter, more disciplined trader in the long run.

Closing Out Your Position

By definition, day traders hold their investment positions only for a single day. This is important for a few reasons:

- Closing out daily reduces your risk of something happening overnight.
- Margin rates — the interest rates paid on money borrowed for trading — are low and in some cases zero for day traders, but the rates go up on overnight balances.
- It's good trade discipline that can keep you from making expensive mistakes.

But like all rules, the single-day rule can be broken and probably should be broken sometimes. In this section, we cover a few longer-term trading strategies you may want to add to your trading business on occasion.

Swing trading: Holding for days

Swing trading involves holding a position for several days. Some swing traders hold overnight, whereas others hold for days or even months. The longer time period gives more time for a position to work out, which is especially important if it is based on news events or if it requires taking a position contrary to the current market sentiment. Although swing trading gives traders more options for making a profit, it carries some risks because the position could turn against you while you're away from the markets.

A tradeoff always exists between risk and return. When you take more risk, you do so in the hopes of getting a greater return. But when you look for a way to increase return, remember that you will have to take on more risk to do it.

Swing trading requires paying attention to some basic fundamentals and news flow. (We discuss fundamental research in Chapter 12.) It's also a good choice for people who have the discipline to go to bed at night instead of waiting up and watching their position in hopes that nothing goes wrong.

Position trading: Holding for weeks

A *position trader* holds a stake in a stock or a commodity for several weeks and possibly even for months. This person is attracted to the short-term price opportunities, but he also believes that he can make more money holding the stake for a long enough period of time to see business fundamentals play out. This increases the risk and the potential return, because a lot more can happen over months than minutes.

Investing: Holding for months or years

An *investor* is not a trader. Investors do careful research and buy a stake in an asset in the hopes of building a profit over the long term. It's not unusual for investors to hold assets for decades, although good ones sell quickly if they realize that they have made a mistake. (They want to cut their losses early, just as any good trader should.)

Investors are concerned about the prospects of the underlying business. Will it make money? Will it pay off its debts? Will it hold its value? They view short-term price fluctuations as noise rather than as profit opportunities.

Many traders pull out some of their profits to invest for the long term (or to give to someone else, such as a mutual fund manager or hedge fund, to invest). It's a way of building financial security in the pursuit of longer goals. This money is usually kept separate from the trading account.

Maxims and Clichés That Guide and Mislead Traders

In this section, we cover a few of the many maxims traders use to think about their trading, such as

- The stock doesn't know you own it.
- Failing to plan is planning to fail.
- Your first loss is your best loss.

A lot more are out there.

Clichés are useful shorthand for important rules that can help you plan your trading. But they can also mislead you because some are really obvious — too obvious to act on effectively. (Yes, everyone knows that you make money by buying low and selling high, but how do you tell what low is and high is?) Here's a run-through of some you'll come across in your trading career, along with our take on what they mean.

Pigs get fat, hogs get slaughtered

Trading is pure capitalism, and people do it for one primary reason: to make money. Sure, a ton of economic benefits come from having well-functioning capital markets, such as better price prediction, risk management, and capital formation. But a day trader just wants to make money.

However, get too greedy and you're likely to get stupid. You start taking too much risk, deviating too much from your strategy, and getting careless about dealing with your losses. Good traders know when it's time to take a profit and move on to the next trade.

This is also a good example of an obvious but tough-to-follow maxim. When are you crossing from being a happy little piggy to a big fat greedy hog that's about to be turned into a pork belly? Just know that if you're deviating from your trading plan because things are going so great, you might be headed for some trouble.

In a bear market, the money returns to its rightful owners

A *bull* market is one that charges ahead; a *bear* market is one that does poorly. Many people think they're trading geniuses because they make money when the entire market is going up. It was easy to make money day trading just about any stock in 2009, when the market recovered from near economic collapse, but it wasn't so easy the year before when the frighteningly out-of-control financial crisis began. It's when the markets turn negative that those people who really understand trading and who know how to manage risk will be able to stay in until things get better, possibly even making nice profits along the way.

The corollary cliché for this is, "Don't confuse brains with a bull market." When things are going well, watch out for overconfidence. It might be time to update your business and trading plans, but it's not to time to cast them aside.

The trend is your friend

When you day trade, you need to make money fast. You don't have the luxury of waiting for your unique, contrary theory to play out. An investor may be buying a stock in the hopes of holding it for decades, but a trader needs things to work now.

Given the short-term nature of the market, the short-term sentiment is going to trump long-term fundamentals. People trading today may be wrong about the direction of foreign exchange, interest rates, or share prices, but if you're closing out your positions tonight, you need to work with the information in the market *today*.

In the short run, traders who fight the market lose money.

Two problems exist with *The trend is your friend*. The first is that by the time you identify a trend, it may be over. Second, there are times when it makes sense to go against the herd, because you can collect when everyone else realizes their mistakes. This is where the psychology of trading comes into play. Are you a good enough judge of human behaviour to know when the trend is right and when it's not?

Buy the rumour, sell the news

Markets react to information. That's ultimately what drives supply and demand. Although the market tends to react quickly to information, it can overreact, too. Lots of gossip gets traded in the markets as everyone looks to get the information they need in order to gain an advantage in the markets. And despite such things as confidentiality agreements and insider-trading laws, many rumours turn out to be true.

These rumours are often attached to such news events as corporate earnings. For whatever reason — good news, analyst research, a popular product — traders might believe that the company will report good quarterly earnings per share. That's the rumour. If you buy on the rumour, you can take advantage of the price appreciation as the story gets more play.

When the earnings are actually announced, one of two things will happen:

- They will be as good as or better than rumoured, and the price will go up. The trader can sell into that and make a profit.
- They will be worse than rumoured, everyone will sell on the bad news, and the trader will want to sell to get out of the loss.

Of course, if the rumour is *bad,* you want to do the opposite: sell on the rumour, and buy on the news. For more information on *short selling* — selling securities in hopes that they fall in price — turn to Chapter 14.

The problem with *Buy the rumour, sell the news* is that rumours are often wrong, and there may be more opportunities to buy on bad news when other traders are panicking, thus driving prices down for a few minutes before sanity sets in. But it's one of those rules that everyone talks about, whether or not they actually follow it.

Cut your losses and ride your winners

We mention in this chapter that you need to cut your losses before they drag you down. No matter how much it hurts and no matter how much you believe you're right, you need to close out a losing position and move on.

But the opposite is not necessarily true. Although good traders tend to be disciplined about selling winning positions, they don't use stops and limits as rigorously on the upside as they might on the downside. They're likely to stick with a profit and see how high it goes before closing out a position.

Note that this conflicts a little with *Pigs get fat, hogs get slaughtered.* (Trading maxims can be so contradictory!) To prevent overconfidence and sloppiness from greed, ride your winners *within reason*. If your general discipline is to risk three ticks on a futures contract in order to make five, and a contract goes up six ticks before you can close it out, you might want to stick with it.

But if you also close out at the end of every day, don't give in to the temptation of keeping that position open just because it's still going up. Keep to your overall discipline.

You're only as good as your last trade

The markets churn on every day with little regard for why everyone trading right now is there. Prices go up and down to match the supply and the demand at any given moment, which may have nothing to do with the actual long-term worth of an item being traded. And it certainly has nothing to do with how much you really, really want the trade to work out.

One of the biggest enemies of good traders is overconfidence. Especially after a nice run of winning trades, a trader can get caught up in the euphoria and believe that he finally has the secret to successful trading under control. While he's checking the real estate listings for that beachfront estate in Maui, BAM! The next trade is a disaster.

Does that mean that the trader is a disaster, too? No, it just means that the markets won this time around.

Most day traders are working in zero-sum markets, which means that for every winner there is a loser. Hence, not everyone can make money every day. The challenge is to maintain an even keel so as not to be distracted by confidence when the trading is going well or by fear when the trading is going poorly. The next trade is a new trade.

A Day in the Life of a Trader

What's it like being a day trader? Wally Trenholm, a day trader in Toronto who's currently developing day trading software and who once sold a business to RIM, answered a few questions about what he does and why he does it. "I wake up before 4 a.m. to watch Europe's open and see what happens in Asia. If things are exciting enough I'll stay awake and concentrate on the markets until 11 a.m. That may sound like a ridiculous schedule, but it works out well for me," he says.

Q: What do you trade, and how long have you been trading?

My trading focuses on futures contracts and options on futures contracts. I have been trading on and off for more than ten years, but I started trading full-time about two years ago. I began with stocks, then moved to options, then to forex before finally coming up with a formula that works best for me. The futures contracts I trade are on high-liquidity assets such as the S&P 500 Index, U.S. Treasuries, the euro, the yen, the Australian dollar, gold, and sometimes oil and natural gas.

I trade the Canadian dollar to compensate for cycles of weakness in my home currency, but I try to avoid trading it for short-term gains as it's hard to view it in a truly objective fashion. However, the Canadian dollar is a great indicator on risk sentiment and even if I don't trade it, I always watch it. If a Canadian dollar trade is brewing then I'm more likely to execute the same trade on the Australian dollar or crude oil instead, since those assets usually move with the Canadian dollar. I don't know why it seems to work better than a plain old Canadian dollar trade, but for me it does.

Q: How did you get started trading?

Until recently, I was an entrepreneur in the technology sector. In 1997, I started a small software company; when I went to my accountant to file my first corporate return, I learned that there was this thing called an RRSP that would give me more money on my personal tax return. Then I found out that some banks would lend you money to put in an RRSP so you could save on your taxes even if you didn't have money to put in the account yourself. I was young and thought I knew what I was doing and it sounded like a great deal, so I signed up. This particular RRSP was "self-directed," which gave me a chance to learn how to lose money in the stock market all on my own.

My bank offered me a non-RRSP account that would allow me to trade options and I thought, wow I can play the upside of a stock that costs $100 and only have to put up $5 to do it? Pretty quickly the money I made from my consulting company ended up in someone else's hands.

I decided to take the markets more seriously and enrolled in the Canadian securities course, a great introductory program that gave me a solid foundation of financial knowledge. It only cost about $1,000.

I took a break from trading to focus on my company, but always planned to get back to it. In 2006 my company was purchased by Research In Motion and all of the sudden I was no longer in debt and had some free cash on hand. Although I was required to work at RIM full-time for the next two years, I opened an Interactive Brokers account and started ramping up my trading as well. I learned how to set up and use the more complicated options strategies available through the IB system. Things started going well, but then, in 2008, the financial crisis hit and it wasn't the best time to cut your teeth on complicated options strategies. I didn't "trade myself into the ground" as they say, but I learned some tough lessons. The biggest lesson was a refresher on what I had learned a decade earlier: If you are going to trade, take it seriously.

After my contract at RIM was up, I finally decided to become a real, full-time independent trader. I read a lot of different books, watched videos, read online articles, tried different strategies, and set up the rule that for every week I lost money, my punishment would be to read another textbook or research another trading topic. That helped with learning technical aspects of trading.

I then decided to use every advantage to compete against other traders. That meant utilizing my true area of expertise: software design and development. I'm in the process of building trading software, partly to help me, but also, if I don't succeed as a trader I can sell my services to other traders or companies.

These days I do most of my trading by hand, but will be increasing my use of automated trading systems as the software I'm working on evolves. For those who don't have programming experience, there are many tools to out there to develop automated trading systems. I just want to build one that works the way I want it to.

Q: Do you close out trades every day, or do you carry some over?

I don't close out trades every day. Since I mostly trade on the U.S. futures markets there is essentially only one market close a week. The markets open Sunday night and close end of business day on Friday and I do not go more than a few hours without checking on them during the entire week. Many of my trades involve options contracts, which usually expire once a month. I do close parts of trades leading into that monthly expiry, but it's unusual for me to exit a position just because the New York markets are closing.

Q: What piece of equipment or software could you not do without?

I don't have any trading software that I am 100 percent happy with. The Interactive Brokers platform has some powerful stuff in it, but the charting isn't all that great. I use one of Thinkorswim.com's charting platforms primarily, but I have issues with that one too. I recently got a Bloomberg terminal and it is amazing, but extremely expensive. As a software developer I am pretty fussy about software and how I think something should work, which is part of the reason why I want to build my own trading application. I do have eight television screens that are constantly showing news or trading information that are pretty important.

Q: What trading strategy do you swear by?

The Elliott Wave Principle for sure. It's a technical analysis method developed by Ralph Nelson Elliott in the 1930s. It's a remarkably elegant mathematical concept that provides a framework to analyze price action on multiple timeframes in a fractal approach, building on concepts taken from Dow Theory.

Another tool that is a close second for me is what traders call "intermarket analysis," which is the study of the relationships between the four main asset classes: stocks, bonds, currencies, and commodities. By viewing the market through these two lenses, I have all I need to trade regardless of what software or brokerage I am using.

Q: What is a typical day like? How easy is it to quit at the end of the day?

My week starts at 6 p.m. on Sunday. I log in to the markets, check Bloomberg.com, Dailyfx.com, and other sites to find out what happened over the weekend. I skim through Sunday talk shows like NBC's *Meet the Press* and ABC's *This Week* and watch *Fareed Zakaria GPS* on my PVR. I also examine the charts and then wait for Asia to open. It's usually pretty slow until Europe opens in the middle of the night, but this is when I get my head around the big events for the week and what price actions on the main four asset classes are saying about where things will go.

At some point I'll go to sleep and wake up, without an alarm clock, before 4 a.m. to watch Europe's open and see what happened in Asia. If things are exciting enough I'll stay awake and concentrate on the markets until around 11 a.m. when most of the U.S. economic data has been released for the day and the market has had its opening direction set. I have around three hours from 11 a.m. to 2 p.m. where I concentrate on other things that need to be addressed during local business hours — like grocery shopping — but I like to be back focusing on the markets by 3 p.m. at the latest. Once the trading day ends in New York at 4 p.m., or sometimes by 6 p.m. if the after-market has anything to offer like an earnings release, my day is over. I replace my Sunday PVR shows with CNBC's *Fast Money,* then repeat that same 24 hours four more times until the week is over.

That may sound like a ridiculous schedule but it works out well for me. I may sleep four hours a night for five nights in a row (some nights even less), but if I am tired and my positions are set than I can sleep as much as I need. If I have something that demands my attention for, say, a week at a time I don't need to ask for vacation, I just do it. And there is a lot of down time as a trader. Sometimes the markets can be very quiet for days on end. Even on busy days there are usually quiet times, often something like 90 minutes of working on the markets and 90 minutes working on something else while watching the markets with my one eye. That something else is usually working on my charting and automated trading system. This keeps me productive in software development, but also keeps me from overtrading. If it was just me and a trading terminal locked in a room for hours on end, my itchy fingers would probably get me into trouble.

I admit that it's not easy to quit at the end of the day. If the markets are open I'm probably trading, or at the very least watching them. When I first got into forex trading I found myself waiting for the weekends to come to an end so I could get back into the markets. A friend of mine told me that when he leaves work at the end of a Friday he says to the other traders on the floor, "Only three more days till Monday!"

Q: What is your secret to managing the stress of trading?

Managing stress is an important part of trading. My goal is to set up a trade as best I can and then stick to the plan. If it works, great, if it fails and I did everything according to plan I try to learn what I can from the situation and improve the next trade plan. If it fails because I went off plan or made another mistake I take a timeout from the market based on how big the loss was and force myself to study a trading-related topic as my punishment. I try to make sure I'm making the best of both successes and failures by turning my monetary losses into clear gains of both knowledge and experience.

Elliott Wave also really helps with stress by defining stop-loss and profit-taking exit points as well as giving you a solid framework to continually evaluate your trading hypothesis. I learned Elliott Wave as a punishment for a really bad week of trading about a year ago and it has literally changed my life as a trader.

Q: What's your best piece of advice for someone considering day trading?

Your mission is to find the trading methodology that will work for you in a sustainable way before you run out of money to trade with. You need to be able to make good decisions, commit to those decisions all while still being flexible and challenging your beliefs when it appears they may be in error. You need to be relentless in learning new concepts and information, disciplined in your execution and risk management, and humble and respectful of the market's ability to alter your financial situation in either direction very quickly. The easiest way to succeed at something is to enjoy doing it, that way the effort it takes to excel doesn't feel like work. I never get tired working towards a goal if I enjoy the journey, and trading will be a lifelong journey for me.

Chapter 3

Signing Up for Asset Classes

In This Chapter

- Finding good assets for day trading
- Seeking securities to trade
- Counting cash and currency
- Making money from mundane commodities
- Deriving profits from derivatives

It's one thing to day trade, but *what* are you going to trade? Stocks, pork bellies, or hockey cards? You have myriad choices, but you have to choose so that you can learn the market, know what changes to expect, and make your trades accordingly.

Although it may be tempting, you can't trade everything. There are only so many hours in a day and only so many ideas you can hold in your head at any one time. Furthermore, some trading strategies (see Chapter 7) lend themselves better to certain types of assets than others. By learning more about all the various investment assets available to a day trader, you can make better decisions about what you want to trade and how you want to trade it.

What Makes a Good Day Trading Asset?

In academic terms, the universe of investable assets includes just about anything you can buy at one price and sell at another, potentially higher price. That means artwork and collectibles, real estate, and private companies would all be considered to be investable assets.

Day traders have a much smaller group of assets to work with. It's not realistic to expect a quick one-day profit on price changes in real estate. Online auctions for collectible items take place over days, not minutes. If you're going to day trade, you want to find assets that trade easily, several times a day, in recognized markets. In other words, you want *liquidity*. As an individual trading your own account, you want assets that can be purchased with relatively low capital commitments. And finally, you may want to use *leverage* — borrowed money — to improve your return (discussed in more detail in Chapter 14), so you want to look for assets that can be purchased using other people's money.

Liquidity

Liquidity is the ability to buy or sell an asset in large quantity without affecting the price levels. Day traders look for *liquid assets* so they can move in and out of the market quickly without disrupting price levels. Otherwise, they may not be able to buy at a good price or sell when they want.

At the most basic level, financial markets are driven by supply and demand. The more of an asset supplied in the market, the lower the price; the more of an asset that people demand, the higher the price. In a perfect market, the amount of supply and demand is matched so that prices don't change. This happens if a high volume of people are trading, so that their supply and demand is constantly matched, or if a very low frequency of trades are happening, so that the price never changes.

You may be thinking, Wait, don't I want big price changes so that I can make money quickly? Yes, you want price changes in the market, but you don't want to be the one causing them. The less liquid a market is, the more likely your buying and selling is going to affect market prices, and the smaller your profit will be.

Volume

Volume is the total amount of a security that trades in a given time period. The greater the volume, the more buyers and sellers are interested in the security, and the easier it is to get in there and buy and sell without affecting the price.

Day traders also look at the relationship between volume and price. This is an important technical indicator, discussed in more detail in Chapter 12. The simple version is this:

- High volume with no change in price levels means an equal match between buyers and sellers.
- High volume with rising prices means more buyers than sellers, so the price will continue going up.
- High volume with falling prices means more sellers than buyers, so the price will keep going down.

Frequency

Another measure of liquidity is *frequency,* or how often a security trades. Some assets, like stock market futures, trade constantly, from the moment the market opens until the very last trade of the day, and then continue into overnight trading. Others, like agricultural commodities, trade only during market hours or only during certain times of the year. Other securities, like stocks, trade frequently, but the volume rises and falls at regular intervals related to such things as *options expiration* (the date at which options on the stock expire).

The more frequently a security trades, the more opportunities you'll have to identify the short-term profit opportunities that make day trading possible.

Volatility, standard deviation, and variance

The *volatility* of a security is how much the price varies over a period of time. It tells you how much prices fluctuate and thus how likely you are to be able to take advantage of that. For example, if a security has an average price of $5 but trades anywhere between $1 and $14, it will be more volatile than one with an average price of $5 that trades between $4 and $6.

One standard measure of volatility and risk is *standard deviation,* which is how much any given price quote varies from a security's average price. The math is shown below (we're sure you're dying to see it), but you can calculate it with most spreadsheet programs and many trading platforms. *N* is the number of price quotes, x_1 is any one price quote, and the funky "X" with the line over it is the average of all the prices over time.

$$\sigma = \sqrt{\frac{1}{N}\sum_{i=1}^{N}\left(x_i - \bar{x}\right)^2}$$

For each of the prices, you calculate the difference between it and the average value. So if the average price is $5, and the closing price today is $8, the difference would be $3. (More likely, the research service that you use would calculate the difference for you; read more about research services in Chapter 7.)

After you have all the differences between the prices and the average, you find the square of these differences. If the difference for one day's price is $8, then the square would be $64. You add up all the squared differences over the period of time that you're looking at and then find the average of them.

That number is called the *variance,* or σ^2. Finally, calculate the square root of the variance, and you have the standard deviation.

The higher the standard deviation, the higher the volatility; the higher the volatility, the more a security's price is going to fluctuate, and the more profit — and loss — opportunities exist for a day trader.

Standard deviation is also a measure of risk that can be used to evaluate your trading performance; we discuss that use of the measure in Chapter 11.

Capital requirements

You don't necessarily need a lot of money to begin day trading, but you do need a lot of money to buy certain securities. Stocks generally trade in *round lots,* which are orders of at least 100 shares. If you want to buy a stock worth $40 per share, you need $4,000 in your account. Your broker will probably let you borrow half of that money, but you still need to come up with the other $2,000.

Options and futures trade by contract, and one contract represents some unit of the underlying security. For example, in the options market, one contract is good for 100 shares of the stock. These contracts also trade in round lots of 100 contracts per order.

No one will stop you from buying a smaller amount than the usual round lot in any given security, but you'll probably pay a high commission and get worse execution for your order. Because the returns on each trade tend to be small anyway, don't take up day trading until you have enough money to trade your target asset effectively. Otherwise, you'll pay too much to your broker without getting much for yourself.

Bonds do not trade in fractional amounts; they trade on a per-bond basis, and each bond has a face value of $1,000. Some trade for more or less than that, depending on how the bond's interest rate differs from the market rate of interest, but the $1,000 is a good number to keep in mind when thinking about capital requirements. Many dealers have a minimum order of 10 bonds, though, so a minimum order would be $10,000.

Marginability

Most day traders make money through a large volume of small profits. One way to increase the profit per trade is to use borrowed money in order to buy more shares, more contracts, or more bonds. *Margin* is money in your account that you borrow against, and almost all brokers will be happy to arrange a margin loan for you, especially if you're going to use the money to make more trades and generate more commissions for the brokerage firm. In Chapter 14, we discuss how margin is used within an investment strategy. Here, though, you want to think about how margin affects your choice of assets for day trading.

Generally, a stock or bond account must hold 50 percent of the purchase price of securities when you borrow the money. So if you want to buy $100 worth of something on margin, you need to have $50 in your account. The price of those securities can go down, but if they go down so much that the account now holds only 30 percent of the value of the loan, you'll get a margin call.

In Canada, margin requirements for each security are set by the Canadian regulators, though brokerage firms sometimes set their own, higher amounts. There are no rules that limit the maximum amount of money you can borrow, but the brokerage firms will lose a lot of money if you don't pay them back. That's why they may set a limit on the loan. Each firm has its own rules, so check with your broker on how they set their margin requirements.

You probably think that the 1929 crash was responsible for the Great Depression of the 1930s, right? Think again. Most economic historians believe that the crash was a distraction. Instead, the real problem was that interest rates fell so rapidly that banks refused to lend money, while prices fell so low that companies had no incentive to produce. It's a situation known as *deflation,* and it's relatively rare, but it is devastating when it occurs.

Most stocks and bonds are marginable (able to be purchased on margin), and the IIROC allows traders to borrow up to 70 percent — you have to put at least 30 percent down — of their value. But not all securities are marginable. Stocks priced below $5 per share, those traded on the OTC Bulletin Board or Pink Sheets (discussed later in this chapter), and those in newly public companies often cannot be borrowed against or purchased on margin. Your brokerage firm should have a list of securities that are not eligible for margin.

If leverage is going to be part of your day trading strategy, be sure the assets you plan to trade are marginable.

Securities and How They Trade

In the financial markets people buy and sell securities every day, but just what are they buying or selling? *Securities* are financial instruments. In the olden days, they were pieces of paper, but now they are electronic entries that represent a legal claim on some type of underlying asset. This asset may be a business, if the security is a stock, or it may be a loan to a government or a corporation, if the security is a bond. In this section, we cover different types of securities that day traders are likely to run across and tell you what you need to jump into the fray.

Day trading in Canada vs. the rest of the world

Nary a day goes by that you don't hear something about the Toronto Stock Exchange. It's up, it's down, Research In Motion's quarterly report sent investors scrambling out of the tech sector — if you watched just the Canadian news you'd think the TSX was the only market on the planet.

In reality, most day traders stay away from Canadian markets. There are really only three places to trade in this country — the TSX, the TSX Venture Exchange, and the Montreal Exchange. That doesn't leave a lot of choice. The markets are also much smaller compared to their U.S. counterparts. Two industries — commodities and financials — make up most of the index, so again choice is limited. Because the markets are small they're less liquid than the NYSE or NASDAQ, making it difficult for traders to make any money.

Fortunately, Canadians have access to a whole swath of markets and products that are based in other countries. A trader can buy an Australian dollar, a stock on the NYSE, or an option on the Chicago Board Options Exchange. And most people do choose to forgo Canadian stocks for American ones, even when trading a Canadian company. Because the U.S. market is more liquid, a trader may want to buy and sell RIM on the NYSE instead of the TSX. In this chapter, we list Canadian and American options; pick what you think is the best place to trade for your style and expertise.

In practice, *asset* and *security* are synonyms, and *derivative* is considered to be a type of asset or security. But to be precise, these three are not the same:

- An asset is a physical item. Examples include a company, a house, gold bullion, or a loan.
- A security is a contract that gives someone the right of ownership of the asset, such as a share of stock, a bond, a promissory note.
- A derivative is a contract that draws its value from the price of a security.

Stocks

A *stock,* also called an *equity,* is a security that represents a fractional interest in the ownership of a company. Buy one share of Microsoft, and you're an owner of the company, just as Bill Gates is. He may own a much larger share of the total business, but you both have a stake in it. Shareholders elect a board of directors to represent their interests in how the company is managed. Each share is a vote, so good luck getting Bill Gates kicked off Microsoft's board.

A share of stock has *limited liability*. That means you can lose all your investment, but no more than that. If the company files for bankruptcy, the creditors cannot come after the shareholders for the money they are owed.

Some companies pay their shareholders a dividend, which is a small cash payment made out of firm profits. Because day traders hold stock for really short periods of time, they don't normally collect dividends.

How stocks trade

Stocks are priced based on a single share, and most brokerage firms charge commissions on a per-share basis. Despite this per-share pricing, stocks are almost always traded in round lots of 100 shares. The supply and demand for a given stock is driven by the company's expected performance.

A stock's price is quoted with a *bid* and an *ask*.

- The bid is the price that other buyers will buy the stock from you if you're selling.
- The ask is the price that other sellers will sell you if you're the one buying.

Bid ask prices on Canadian exchanges are a centralized quote — they represent the best bid and ask prices from all participants on the market. In the U.S. it's the broker who sets the bid ask price — and often profits off the spread — but in Canada quotes are posted for everyone to see regardless of broker.

Here's an example of a price quote:

```
MSFT $27.70 $27.71
```

That's a quote for Microsoft (ticker symbol: MSFT on the NASDAQ). The bid is listed first: $27.70; the ask is $27.71. That's the smallest spread you'll ever see! The spread here is so small because Microsoft is a liquid stock, and no big news events at the moment might change the balance of buyers and sellers.

If your American trading buddy is talking about how his broker takes a cut of the spread, don't panic and wonder why you haven't noticed those same fees. In Canada brokers make money off commission — it's unlikely they're taking a percentage of the spread.

We tend to use the words *broker* and *dealer* interchangeably, but a difference does exist. A broker simply matches buyers and sellers of securities, whereas a dealer buys and sells securities out of its own account. Almost all brokerage firms are both brokers and dealers.

Where stocks trade

Stocks trade mostly on organized *exchanges* such as the Toronto Stock Exchange and the New York Stock Exchange, but more and more they trade on electronic communications networks, also called alternative trading systems, some of which are operated by the exchanges themselves. Brokerage firms either belong to the exchanges themselves or work with a correspondent firm that handles the trading for them, turning over the order in exchange for a cut of the commission.

When you place an order with your brokerage firm, the broker's trading staff executes that order wherever it can get the best deal. But is that the best deal for you? You'll be happy to know, that yes it is. Canadian dealers have an obligation to get the best execution for their client — it's written right in the rules set out by the regulators.

The financial markets are in a state of flux, with a lot of mergers and acquisitions among the exchanges. The information here might be obsolete when you read it, which really is fascinating. It wasn't so long ago that these exchanges were staid organizations run like private clubs.

Toronto Stock Exchange (TSX)

The TSX is *the* Canadian exchange. If a Canadian company wants the public's cash, it's going to list on the TSX — and almost all major corporations in the Great White North do. However, not all companies can trade on the exchange — you definitely won't see the corner store take out an IPO, and even larger businesses can't automatically list. More than 1,400 companies are listed on the exchange, with a total market cap — the total dollar market value of a company's outstanding shares — of more than $1.8 trillion.

All the companies listed on the exchange paid a fee to be there. Depending on the size of the company, businesses have to pay between $10,000 and $200,000 to list. In most cases companies are assigned a three-letter ticker symbol — Research In Motion uses RIM, for example — but not always. Gold company Kinross's symbol is, appropriately, K, and Toronto Dominion Bank can be found under TD. Some companies, like Toronto-based media company Torstar, have a .B after their symbol (TS.B), which means investors can purchase only non-voting class B shares.

Companies have to meet a number of requirements to list, and the requirements vary depending on the industry. You can find out all about the wonderful world of listing at `www.tmx.com`, but here are the basics: Company execs have to show they're successful, or, if it's a new venture, that the management has a record of experience. Companies must also have a certain amount of assets, though it varies per sector — tech businesses, for example, require a minimum of $10 million in their treasury.

Bringing the TSX into the 21st century

The TSX is 149 years old. In 1861, 24 men got together at Toronto's Masonic Hall and started the exchange. Membership cost $5, there were only 18 listed securities, and trading was limited to one 30-minute session a day. In 1997, TSX closed its trading floor and went virtual — becoming, at that time, the largest floorless exchange in North America.

In 1999, Canada's trading landscape underwent a major change. At the time there were stock exchanges in most big Canadian cities, but that year it was decided the TSX would become the sole place to trade senior equities. The Montreal Exchange stuck to derivatives, and the rest of the exchanges formed the Canadian Venture Exchange (CDNX). Two years later the TSX Group (the company that owns and operates the TSX) bought the CDNX, and in 2002 renamed it the TSX Venture Exchange (TSXV). Since then the TSX Group has become a public company itself, attracted international listings, merged with the Montreal Exchange, and changed its name to the TMX Group.

TSX Venture Exchange (TSXV)

The Calgary-based TSX Venture Exchange operates like the TSX, but it's for junior companies or new businesses looking for startup capital. More than 2,100 companies are listed on the exchange, with a total market cap of nearly $40 billion. The mining industry makes most use of the TSXV — 53 percent of the companies are from that sector — and oil and gas companies come in a distant second. Some of these companies will eventually move to the TSX, and others will close shop and delist. Because it's mostly for smaller operations it's a slightly more volatile place to invest.

The TSXV is a good place for traders to play resource-based companies, because that's what makes up most of the index.

Alternative trading systems (ATS) and electronic communication networks (ECN)

Once upon a time the TSX was the only exchange in town. That monopoly meant it could charge brokers high fees for trades. And, if something went wrong with the TSX's software — like it did in December 2008, when a technical glitch cancelled an entire day of trading — investors would be out of luck. Alternative trading systems, also called electronic communication networks, have been around since the turn of the century, but only recently have they begun to be a viable alternative to the standard exchanges. Some people expect 40 percent of all trades will be made on alternative trading systems by 2012; it was about 10 percent in 2009.

Canada has a number of alternative trading systems — Alpha ATS, Pure Trading, Chi-X Canada, and OMEGA ATS, to name a few — and all list the exact same securities as the TSX, but at different prices. Share prices don't vary too much, though; RIM's open price could be $46.15 and Alpha ATS lists it at $46.50. Luckily, traders don't have to worry about the different exchanges because the broker will automatically sort through every exchange and buy the stock at the best price. A good chance exists you won't even know that you purchased a stock on Chi-X instead of the TSX.

Some traders swear like sailors as they rapidly buy and sell, but one F-word is worse than anything you'd hear a few minutes to close: *fees*. Brokers have to pay them every time they trade, and those costs are often passed down to the trader. When the TSX had a monopoly it could charge whatever it wanted; alternative trading systems were created in part to bring those fees down. Fortunately, fees have fallen, and as alternative trading systems gain more ground they could drop more. That's good news for traders who will hopefully see commission costs tumble as brokers pass on their savings to their customers.

The New York Stock Exchange (NYSE)

Why is an American exchange listed in a Canadian day traders book? Because most day traders spend money on U.S. exchanges. It's important to know just as much about them — if not more — than the TSX. The New York Stock Exchange is the Big Kahuna of stock exchanges. Most of the largest U.S. corporations trade on it, and, like the TSX, they pay a fee for that privilege. The more than 2,000 companies listed on the exchange also have ticker symbols with three or fewer letters; many old companies have one-letter symbols, like F for Ford and T for AT&T.

Two of the largest companies in the world, Intel and Microsoft, are not listed on the New York Stock Exchange, and supposedly, exchange officials had told both companies that if they moved to the NYSE they could have the ticker symbols I and M, which were unassigned for decades. However, in 2007 the NYSE gave the M symbol to Macy's, formerly Federated Stores, so for now the computer giant is out of luck.

To be listed on the New York Stock Exchange, a company generally needs to have at least 2,200 shareholders, trade at least 100,000 shares a month, carry a *market capitalization* (number of shares outstanding multiplied by price per share) of at least $100 million, and post annual revenues of at least $75 million.

The New York Stock Exchange is more than 200 years old, and has been going through some big corporate changes in order to stay relevant. Unlike its Canadian counterpart, it's a *floor-based exchange*. The trading area is a big open space in the building, known as the *floor*. The floor broker, who works for the member firm, receives the order electronically and then takes it over to the trading post, which is the area on the floor where the stock in question trades. At the trading post, the floor broker executes the order at the best available price.

The American Stock Exchange (AMEX)

The American Stock Exchange is a floor-based exchange also headquartered in New York City. Like the New York Stock Exchange, floor brokers receive orders and take them to trading posts to be filled. AMEX specializes in commodity companies — those that mine metals or pump out oil — but some other types of businesses are also listed on it. Listed companies have two- or three-letter ticker symbols and generally are profitable, have a market capitalization (number of shares outstanding multiplied by price per share) of at least $75 million, and have a price per share of at least $2.00. These companies tend to be smaller and more speculative than New York Stock Exchange companies.

NASDAQ

NASDAQ used to stand for the National Association of Securities Dealers Automated Quotation System, but now it's just a name, not an acronym, pronounced just like it's spelled. When NASDAQ was founded, it was an electronic communication network (more on those below) that handled — like the TSXV — companies that were too small or too speculative to meet New York Stock Exchange or American Stock Exchange listing requirements. What happened was that brokers liked using the NASDAQ network, while technology companies (Microsoft, Intel, Oracle, Apple) that were once small and speculative became international behemoths. But the management teams of these companies saw no reason to change how they were listed.

NASDAQ companies have four-letter ticker symbols. When a customer places an order, the brokerage firm looks to see whether a matching order is on the network. Sometimes, it can be executed electronically; in other cases, the brokerage firm's trader needs to call other traders at other firms to see whether the price is still good. A key feature of NASDAQ is its *market makers,* who are employees of member brokerage firms who agree to buy and sell minimum levels of specific stocks in order to ensure some basic level of trading is taking place.

NASDAQ divides its listed companies into three categories:

- **The NASDAQ Global Select Market** includes the 1,000 largest companies on the exchange and has high governance and liquidity standards for participating firms.

- **The NASDAQ Global Market** includes companies that are too small for the Global Select Market, but that in general have a market capitalization of at least $75 million, at least 1.1 million shares outstanding, at least 400 shareholders, and a minimum price per share of $5.00.
- **The NASDAQ Capital Market** is for companies that do not qualify for the NASDAQ Global Market. To qualify here, companies need a market capitalization of at least $50 million, at least one million shares outstanding, about 300 shareholders, and a minimum price per share of $4.00.

Day traders will find that NASDAQ Global Select Market companies are the most liquid. They may also notice changes in trading patterns when a company is close to being moved between categories. An upgrade is a sign of good news to come and increased market interest. A downgrade means that the company most likely isn't doing well and will be of less interest to investors.

Over-the-Counter Bulletin Board (OTC BB)

The Over-the-Counter Bulletin Board is the market for companies that are reporting their financials to the provincial securities commissions (and, in the States, the U.S. Securities and Exchange Commission) but that do not qualify for listing on the TSXV or NASDAQ. Canada's OTC market is tiny; you can buy these types of companies on the TMX Group — run NEX. The exchange is for companies that have low levels of business activity or aren't active anymore. In other words, they're too small to trade on other exchanges.

In many cases, a Bulletin Board listing is often a last hurrah before oblivion.

Pink Sheets

Pink Sheets are essentially the American version of the NEX, though it's not run by any major exchange. Want to know where it got its colourful name? Once upon a time, there were few electronic networks, and there was not room for many companies to trade on them. Smaller companies did not trade daily. To find current prices, brokerage firms subscribed to a price service that sent out a weekly newsletter listing the prices for those companies. The newsletter was printed on pink paper, so it became known as the Pink Sheets.

Over the years, NASDAQ expanded and added more listing opportunities for companies, and the Over-the-Counter Bulletin Board was created for companies that had to file with the SEC but did not qualify for listing. The universe of companies that did not qualify for one of these quotation systems was very small. The Pink Sheets went online (`www.pinksheets.com`) so that people could get more regular price information.

Pink Sheet companies do not have listing requirements. Most do not qualify for listing on the NASDAQ or OTC BB, usually because they're not current on their filings with the SEC. These companies have four- or five-letter ticker symbols and are sometimes shown with the suffix .PK after the ticker. Orders for Pink Sheet companies are placed through brokerage firms that use the service to find prices and match buyers and sellers.

Although Pink Sheets is a U.S.-based company, Canadian businesses are listed on it as well — especially tiny mining companies. One company you'll probably be surprised to find on the site is the once-mighty Nortel Networks. Years ago, the former tech giant accounted for more than a third of the value of the entire S&P/TSX Composite Index; a few months after it filed for bankruptcy in January 2009 it delisted from the TSX and the NYSE. You can now buy it for less than a penny under the ticker NRTLQ.

Not all Pink Sheet companies are legitimate. Because of the minimal listing requirements, the Pink Sheets tend to be the hangout for the penny stock (those trading at less than $1.00 per share), the fraudulent company, and the security that's easily manipulated by a boiler-room operator. It can be a tough crowd, and a lot of people get burned.

Bonds

A *bond* is a loan. The bond buyer gives the bond issuer money. The bond issuer promises to pay interest on a regular basis. The regular coupon payments are why bonds are often called *fixed income investments*. Bond issuers repay the money borrowed — the principal — on a predetermined date, known as the *maturity*. Bonds generally have a maturity of more than ten years; shorter-term bonds are usually referred to as *notes,* and bonds that will mature within a year of issuance are usually referred to as *bills*. Most bonds in North America are issued by corporations (corporate bonds) or by the federal governments (called government bonds in Canada and Treasury bonds in the States). Some local governments in the U.S. also issue municipal bonds, but that's much less common in Canada.

The interest payments on a bond are called *coupons*. You've probably seen "car for sale" or "apartment for rent" signs with little slips of paper carrying a phone number or e-mail address cut into the bottom. If you're interested in the car or the apartment, you can rip off the slip and contact the advertiser later. Bonds used to look the same. The bond buyer would receive one large certificate good for the principal, with a lot of smaller certificates, called coupons, attached. When a payment was due, the owner would cut off the matching coupon and deposit it in the bank. (Some old novels refer to rich people as "coupon clippers," meaning that their sole labour in life was to cut out their bond coupons and cash them in. Nowadays, bond payments are handled electronically, so the modern coupon clipper is a bargain hunter looking for an extra 50 cents off a jar of peanut butter.)

Over the years, enterprising financiers realized that some investors needed regular payments, but others wanted to receive a single sum at a future date. So they separated the coupons from the principal. The principal payment, known as a *zero-coupon bond,* is sold to one investor, while the coupons, called *strips,* are sold to another investor. The borrower makes the payments just like with a regular bond. (Regular bonds, by the way, are sometimes called *plain vanilla.*)

The borrower who wants to make a series of payments with no lump-sum principal repayment would issue an *amortizing* bond to return principal and interest on a regular basis. If you think about a typical mortgage, the borrower makes a regular payment of both principal and interest. This way, the amount owed gets smaller over time so that the borrower does not have to come up with a large principal repayment at maturity.

Other borrowers would prefer to make a single payment at maturity, so they issue *discount bonds*. The purchase price is the principal reduced by the amount of interest that otherwise would be paid.

If a company goes bankrupt, the bondholders get paid before the shareholders. In some bankruptcies, the bondholders take over the business, leaving the current shareholders with nothing.

How bonds trade

Bonds often trade as single bonds, with a face value of $1,000, although some brokers will only take on minimum orders of ten bonds. They don't trade as frequently as stocks do because most bond investors are looking for steady income, so they hold their bonds until maturity. Bonds have less risk than stocks, so they show less price volatility. The value of a bond is mostly determined by the level of interest rates in the economy. As rates go up, bond prices go down; when rates go down, bond prices go up. Bond prices are also affected by how likely the loan is to be repaid. If traders don't think that the bond issuer will pay up, then the bond price will fall.

Generally speaking, only corporate (and municipal in the U.S.) bonds have repayment risk. It's possible that the U.S. government could default, but that's unlikely as long as it can print money. Most international government bonds have similarly low default risk, but some countries *have* defaulted. The most notable was Russia, which refused to print money to repay its debts in the summer of 1998. This caused huge turmoil in the world's financial markets, including the collapse of a major hedge fund, Long-Term Capital Management.

The global financial crisis also put many countries at risk, especially in Europe. In 2010 fears spread that Greece would default on its loans after Standard & Poor's — a U.S.-based company that rates borrowers — downgraded the country's debt rating to junk bond status. That sent stock markets plunging and spread fear that other financially strapped European countries, like Spain and Portugal, would default too. So, as you can see, just because a bond is issued by a government doesn't mean your investment is guaranteed.

In the past, investment banks and governments would sell new bonds directly to institutional investors, like pension plans or mutual funds. Now, anyone can buy bonds — but because they are usually purchased in large quantities, it's rare that a retail investor would buy a few bonds to complement her stocks. Traders, though, have more access to the bond market thanks to their broker. The broker will buy hundreds of thousands of dollars in bonds (or much more) and then sell them piecemeal to traders. Most bonds trade over-the-counter, meaning dealers trade them among themselves rather than on an organized exchange.

A bond price quote looks like this:

```
3 3/4 Mar 11 n 99:28 99:29
```

This is a U.S. Treasury note maturing in March 2011 carrying an interest rate of 3.75 percent. Similar to stocks, the numbers right after the "n" (for *note*) list the bid and ask. The first number is the bid, and it's the price at which the dealer will buy the bond from you if you're selling. The second number is the ask, and it's the price the dealer will charge you if you're buying. The difference is the spread, and that's the dealer's profit.

But wait, there's more: corporate bonds trade in eighths of a percentage point, and government bonds trade in 32nds. The bid of 99:28 means that the bond's bid price is 99 $\frac{28}{32}$ percent of the face value of $1,000, or $998.75.

Why on earth do bonds trade in eighths or fractions of eighths? Do traders just like to show off their math skills? No, it goes back to before the American Revolution. The dominant currency in most of the Americas then was the Spanish doubloon, a large gold coin that could be cut into fractions to make trade easier. Like a pie, it would be cut into eight equal pieces, so prices throughout the colonies were often set in eighths. (In Robert Louis Stevenson's book *Treasure Island,* the parrot keeps squawking "Pieces of eight! Pieces of eight!" This is why.)

The fractional pricing convention carried over to North American securities markets, and has persisted because it guarantees dealers a bigger spread than pricing in decimals. After all, $\frac{1}{32}$ of a dollar is more than $\frac{1}{100}$. U.S. and

Canadian stocks were priced in sixteenths until 2001. You'll notice a difference between the U.S. and Canadian bond markets though. If you're purchasing an American bond it will be priced using the old convention, but buy a Canadian bond and you'll be dealing in decimals.

Most bonds are not suitable for day traders. Only government bonds have enough consistent trading volume to attract a day trader. Because of the capital required to trade and the relatively low liquidity of many types of bonds, many traders prefer to use *futures* to bet on interest rates. We discuss futures in detail later in this chapter.

Are you one of those day traders who wants to buy or sell bonds anyway? Or do you just want to know more about the market? Then read on.

Listed bonds

Some larger corporate bonds are traded on the TSX, the New York Stock Exchange, and the American Stock Exchange. When you want to buy or sell them you place an order through your brokerage firm, which sends an order to the floor broker. The process is almost identical to the trading of listed stocks.

Over-the-counter trading

Most corporate and municipal bonds trade over-the-counter, meaning no organized exchange exists. Instead, brokerage firms use electronic price services to find out where the buyers and sellers are for different issues. Over-the-counter bonds don't trade much. Buyers often give their quality, interest rate, and maturity requirements to their broker, and the broker waits until a suitable bond comes to market.

Treasury dealers

Unlike the corporate and municipal bond market, the Treasury market is one of the most liquid in the world. The best way to buy a new Treasury bond is directly from the government, because no commission is involved. You can get more information from the government of Canada's Web site, `http://csb.gc.ca`, or the U.S. Treasury Department's Web site, `www.savingsbonds.gov`. Both have information on different government bonds for various purchasers.

After the bonds are issued, they trade on a secondary market of Treasury dealers. These are large brokerage firms registered with the government that agree to buy and sell bonds and maintain a stable market for the bonds. If your brokerage firm is not a Treasury dealer, it has a relationship with one that it can send your order to.

Treasury dealers do quite a bit of day trading in Treasury bonds for the firm's own account. After all, the market is liquid enough that day trading is possible. Few individual day traders work the Treasury market, though, because it requires a great deal of capital and leverage to make a high return.

Exchange traded funds (ETFs)

Exchange traded funds are a cross between mutual funds and stocks, and they offer a great way for day traders to get exposure to market segments that might otherwise be difficult to trade. A money management firm buys a group of assets — stocks, bonds, or others — and then lists shares that trade on the market. (One of the largest organizers of exchange traded funds is iShares, `www.ishares.com`.) In most cases, the purchased assets are designed to mimic the performance of an index, and investors know what those assets are before they purchase shares in the fund.

Exchange traded funds are available on the big market indexes, like the S&P/TSX Composite Index, the S&P/TSX 60, the S&P 500, and the Dow Jones Industrial Average. They are available in a variety of domestic bond indexes, international stock indexes, foreign currencies, and commodities.

How exchange traded funds trade

For day traders, the advantage of exchange traded funds is that they can be bought and sold just like stocks, discussed earlier in this chapter. Customers place orders, usually in round lots, through their brokerage firms. The price quotes come in decimals and include a spread for the dealer.

Where exchange traded funds trade

The firm that sets up the exchange traded fund gets to choose the market where it will trade, as long as the fund meets the exchange's requirements for size, liquidity, and financial reporting. Exchange traded funds trade on the TSX, NYSE, the AMEX, and NASDAQ.

Cash and Currency

Cash is king, as they say. It's money that's readily available in your day trading account to buy more securities. For the most part, the interest rate on cash is very low, but if you're closing out your positions every night, you'll always have a cash balance in your brokerage account. The firm will probably pay you a little interest on it, so it will contribute to your total return.

Money market accounts are boring. For day trading excitement, cash can be traded as foreign currency. Every day, trillions (yes, that's trillions with a *t*) of dollars are exchanged, creating opportunities to make money as the exchange rates change. Currency is a bigger, more liquid market than the U.S. stock and bond markets combined. It's often referred to as the *forex* market, short for *foreign exchange*.

How currency trades

The exchange rate is the price of money. It tells you how many dollars it takes to buy yen, pounds, or euros. The price that people are willing to pay for a currency depends on the investment opportunities, business opportunities, and perceived safety in each nation. If American businesses see great opportunities in Thailand, for example, they'll have to trade their dollars for baht in order to pay rent, buy supplies, and hire workers there. This will increase the demand for baht relative to the dollar, and it will cause the baht to go up in price relative to the dollar.

Exchange rates are quoted on a bid-ask basis, just as are bonds and stocks. A quote might look like this:

```
USDJPY=X 118.47 118.50
```

This is the exchange rate for converting the U.S. dollar into Japanese yen. The bid price of 118.47 is the amount of yen that a dealer would give you if you wanted to sell a dollar and buy yen. The ask price of 118.50 is the amount of yen the dealer would charge you if you wanted to buy a dollar and sell yen. The difference is the dealer's profit, and naturally, you'll be charged a commission, too.

Note that with currency, you're a buyer and a seller at the same time. This can increase the profit opportunities, but it can also increase your risk.

Day traders can trade currencies directly at current exchange rates, which is known as *trading in the spot market*. They can also use currency exchange traded funds (discussed earlier) or currency futures (discussed later in this chapter) to profit from the changing prices of money.

Where currency trades

Spot currency — the real-time value of money — does not trade on an organized exchange. Instead, banks, brokerage firms, hedge funds, and currency dealers buy and sell among themselves all day, every day.

Day traders can open dedicated forex accounts through their broker or a currency dealer (one is Forex.ca) and then trade as they see opportunities during the day.

How the Canadian dollar is traded

The most common currency transaction is the euro against the U.S. dollar, mainly because Europe is one of the largest trading blocs in the world and a lot of business is done between those two countries. But Canadians often trade the loonie against the greenback for two reasons: America's our biggest trading partner, and it's just what we know. You can, of course, trade the Canadian dollar against any other currency too.

Beginners may want to stick to the Canada–U.S. relationship, simply because most news outlets in the Great White North report on currency fluctuations relative to the American buck. Understanding how to trade the loonie against the yen takes a bit more work.

Commodities and How They Trade

Commodities are basic, interchangeable goods sold in bulk and used to make other goods. Examples include oil, gold, wheat, and lumber. Commodities are popular with investors as a hedge against inflation and uncertainty. Stock prices can go to zero, but people still need to eat! Although commodity prices usually tend to increase at the same rate as in the overall economy, so they maintain their real (inflation-adjusted) value, they can also be susceptible to short-term changes in supply and demand. A cold winter increases demand for oil, a dry summer reduces production of wheat, and a civil war could disrupt access to platinum mines.

Day traders aren't going to buy commodities outright — if you really want to haul bushels of grain around all day, you can do that without taking on the risks of day trading. You'd get more exercise, too. Instead, day traders who want to play with commodities can look to other investments. The most popular way is to buy futures contracts, which change in price with the underlying commodity (discussed later in this chapter). Increasingly, many trade commodities through exchange traded funds (see earlier section) that are based on the value of an underlying basket of commodities.

Derivatives and How They Trade

Derivatives are financial contracts that draw their value from the value of an underlying asset, security, or index. For example, an S&P/TSX 60 futures contract would give the buyer a cash payment based on the price of the S&P/TSX 60 index on the day that the contract expires. The contract's value thus depends on where the index is trading. You're trading not the index itself, but rather a contract with a value derived from the price of the index. The index value changes all the time, so day traders have lots of opportunities to buy and sell.

Types of derivatives

Day traders are likely to come across three types of derivatives. Options and futures trade on dedicated derivatives exchanges, whereas warrants trade on stock exchanges.

Options

An *option* is a contract that gives the holder the right, but not the obligation, to buy or sell the underlying asset at an agreed-upon price at an agreed-upon date in the future. An option that gives you the right to buy is a *call,* and one that gives you the right to sell is a *put.* A call is most valuable if the stock price is going up, whereas a put has more value if the stock price is going down.

Here's one way to remember the difference: you *call up* your friend to *put down* your enemy.

For example, a MSFT 2011 Mar 22.50 call gives you the right to buy Microsoft at $22.50 per share at the expiration date on the third Friday in March, 2011. (Did you know that traders refer to Microsoft as "Mr. Softy"? Clever, huh?) If Microsoft is trading above $22.50, you can exercise the option and make a quick profit. If it's selling below $22.50 you could buy the stock cheaper in the open market, so the option would be worthless.

You can find great information on options, including online tutorials, on the Montreal Exchange's Web site, www.m-x.ca. For an American perspective visit the Chicago Board Options Exchange's Web site, www.cboe.com.

Futures

A *futures* contract gives one the obligation to buy a set quantity of the underlying asset at a set price and a set future date. These started in the agricultural industry because they allowed farmers and food processors to lock in their prices early in the growing season, reducing the amount of uncertainty in their businesses. Futures have now been applied to many different assets, ranging from pork bellies (which really do trade — they are used to make bacon) to currency values. A simple example is a locked-in home mortgage rate; the borrower knows the rate that will be applied before the sale is closed and the loan is finalized. Day traders use futures to trade commodities without having to handle the actual assets.

Most futures contracts are closed out with cash before the settlement date. Financial contracts — futures on currencies, interest rates, or market index values — can only be closed out with cash. Commodity contracts may be settled with the physical items, but almost all are settled with cash. No one hauls a side of beef onto the floor of the Chicago Board of Trade!

Warrants

A *warrant* is similar to an option, but it's issued by the company rather than sold on an organized exchange. (After they are issued, warrants trade similarly to stocks.) A warrant gives the holder the right to buy more shares in the company at an agreed-upon price in the future.

A cousin of the warrant is the *convertible bond,* which is debt issued by the company. The company pays interest on the bond, and the bondholder has the right to exchange it for stock, depending on where interest rates and the stock price are. Convertibles trade on the stock exchanges.

Contract for difference (CFD)

A *contract for difference* allows traders to get exposure to an underlying asset, such as a share, index, currency, or commodity, without actually owning the asset itself. Because you don't own the asset commissions are often less — CMC Markets, one of the main CFD brokers, charges $5 for buying a contract on a stock; if you bought the actual stock through a discount broker you'd pay anywhere between $7 and $20.

CFDs are similar to futures contracts, but they have no fixed expiry date or contract size. A trader makes money depending on what the difference is between the initial contract price and the time the CFD is sold.

Buying and selling derivatives

Derivatives trade a little differently than other types of securities because they are based on promises. When someone buys an option on a stock, they aren't trading the stock with someone right now, they're buying the right to buy or sell it in the future. That means that the option buyer needs to know that the person on the other side is going to pay up. So, the derivatives exchanges have systems in place to make sure that those who buy and sell the contracts will be able to perform when they have to. Requirements for trading derivatives are different than in other markets.

How derivatives trade

Remember marginability from early in this chapter? Well, the word *margin* is used differently when discussing derivatives, but that's in part because derivatives are already leveraged — you aren't buying the asset, just exposure to the price change, so you can get a lot of bang for your buck. (We cover the risks and rewards of leverage in detail in Chapter 14.)

Margin in the derivatives market is the money you have to put up to ensure that you'll perform on the contract when it comes time to execute it. In the stock market, margin is collateral against a loan from the brokerage firm. In the derivatives markets, margin is collateral against the amount you might have to pay up on the contract. The more likely it is that you will have to pay the party who bought or sold the contract, the more margin money you will have to put up. Some exchanges use the term *performance bond* instead.

To buy a derivative, you put up the margin with the exchange's clearing house. That way, the exchange knows you have the money to make good on your side of the deal — if, say, a call option that you sell is executed, or you lose money on a currency forward that you buy. Your brokerage firm will arrange for the deposit.

At the end of each day, derivatives contracts are *marked-to-market,* meaning that they are revalued. Profits are credited to the trader's margin account, and losses are deducted. If the margin falls below the necessary amount, the trader will get a call and have to deposit more money.

By definition, day traders close out at the end of every day, so their options are not marked-to-market. The contracts will be someone else's problem, and the profits or losses on the trade go straight to the margin account, ready for the next day's trading.

Where derivatives trade

Traditionally, derivative trading involves *open-outcry* on physical exchanges. Traders on the floor get orders and execute them among themselves, shouting and using hand signals to indicate what they want to do. No central trading post or market maker controls the activities or guarantees a market. Most traders are employees of large commodities brokerage firms, but some are independent. No matter who employs them, traders may be executing someone else's orders for a fee, or they may be working for proprietary accounts.

Open-outcry has fewer economies of scale than the electronic trading systems that dominate activity in other assets. That's why there are more derivatives exchanges in the United States than active stock exchanges. Still, all the exchanges offer some electronic trading services, and that has become more and more popular. It's also causing much restructuring and consolidation among the exchanges. In July 2007 the Chicago Board of Trade merged with the Chicago Mercantile Exchange because floor traders at both exchanges were losing market share to electronic trading.

Getting to know the CME Group

The CME Group is the largest futures exchange in the world. It was formed in July 2007, after the Chicago Board of Trade merged with the Chicago Mercantile Exchange; in 2008 it acquired the fuels and metals–focused New York Mercantile Exchange (NYME) and the Commodity Exchange (COMEX). Even though these exchanges are owned by one company, they still have separate locations and traders access the individual exchanges. We listed each exchange separately in this chapter, but you can find information on all of them at CMEgroup.com.

Sometimes, the people in the pits start messing around with each other, and that can cause unusual volatility in the trading of the securities. Day traders who deal in commodities will often notice short periods of irrational trading for those derivatives that trade primarily in pits. The more human involvement, the less efficient a market will be.

Montreal Exchange (MX)

Most day traders will access American exchanges to trade derivatives, but some instruments can be bought and sold right here in Canada, on the TMX Group's Montreal Exchange. The MX is Canada's oldest exchange, starting up in 1832. In the early 1900s Montreal was Canada's financial centre; it used to execute many more trades than its Toronto counterpart. The ME was, at one time, so integral to Canada's financial markets that the terrorist group Front de libération du Québec bombed it in 1969. Over time the exchange began trading options and futures. In 1999 the TSX became the recognized place to sell stocks, and the MX became Canada's main derivatives exchange. Nine years later the MX merged with the TSX Group to form the TMX Group. These days, the MX's business is primarily in equity, exchange traded funds, and currency options, and index, interest rate, and energy derivatives.

Chicago Board of Trade (CBOT)

At the top of the Chicago Board of Trade's building is a statue of Ceres, the Greek goddess of grain. That's because this is the centre of futures trading in corn, wheat, rice, oats, and soybeans. The Board of Trade has branched out over the years and now offers futures contracts on financial commodities like Treasury bonds and the Dow Jones Industrial Average. Recently, it added trading in ethanol futures, an expansion from its history with corn. When a brokerage firm gets a customer order for a future traded on the Board of Trade it can send it to floor brokers to fill in the trading pits, or it can use the exchange's electronic trading system.

Chicago Mercantile Exchange (CME)

Futures in non-grain agricultural products, such as milk, butter, cattle, pork bellies, and fertilizer, trade at the Chicago Mercantile Exchange, known more colloquially as "the Merc." Other key futures traded here include foreign exchange, interest rates, and the Standard & Poor's and NASDAQ indexes. The Merc has also added some alternative products such as futures in weather and real estate. When brokerage firms receive orders for the Merc's futures they send them to floor brokers, who can fill them in the trading pits, or they can use the Merc's electronic trading system.

New York Mercantile Exchange (NYMEX)

Fuels and metals trade at the New York Mercantile Exchange, which is the largest physical commodities exchange in the United States. Most trading takes place in open-outcry pits, but an electronic system is available for overnight trading.

New York Board of Trade (NYBOT)

The New York Board of Trade was founded in 1998, when the Coffee, Sugar, and Cocoa Exchange merged with the New York Cotton Exchange. Here, traders can buy and sell futures and options on those commodities as well as on orange juice, the New York Stock Exchange, the U.S. dollar, and the euro. Orders are filled in the trading pits or through an electronic trading system.

Chicago Board Options Exchange (CBOE)

The Chicago Board Options Exchange, often known by the acronym CBOE (pronounced *see-bow*), is the largest options market in the United States. This is where orders for stock options are traded. Brokerage firms use floor brokers in the trading pits or the CBOE's electronic trading system to handle customer orders.

Chapter 4

Investing, Trading, and Gambling

In This Chapter

- Taking on risk and getting a return
- Investing for the long haul
- Trading for the day
- Gambling it all away
- Managing the risks you take

Day trading isn't investing, nor is it gambling — at least not if done right. But the lines among the three can be thin, and if you know where they are you'll be in a better position to follow your trading strategy and make more money. And if you can avoid the trap of gambling, you'll be better able to preserve your trading capital.

The difference between investing and gambling is the *risk and return tradeoff.* In investing, the odds are generally in your favour, but that doesn't mean you're going to make money. Some day traders end up gambling, and then the odds are moving against them. And unlike in the finer establishments in Las Vegas, no one is going to bring the failed day trader free drinks to help ease the pain. A lot comes down to personality; if you are on a casino's "do not admit" list, you probably aren't a great candidate for day trading.

This chapter starts off with a lot of gory details about risk and return. It helps you understand how the securities markets price risk and reward those who are willing to take it. Then we explain the differences in risk and reward for investors, traders, and gamblers to give you better information to help you plan your day trading.

Understanding Risk and Return

Investors, traders, and gamblers have this in common: They are putting some of their money at risk and they expect to get a return. Ideally, that return comes in the form of cold, hard cash — but at a casino, you might get your return in the form of tickets to a Celine Dion concert after you lose a lot of money at the tables.

Trading is a business: The more you know about the potential risks and the sources of your potential return, the better off you'll be. Your risk is that you won't get the return you expect, and your reward is that you get fair compensation for the risk you take.

What is risk, anyway?

Risk is the measurable likelihood of loss. The riskier something is, the more frequently a loss will occur, and the larger that loss is likely to be. Playing in traffic is riskier than driving in traffic, and skydiving is riskier than gardening. This doesn't mean that you can't have losses in a low-risk activity or big gains in a high-risk one. It just means that with the low-risk game, losses are less likely to happen, and those that do are likely to be small.

What's the difference between risk and uncertainty? Risk involves the known likelihood of something good or bad happening so that it can be priced. What's the likelihood of your living to be 100? Or of getting into a car accident tonight? Your insurance company knows, and it figures your rates accordingly. What's the likelihood of aliens from outer space arriving and taking over the Earth? Who knows! It could happen, but that event is uncertain, not risky — at least until it happens.

The ability to measure risk made modern business possible. Until mathematicians were able to use statistics to quantify human activities, people assumed that bad things were simply the result of bad luck or, worse, the wrath of the gods. But when they could understand probability, it could be applied and used. If a sailor agreed to join a voyage of exploration, what was the probability that he would return home alive? And what would be fair compensation to him for that risk? What was the probability of a silo of grain going up in flames? And how much should the farmer charge the grain buyers for the risk that he was taking, and how much should someone else charge to insure the farmer against that fire?

Considering the probability of a loss

Whenever you take risk, you take on the probability of loss. If you know what that probability is, you can determine whether the terms you are being offered are fair and you have a reasonable expectation for the size of the loss.

One way to determine whether the terms of your day trading strategy are fair is through *backtesting*, which we discuss in Chapter 11.

Imagine that you are presented with this opportunity: You put up \$10. You have an 80-percent chance of getting back \$11 and a 20-percent chance of losing everything. Should you take it? To find out, you multiply the expected return by the likelihood and add them together: (80% × \$11) + (20% × \$0) = \$8.80. Your expected return of \$8.80 is less than the \$10 cost of this contract, so you should pass on it.

Now, suppose you are offered this opportunity: You put up \$10. You have a 90-percent chance of getting back \$11 and a 10-percent chance of getting back \$6. Your expected return is (90% × \$11) + (10% × \$6) = \$10.50. This contract would be in your favour, so you should take it.

Now here's a third proposition: You put up \$10. You have a 90-percent chance of getting back \$13.89 and a 10-percent chance of losing \$20 — even more than you put up. Your expected return is (90% × \$13.89) + (10% × –\$20) = \$10.50. It's the same expected return as the proposition above, but do you like it as much?

When thinking about loss, most people tend to put too much weight on the absolute dollar amount that they can lose, rather than thinking about the likelihood. The problem is that the markets don't trade on your personal preferences. This is one of the psychological hurdles of trading that those who are successful can overcome. Can you? (You can find some tips on this in Chapter 8.)

Working with limited liability (usually)

Securities markets rely on the concept of *limited liability*. That is, you cannot lose any more money than you invested in the first place. If you buy a stock, it can go down to zero, but it can't go any lower. If the company goes bankrupt, no one can come to you and ask you to cover the bills. On the other hand, the most the stock can go up in price is infinity, so the possible return for your risk is huge. (Research In Motion has grown more than 650 percent since it came public, which isn't quite infinity, but we sure wish we had taken that proposition.)

Most day trading strategies have the same limited liability: You can lose what you trade, and no more. Some strategies have unlimited liability, however, such as selling short or using leverage. If you sell a stock short (borrow shares and then sell them in hopes that the stock goes down in price, allowing you to repay the loan with cheaper shares, a strategy we discuss in Chapter 14), and if the stock goes up to infinity, you have to repay the loan with those infinitely valued shares! Most likely, you're going to close out your position before that happens, but keep in mind that even if you close out your positions every night like a good day trader should, some strategies have the potential to cost you more money than you have in your trading account.

To protect themselves and to protect you against losing more money than you have, brokerage firms and options exchanges will require you to keep enough funds in your account to cover shortfalls (known as *margin,* discussed in Chapter 3). You will have to be approved before you can trade in certain securities. For example, anyone trading options has to fill out an agreement that the brokerage firm must first approve and then keep on file.

Playing the zero-sum game

Many day trading strategies are *zero-sum games,* meaning that for every winner on a trade, there is a loser. This is especially true in options markets. Now, the person on the other side of the trade might not mind being a loser; she may have entered into a trade to *hedge* (protect against a decline in) another investment and is happy to have a small loss instead of a much larger one.

The problem for you as a day trader is that little wiggle room exists in a zero-sum game. Every trade you make is going to win or lose, and your losses may exactly offset your winners. If your strategy takes place in a market that is a zero-sum game, such as the options market, make sure that you've tested your strategy thoroughly (see Chapter 11 for more on that) so that you know whether your odds are better than even.

Finding the probability of not getting the return you expect

In addition to absolute measures of risk and liability, consider another factor: *volatility.* That's how much a security's price might go up or down in a given time period.

The math for measuring volatility is based on standard deviation (discussed in Chapters 3 and 11). A standard deviation calculation starts with the average return over a given time period. This is the *expected* return — the return that, on average, you'll get if you stick with your trading strategy. But any given week, month, or year, the return might be very different from what you expect. The more likely you are to get what you expect, the less risk you take in the form of volatility.

Standard deviation shows up many times in trading, and we give a detailed explanation of it in Chapter 11. The key thing to know is this: The higher the standard deviation of the underlying securities, the more risk you take with your trade. However, the same volatility creates trading opportunities for day traders to exploit. A security with a low standard deviation isn't going to offer you many chances to make money over the course of a day.

Standard deviation is used to calculate another statistic: beta. *Beta* tells you how risky a security is relative to the risk of the market itself. If you buy a stock with a beta of more than 1, then that stock is expected to go up in price by a larger percentage than the market when the market is up, and it's expected to go down by a larger percentage than the market when the market is down.

High-beta stocks, and options on high-beta stocks, are riskier than low-beta stocks, but they offer a greater potential for return.

The word *beta* comes from the capital assets pricing model, an academic theory that says that the return on an investment is a function of the risk-free rate of return (discussed in the next section), the extra risk of investing in the market as a whole, and then the volatility — beta — of the security relative to the market. Under the capital assets pricing model, no other sources of risk and return exist. Any other sources would be called *alpha,* but in theory, alpha doesn't exist. Not everyone agrees with that, but the terms alpha and beta have stuck.

Getting rewarded for the risk you take

When you take risk, you expect to get a return. That's fair enough, right? That return comes in a few different forms related to the risk taken. Although you might not really care how you get your return as long as you get it, thinking about the breakdown of returns can help you think about your trading strategy and how it works for you.

Opportunity cost

The *opportunity cost* of your money is the return you could get doing something else. Is your choice day trading or staying at your current job? Your opportunity cost is your current salary and benefits. You'd give up that money if you quit to day trade. Is the opportunity cost low enough that it's worth your while? It may be. Just because taking advantage of an opportunity carries a cost doesn't mean that the opportunity isn't worth it.

When you trade, you want to cover your opportunity cost. Your cost will be different than someone else's, but if you know what it is up front, you'll have a better idea of whether your return is worth your risk.

You can think about opportunity cost in another way, too. When you make one trade, you give up the opportunity to use that money for another trade. That means you want to trade only when you know the trade is going to work out, more likely than not. That's why you need to plan your trades (see Chapter 2) and backtest (run a simulation using your strategy and historical securities prices) and evaluate your performance (see Chapter 11) so that you know you're trading for the right reasons, and not just out of boredom.

Risk-free rate of return and the time value of money

The value of money changes over time. In most cases, this is because of *inflation,* which is the general increase in price levels in an economy. But it's also because you give up the use of money for some period of time. That's why any investment or trading opportunity should include compensation for the *time value of your money.*

In day trading, your return from time value is small, because you hold positions for only a short period of time and close them out overnight. Still, some time component is relevant to the money you make. That smallest return is known as the *risk-free rate of return.* That's what you demand for giving up the use of your money, even if you know with certainty that you'll get your money back. In practice, investors think of the risk-free rate of return as the rate on Canadian or U.S. government Treasury bills, which are bonds that mature in less than one year. This rate is widely quoted in newspapers and electronic price quote systems.

If you cannot generate a return that's at least equal to the risk-free rate of return, you shouldn't be trading.

Risk–return tradeoff

Economists say there's no such thing as a free lunch. Whatever return you get, you get because you took some risk and gave up another opportunity for your time and money. In that sense, making money is all about work and risk.

This is known as the *risk–reward tradeoff.* The greater the potential reward, the greater the amount of risk you're expected to take, and thus the greater potential you have for loss. But if you understand the risks you're taking up front, you may well find that they are worth taking. That's why you have to think about the risks and rewards up front.

The magic of market efficiency

The reason why a balance between risk and reward exists is that markets are reasonably efficient. This efficiency means that prices reflect all known information about the companies and the economy, and it means that all participants understand the relative tradeoffs available to them. Otherwise, you'd have opportunities to make a riskless profit, and that just won't do according to the average economist. "You can't pluck nickels out of thin air," they like to say. In an efficient market, if an opportunity exists to make money without risk, someone would have taken advantage of that already.

The oldest economics joke ever told

So now that you're wise to the ways of risk and return, this joke should make sense to you:

Two economists are walking down the street. One sees a $20 bill on the sidewalk and stops to pick it up. "Don't bother," says the other. "If it were real, someone would have taken it already."

"Don't be so sure," says the first economist. He picks it up, sees that it is real, then turns to his friend and says, "How about if I buy you a free lunch?"

It works like this: You have information that says Company A is going to announce good earnings tomorrow, so you buy the stock. Your increased demand causes the price to go up, and pretty soon, the stock price is where it should be given that the company is doing well. The information advantage is rapidly eliminated. And in most cases, everyone gets the news — or hears the rumour — of the good earnings at the same time, so the price adjustment happens quickly.

Wouldn't it be great if you could get the news of a good earnings report before everyone else, to make a quick trading profit? Yep. At least until the RCMP show up and haul you off to prison — talk about your opportunity costs! It's illegal to trade on *material inside information* (which would be information that is not generally known that would affect the price of the security). Canada's provincial securities commissions, the Investment Industry Regulatory Organization of Canada and the individual brokers monitor trading for patterns that suggest illegal trading based on inside information. They want all investors and traders to feel confident that the investment business is fair. Be very wary of tips that seem too good to be true.

Now, you'll notice in the example that it was the activity of traders that caused the price of Company A's stock to go up to reflect the expected good earnings report. The markets may be more or less efficient, but that doesn't mean they work by magic. Price changes happen because people act on news, and those who act the fastest are day traders.

In economic terms, *arbitrage* is a riskless profit. A hard-core believer in academic theory would say that arbitrage opportunities don't exist. In practice, though, they do. Here's how it works: although Company A is expected to have a good earnings announcement tomorrow, you notice that the stock price has gone up faster than the price of a call option on Company A, even though premium should reflect the stock price. So, you sell Company A (borrowing shares and selling it short if you have to), and then use the proceeds to buy the option. When the option price goes up to reflect the stock price, you can sell it and lock in a riskless profit — at least, before your trading costs are considered. We discuss arbitrage in more detail in Chapter 15.

Investing

Investing is the process of putting money at risk in order to get a return. It's the raw material of capitalism. It's the way that businesses get started, roads get built, and explorations get financed. It's how our economy matches people who have too much money, at least during part of their lives, with people who need it in order to grow society's capabilities.

Investing is heady stuff. And it's very much focused on the long term. Good investors do a lot of research before committing their money, because they know that it will take a long time to see a payoff. That's okay with them. Investors often invest in things that are out of favour, because they know that with time others will recognize the value and respond in kind.

One of the best investors of all time is Warren Buffett, Chief Executive Office of Berkshire Hathaway. His annual letters to shareholders offer great insight. You can read them at `www.berkshirehathaway.com/letters/letters.html`.

What's the difference between investing and saving? When you save, you take no risk. Your compensation is low — it's just enough to cover the time value of money. Generally, the return on savings equals inflation and no more. In fact, a lot of banks pay a lot less than the inflation rate on a federally insured savings account, meaning that you're paying the bank to use your money.

In contrast to investing, day trading moves fast. Day traders react only to what's on the screen: no time to do research, and the market is always right when you are day trading. You don't have two months or two years to wait for the fundamentals to work out and the rest of Wall Street to see how smart you were. You have today. And if you can't live with that, you shouldn't be day trading.

Trading

Trading is the act of buying and selling securities. All investors trade, because they need to buy and sell their investments. But to investors, trading is a rare transaction, and they get more value from finding a good opportunity, buying it cheap, and selling it at a much higher price sometime in the future. But traders are not investors.

Traders look to take advantage of short-term price discrepancies in the market. In general, they don't take a lot of risk on each trade, so they don't get a lot of return on each trade, either. Traders act quickly. They look at what the market is telling them and then respond. They know that many of their trades will not work out, but as long as more than half work, they'll be okay. They don't do a lot of in-depth research on the securities they trade, but they know the normal price and volume patterns well enough that they can recognize potential profit opportunities.

Trading keeps markets efficient, because it creates the short-term supply and demand that eliminates small price discrepancies. It also creates a lot of stress for traders, who must react in the here and now. Traders give up the luxury of time in exchange for a quick profit.

Speculation is related to trading, in that it often involves short-term transactions. Speculators take risks assuming a much greater return than might be expected, and a lot of what-ifs may have to be satisfied for the transaction to pay off. Many speculators hedge their risks with other securities, such as options or futures.

Gambling

A *gambler* puts up money in the hopes of a payoff if a random event occurs. The odds are always against the gambler and in favour of the house, but people like to gamble because they like to hope that if they hit it lucky, their return will be as large as their loss is likely.

Some gamblers believe that the odds can be beaten, but they are wrong. (Certain card games are more games of skill than gambling, assuming you can find a casino that will play under standard rules. Yeah, you can count cards when playing blackjack with your friends, but it's a lot harder in a professionally run casino.) They get excited about the potential for a big win and get caught up in the glamour of the casino, and soon the odds go to work and drain away their stakes.

A *fair lottery* takes place when the expected payoff is higher than the odds of playing. You won't find it at most casinos, although sometimes the odds in a sports book or horse race favour the bettor, at least in the short term. A more common example takes place in lotteries when the jackpots roll over to astronomical amounts. Canadian lotteries don't get high enough to fit this description, but if you're travelling through the States you may want to pick up a multi-state Mega Millions ticket. In March of 2007, the lottery had a jackpot of $390 million, but the odds of winning were 1 in 175 million. This means that a $1.00 ticket had an expected value of $2.28, making it a fair proposition.

Trading is not gambling, but traders who are not paying attention to their strategy and its performance can cross over into gambling. They can view the blips on their computer screen as a game. They can start making trades without any regard for the risk and return characteristics. They can start believing that how they do things affects the trade. And pretty soon, they are using the securities market as a giant casino, using trading techniques that have odds as bad as any slot machine.

Managing the Risks of Day Trading

Now that you know more about the risks, returns, and related activities of day trading, you can think more about how you're going to run your day trading business. Before you flip through the book to find out how to get started, consider two more kinds of risk you need to be aware of:

- Business risk
- Personal risk

Business risk

Business risk is the uncertainty of the timing of your cash flow. Not every month of trading is going to be great, but your bills will come due no matter what. You'll have to pay for subscriptions while keeping the lights turned on and the computer connected to the Internet. Taxes come due four times a year, and keyboards hold a mysterious attraction for carbonated beverages, causing them to short out at the most inopportune times.

Regardless of what happens to your trading account, you need cash on hand to pay your bills or you'll be out of business. The best way to protect yourself is to start out with a cash cushion just for covering your operating expenses. Keep it separate from your trading funds. Replenish it during good months.

Personal risk

The *personal risk* of trading is that it becomes an obsession that crowds out everything else in your life. Trading is a stressful business, and the difference between those who succeed and those who fail is psychological. And, in fact, the personal risk is so great that we devote an entire chapter to managing it — go to Chapter 8 if anything you have read in this chapter alarms you.

Chapter 5

Fun with Regulation

In This Chapter

- Looking at a history of day trading and regulations
- Wondering who all these regulators are, anyway
- Considering some basic brokerage requirements
- Handling hot tips
- Trading with other people

The financial markets are wild and woolly playgrounds for capitalism at its best. Every moment of the trading day, buyers and sellers get together to figure out what the price of a stock, commodity, or currency should be at that moment given the supply, the demand, and the information out there. It's beautiful.

One reason why the markets work so well is that they are regulated. That may seem like an oxymoron: Isn't capitalism all about free trade, unfettered by any rules from nannying bureaucrats? Ah, but for capitalism to work, people on both sides of a trade need to know that the terms will be enforced. They need to know that the money is in their account and safe from theft. And they need to know that no one has an unfair advantage. *Regulation* creates the trust that makes markets function.

Day traders may not be managing money for other investors, and they may not answer to an employer, but that doesn't mean they don't have rules to follow. They have to comply with applicable securities laws and exchange regulations, some of which specifically address those who make lots of short-term trades. Likewise, brokers and advisers who deal with day traders have regulations that they need to follow, and understanding them can help day traders make better decisions about whom to deal with. In this chapter, you find out who does the regulating, what they look at, and how it all affects you.

How Regulations Created Day Trading

Canada's regulatory system is very different from that in the U.S., though it all stems from the same place. The American system came first, and so we borrowed many rules from our southern neighbours. Things have developed significantly since then, and although many similarities exist you'll also find a lot of differences. But first, a quick course in American history is in order so you can see how regulation in fact helped create trading.

With the advent of the telegraph, traders could receive daily price quotes. Many cities had *bucket shops,* which were storefront businesses where traders could bet on changes in stock and commodity prices. They weren't buying the security itself, even for a few minutes, but were instead placing bets against others. These schemes were highly prone to manipulation and fraud, and they were wiped out after the stock market crash of 1929.

After the 1929 crash, small investors could trade off the ticker tape, which was a printout of price changes sent by telegraph, or wire. In most cases, they would do this by going down to their brokerage firm's office, sitting in a conference room, and placing orders based on the changes they saw come across the tape. Really serious traders could get a wire installed in their own office, but the costs were prohibitive for most individual investors. In any event, traders still had to place their orders through a broker rather than having direct access to the market, so they could not count on timely execution.

Another reason why so little day trading happened back then is that until 1975 all American brokerage firms charged the same commissions. That year, the U.S. Securities and Exchange Commission (SEC) ruled that this amounted to price fixing, so brokers could then compete on their commissions. Some brokerage firms, such as Charles Schwab, began to allow customers to trade stock at discount commission rates, which made active trading more profitable. (Today, Canadian fees are all over the map — and getting cheaper, so compare commission prices before you settle on a broker.)

The system of trading off the ticker tape more or less persisted until the stock market crash of 1987. Brokerage firms and market makers were flooded with orders, so they took care of their biggest customers first and pushed the smallest trades to the bottom of the pile. After the crash, the exchanges and the SEC called for several changes that would reduce the chances of another crash and improve execution if one were to happen. One of those changes was the Small Order Entry System, often known as SOES, which gave orders of 1,000 shares or fewer priority over larger orders.

Similar regulation was developed in Canada at about the same time. The Order Exposure Rule was created to make sure smaller orders were given the same priority as larger ones. Here, 50 standard trading units or fewer (about 5,000 shares) have to be immediately entered on a market place. Brokers can't fill their larger orders first.

In the 1990s, when Internet access became widely available, this became less of a problem because traders could place orders in real time. But the rule still applies. Brokers could, theoretically, wait to execute Internet orders so they could deal with their 100,000-share trades first. Of course, that would be terrible for business — and with so much competition, fast execution is a selling point. Still, this rule, plus the speed of the Internet, put traders on the same footing as brokers and made day trading look like a pretty good way to make a living.

Who Regulates What?

In Canada, financial markets get regulatory oversight from various bodies, but most of the rules come from the provincial security commissions (such as the Ontario Securities Commission; OSC) and the Investment Industry Regulatory Organization of Canada (IIROC). Both have similar goals: to ensure that investors and traders have adequate information to make decisions, and to prevent fraud and abuse.

Unlike in the United States, which has the Securities and Exchange Commission, Canada has no national regulator. IIROC governs dealers (the institutions whose trading software you're using) across the country, and the securities commissions enforce the provincial Securities Act and Commodity Futures Act. The commissions' mandate, says the OSC's Web site, is to protect investors from "unfair, improper or fraudulent practices and to foster fair and efficient capital markets and confidence in capital markets."

Both IIROC and Canada's other self-regulatory organization, the Mutual Fund Dealers Association (MFDA), which oversees dealers who sell only mutual funds, police their own members, but the former self-regulatory organization (SRO) does a lot more. IIROC regulates the TSX, the Canadian National Stock Exchange, and various alternative trading systems such as Bloomberg Tradebook and Omega ATS.

When it comes to equity exchanges, IIROC's main job is to make sure nothing fishy is happening. The organization monitors trading activity and can place halts or delays if market integrity is compromised. It also enforces Universal Market Integrity Rules — the rules in Canada that govern trading.

IIROC also monitors how securities are traded in order to look for patterns that might point to market manipulation or insider trading. It works with brokerage firms to make sure they know who their customers are and that they have systems in place to make certain these customers play by the rules.

Because the stock and corporate bond markets are the most popular markets and have a relatively large number of relatively small issuers, regulators are active and visible. Not just one government is issuing currency — a whole bunch of companies issue shares of stock. When it turns out that one of these companies has fraudulent numbers the headlines erupt, and suddenly everyone cares about what the regulators are up to. That's just the first layer in regulating this market.

As we write this, serious talk is happening in the hallowed halls of the Legislature about creating a single national securities regulator in Canada, much like the SEC in the United States. Governments have been debating the question of whether Canada needs one for decades, so the chances of it happening soon are slim. However, if you're reading this book a few years after its publication date, be aware that some of what we've written here may be obsolete.

Provincial securities commissions

Each province has its own agency to ensure the markets work efficiently. Although rules may vary, they all share a common goal: to keep capital markets safe from fraud. Each commission governs its own jurisdiction, but they do work together. The commissions also work with the SEC or other governing bodies when fraud crosses country borders.

The provincial securities commissions have various functions, including:

- Regulating provincial capital markets by enforcing the provincial Securities Act and, depending on where, the Commodity Futures Act. The commissions ensure that any companies that have securities listed on exchanges in their jurisdiction report their financial information accurately and on time, so that investors can determine whether investing in the company makes sense for them
- Working with various stakeholders — retail investors, pensions funds, dealers, advisers, stock exchanges, alternative trading systems, SROs, and more — in ensuring compliance, investor protection, and keeping fair and efficient markets.
- Prosecuting firms and individuals who violate securities law. Although the commissions spend a lot of time investigating allegations of misconduct, they hold hearings over takeover bids and other regulatory issues, too.

Investment Industry Regulatory Organization of Canada (IIROC)

`www.iiroc.ca`

IIROC is a relatively new organization. It was created in 2008 when the Investment Dealers Association and Market Regulation Services merged. The

IDA was an SRO that oversaw Canadian dealers, and MRS provided regulation services for Canadian markets. The union has brought better oversight to the industry, making it more difficult for nefarious crooks to take advantage of investors.

The new SRO oversees investment dealers in Canada that trade stocks, bonds, mutual funds, options, forex, and other securities. It also looks after trading activity on debt and equity markets. It has 206 member firms, with about 28,000 people who are registered to sell securities. IIROC administers background checks and licensing exams, regulates securities trading and monitors how firms comply, and provides information for investors so that they are better informed about the investing process.

IIROC also requires advisers to know as much as they can about their clients, via Know Your Client forms. This includes determining whether an investment strategy is suitable for them. We discuss suitability later in this chapter under "Are you suitable for day trading?" — for now, just know that it's an IIROC function.

The first thing a day trader should do is check IIROC and MFDA's media release pages and the security commissions' registration sites. Every time a disciplinary hearing against a firm or adviser takes place, the progress of the proceedings is posted on the site. Find out whether the firm you want to trade with has violated any regulations. The security commissions' registrations sites allow you to type in the name of a person or firm and see whether they are in fact registered, what category they're registered in, and if any conditions were attached to that registration. These tools help ensure you're not dealing with a criminal.

Mutual Fund Dealers Association of Canada (MFDA)

`www.mfda.ca`

Unlike IIROC, which oversees dealers who trade stocks and bonds, the MFDA represents members who work only with mutual funds. Despite operating under its own set of rules, it shares many of the same goals as IIROC. It regulates operations, standards, and business conduct of its members and tries to improve investor protection. It can fine members for violating rules, and works with authorities when criminal charges are laid.

The MFDA represents 140 firms, or 81,262 advisers, with about $284 billion in assets under administration. It's highly unlikely the brokerage firm you use will be an MFDA member. Because you're trading more than just mutual funds, you'll be working in an IIROC environment.

The exchanges

It wasn't long ago that each major city had its own exchange. But through mergers and an agreement that Toronto would host a central stock exchange, the TSX became the main exchange in the country. However, depending on what you trade, the TSX is not the only game in town — you'll also find the Toronto Venture Exchange (TSXV), the Montreal Exchange (MX), and other exchanges and alternative trading systems.

Canada's main exchanges are owned by the TMX Group. It oversees the TSX, the TSXV, the MX, the Natural Gas Exchange (NGX), the Boston Options Exchange (BOX), and a few others. The group has outsourced its regulation duties of the TSX and TSXV to IIROC, and the others regulate trading activity in-house.

Brokerage Basics for Firm and Customer

No matter how they are regulated, brokers and futures commission merchants have to know who their customers are and what they are up to. That leads to some basic regulations about suitability and money laundering — and extra paperwork for you. Don't be too annoyed by all the paperwork you have to fill out to open an account, though — your brokerage firm has even more.

Are you suitable for day trading?

Brokerage firms have to make sure the activity surrounding their customers is appropriate. The firms need to know their customers and be sure that any recommendations are suitable. When it comes to day trading, firms want to be sure their customers are dealing with *risk capital* — money they can afford to lose. They also want to be sure that their customers understand the risks they are taking. Depending on the firm, and what you're trying to do, you might have to submit financial statements, sign a stack of disclosures, and verify that you have had previous trading experience.

It's no one's business but your own, of course, except that the regulators want to make sure that firm employees aren't talking customers into taking on risks they should not be taking. Sure, you can lie about it. You can tell the broker you don't *need* the $25,000 you're putting in your account, even if that's the money paying for your kidney dialysis. But when it's gone, you can't say you didn't know about the risks involved.

Staying out of the money Laundromat

Money laundering is a way to receive money acquired from illegal activities. Your average drug dealer, Mafia hit man, or corrupt politician doesn't accept credit cards, but he really doesn't want to keep lots of cash in his house. How can he collect interest on his money if it's locked in a safe in his closet? And besides, his friends are an unsavory sort. Can he trust them to stay away from his cache? If this criminal fellow takes all that cash to the bank, those pesky bankers will start asking a lot of questions, because they know that most people pursuing legitimate business activities get paid through cheques or electronic direct deposit.

Hence, the felon with funds will look for a way to make it appear that the money is legitimate. It happens in all sorts of ways, ranging from making lots of small cash deposits to engaging in complicated series of financial trades and money transfers, especially between countries, that become difficult for investigators to trace. Sometimes these transactions look a lot like day trading, and that means that legitimate brokerage firms opening day trade accounts should be paying attention to who their customers are.

Fighting money laundering took on urgency after the September 11, 2001 attacks, because it was clear that someone somewhere had given some bad people a lot of cash to fund the preparation and execution of their deadly mission. Several nations increased their oversight of financial activities during the aftermath of the strikes on the World Trade Center and Pentagon. That's why one piece of paperwork from your broker will be the anti–money laundering disclosure. The Financial Transactions Reports Analysis Centre of Canada (FINTRAC) is the government body that looks after money laundering activities, but brokers track this as well. If they suspect a trader is laundering money they'll report it to FINTRAC, which will then investigate.

In order for your brokerage firm to verify that it knows who its customers are and where their money came from, you'll probably have to provide the following when you open a brokerage account:

- Your name
- Date of birth
- Street address
- Place of business
- Social Insurance Number
- Driver's licence and passport
- Copies of financial statements

Money laundering: Al Capone or Watergate?

Although some believe that the term *money laundry* dates back to Al Capone's attempts to evade taxes by owning laundries — businesses that had a large number of small cash transactions — the U.S. Federal Reserve Board says the term didn't come into use until the Watergate scandal, when Nixon's campaign staff had to hide the money used to pay the people who broke into his opponent's psychiatrist's office.

Rules for day traders

Here's the problem for regulators: Many day traders lose money, and those losses can be magnified by the use of *leverage strategies* (trading with borrowed money, meaning that you can lose more money than you have in the quest for large profits; we discuss this in detail in Chapter 14). If the customer who lost the money can't pay up, then the broker is on the hook. If too many customers lose money beyond what the broker can absorb, then the losses ripple through the financial system, and that's not good.

IIROC has a long list of rules that its member firms have to meet in order to stay in business. The organization sets margin requirements and, depending on the type of account, the requirements are stricter to reflect the greater risk. You can read through all the rules by visiting this link: `iiroc.ca/English/ComplianceSurveillance/RuleBook/Pages/UMIR.aspx`.

The rules set by IIROC are minimum requirements. Brokerage firms are free to set higher limits for account size and borrowing in order to manage their own risks better.

Tax reporting

If you're a long-term investor receiving dividends, your online broker will send you a slip at the end of the year detailing how much income you've made. Traders will also receive tax forms if they received dividends or interest income — this mostly applies to people who hold overnight positions. Brokers may also send out a summary of trades to help track capital gains and losses. We cover tax issues in Chapter 10.

Hot Tips and Insider Trading

The regulations are very clear for things about suitability and money laundering. You get a bunch of forms, you read them, you sign them, you present documentation, and everyone is happy. The rules that keep the markets functioning are clear and easy to follow.

Another set of rules also keeps markets functioning — namely, that no one has an unfair information advantage. If you knew about big merger announcements, interest rate decisions by the Bank of Canada, or a new sugar substitute that would eliminate demand for corn syrup, you could make a lot of money in the stock market, trading options on interest rate futures, or playing in the grain futures market.

Insider trading is a broad term. Any non-public information that a reasonable person would consider when deciding whether to buy or sell a security could apply, and that's a pretty vague standard — especially because the whole purpose of research is to combine bits of immaterial information together to make investment decisions.

Day traders can be susceptible to hot tips, because they are buying and selling so quickly. If these hot tips are actually inside information, though, the trader can become liable. If you get great information from someone who is in a position to know — an officer, a director, a lawyer, an investment banker — you may be looking at stiff penalties. According to the Canada Business Corporations Act, courts can assess civil penalties of "any measure of damages it considers relevant in the circumstances." A criminal conviction can land someone in jail for up to ten years.

Insider trading is difficult to prove, so federal regulators use other tools to punish those it suspects of making improper profits. In the United States, Martha Stewart wasn't sent to prison on insider trading charges; she was charged with obstructing justice by lying to investigators about what happened.

Whenever a big announcement is made, such as a merger, the exchanges go back and review trading for several days before to see whether any unusual activities occurred in relevant securities and derivatives. Then they start tracing them back to the traders involved through the brokerage firms to see whether it was coincidence or part of a pattern.

The bottom line is this: You may never come across inside information. But if a tip seems too good to be true, it probably is — so be careful.

Taking on Partners

After your day trading proves to be wildly successful, you might want to take on partners to give you more trading capital and a slightly more regular income from the management fees. You can do it, but it's a lot of work.

If you start trading as a business a good chance exists you'll have to register with your provincial securities commission as a dealer, an investment fund manager, or perhaps something else depending on what you're doing. What triggers registration is complicated. If you're thinking about bringing people on board, it's best to call your securities commission or a lawyer and ask them what you need to do. You may also want to read part 25.1 of the Ontario Securities Act (`www.e-laws.gov.on.ca/html/statutes/english/elaws_statutes_90s05_e.htm#BK55`) to find out which category you'd fall under.

Registration is not a do-it-yourself project. An error or omission may have tremendous repercussions down the line, from fines to jail time. If you want to take on partners for your trading business, spend the money for qualified legal advice. It will protect you and show prospective customers that you're serious about your business.

Part II
Day Trading Tools

"No, day trading hasn't interfered with my regular practice at all. In fact, I'm preparing to make a trade now."

In this part . . .

Day trading is first and foremost a business, and here you'll learn how to get set up for success. This part includes information on how to set up your office and find brokerage services; where to get the support services you need to research trades; and how to get through the treacherous days with your sanity intact and your positions under control. You'll find how to pay taxes, and figure out how well your time, energy, and trading is paying off.

Chapter 6

Setting Up Your Accounts and Office

In This Chapter

- Knowing what to look for in a brokerage firm
- Choosing among the many brokers you have to pick from
- Getting equipped to trade
- Playing in a trading arcade

Day trading is possible only because technology costs have come down dramatically over the years. That makes it feasible to set up shop in the comfort of your home. But remember: This is a home business, so you do need to set up for it.

Sure, some days you can sit and trade from your laptop in a coffee shop, but to end up doing that well, you first need to commit to the space and the equipment at home. If you skimp on your Internet connection, for example, you can't be upset if it's unable to handle the data on a big market day. When your PC goes down, you'd better have a way to get it back up fast if you have open positions. And if the responsibility seems overwhelming, maybe you should look for a *trading arcade* — an office space for traders — and move your operation there.

In this chapter, we list different brokers that handle day traders, go over the basics of your office setup, and give you some advice on finding a trading arcade.

Choosing a Brokerage

If you're going to trade, you need a brokerage account. Chapter 3 covers some of the basics of different types of securities and where they trade. That's the first place to start.

If you're going to trade stocks, you need a full-service broker that has access to the Toronto Stock Exchange, NASDAQ, the New York Stock Exchange, and other major exchanges.

Many day traders pursue two or three strategies, which may require holding different brokerage accounts. That's not unusual. If you're going to trade grain futures and tech stocks both, you might want one account with a futures brokerage and another account with a stock brokerage that offers fast execution.

Direct access to pricing and trading

All brokerage firms offer *price quotes*: a summary of the current bid and offer prices for selling or buying the security in question. But not all of these price quotes are the same. Some are offered in *real time* — meaning that you see the prices as soon as your modem can transmit the change to you. Others are delayed, sometimes by seconds, sometimes by minutes. If you are buying a bond with plans to hold it for ten years, then the difference in price between now and 15 minutes ago probably isn't material. But if you are looking to day trade in the bond market using short-term changes in treasury futures, then a delay of even 30 seconds might be the difference between your strategy succeeding or failing.

Direct-access brokers allow you to see the price quotes in real time so that you can act on them immediately, and they allow you to work through different electronic communications networks rather than going through the firm's own traders. Almost all day trading strategies need direct access in order to maximize profitability.

A traditional retail brokerage, by contrast, offers customers more research and advice and may even improve order execution by waiting until market conditions are more favourable. That's fine for investors, but not so good for day traders.

In addition to different levels of market access, brokerage firms offer different types of price quotes with different amounts of detail. Read on for descriptions and pictures to see what you need for your strategy.

Faster, detailed price quotes are valuable to traders, so brokerage firms usually charge more for them. Don't skimp on price services at the expense of your trading profitability.

Level 1 quotes

Level I quotes give you the current bid and ask (or bid and offer) prices for a given security. The *bid,* of course, is the price at which the broker buys the security from you, and the *ask,* also called *offer* in some markets, is the price at which the broker offers to sell the security to you. A level I quote also shows the size of the most recent buy and sell orders.

Most brokerage firms offer real-time level I quotes for free, but these numbers do not have enough detail for day trading.

Level II quotes

Level II quotes tell you not only what the current bid and offer prices are, but also who the other buyers and sellers are — the brokerage firms who are buying and selling the security — and what size orders they have at different prices (Figure 6-1). This information can help you gauge the volatility and direction of trading in the market, and that can help you make more profitable trades. Most brokerage firms that specialize in day trading offer level II quotes in most markets.

SYMBOL	AMAT	Applied Materials (NGS)			
LAST SALE	20.15 q	NASDAQ Bid Tick (+)			
NATIONAL BBO	20.15 q	20.16 q	6900 × 3000		
MPID	**Bid**	**Size**	**MPID**	**Ask**	**Size**
NSDQ	20.15	3000	NSDQ	20.16	2000
ARCX	20.15	2600	ARCX	20.16	1900
BEST	20.15	1500	TDCM	20.16	1000
NITE	20.15	1400	OPCO	20.17	2100
CINN	20.15	1200	BARD	20.17	1000
BOFA	20.15	1000	CLYP	20.18	2000
AUTO	20.14	5000	SCHB	20.18	1500
LEHM	20.14	1000	NITE	20.18	1100
ABLE	20.14	1000	DAIN	20.18	100
SCHB	20.14	500	TEJS	20.18	100
GSCO	20.14	100	GSCO	20.18	100
RAJA	20.12	1200	MSCO	20.19	1500
TDCM	20.12	1000	JPMS	20.19	100
MONR	20.12	1000	BEST	20.20	1200
SWST	20.12	1000	NFSC	20.20	1000
NORT	20.12	400	FBRC	20.20	800
JPMS	20.12	100	FACT	20.20	100
PERT	20.11	800	UBSW	20.21	1100
PIPR	20.11	100	GSCO	20.21	1000
PRUS	20.10	500	FBCO	20.21	100
FBCO	20.09	1400	LEHM	20.21	100
COWN	20.09	800	RHCO	20.21	100
HDSN	20.09	400	WCHV	20.22	1200
UBSW	20.09	400	GLBT	20.22	1000

Figure 6-1: A NASDAQ level II quote looks like this.

TotalView quotes

TotalView quotes show all orders in the U.S. market for a given security, both attributed to market makers and anonymous (Figure 6-2). This gives traders the most detailed information about what's happening in the market. It may be overkill for some trading strategies, but vital to the success of most. You'll have a better idea of how much information your trading strategies need after you test them using the advice in Chapter 11.

SYMBOL	AMAT	Applied Materials (NGS)	
LAST SALE	20.15 q	NASDAQ Bid Tick (+)	
NATIONAL BBO	20.15 q	20.16 q	6900 × 3000

Bid Price	Total Depth	Ask Price	Total Depth
20.15	10700	20.16	4900
20.14	56100	20.17	9100
20.13	26300	20.18	13400
20.12	9900	20.19	11200
20.11	1700	20.20	8700

MPID	Bid	Size	MPID	Ask	Size
NSDQ	20.15	3000	NSDQ	20.16	2000
ARCX	20.15	2600	ARCX	20.16	1900
BEST	20.15	1500	TDCM	20.16	1000
NITE	20.15	1400	NSDQ	20.17	6000
CINN	20.15	1200	OPCO	20.17	2100
BOFA	20.15	1000	BARD	20.17	1000
NSDQ	20.14	28500	NSDQ	20.18	5000
BEST	20.14	12500	OPCO	20.18	2500
NITE	20.14	7500	CLYP	20.18	2000
AUTO	20.14	5000	SCHB	20.18	1500
LEHM	20.14	1000	NITE	20.18	1100
ABLE	20.14	1000	TDCM	20.18	1000
SCHB	20.14	500	DAIN	20.18	100
GSCO	20.14	100	TEJS	20.18	100
NSDQ	20.13	10000	GSCO	20.18	100
GSCO	20.13	8800	NSDQ	20.19	5500
SCHB	20.13	7500	NITE	20.19	3000
NSDQ	20.12	2200	MSCO	20.19	1500
BEST	20.12	2000	OPCO	20.19	1000
RAJA	20.12	1200	JPMS	20.19	100
LEHM	20.12	1000	SCHB	20.19	100
TDCM	20.12	1000	BAR	20.19	4000
MONR	20.12	1000	BEST	20.20	1200
SWST	20.12	1000	NFSC	20.20	1000
NORT	20.12	400	NSDQ	20.20	1000
JPMS	20.12	100	FBRC	20.20	800
PERT	20.11	800	SCHB	20.20	500
GSCO	20.11	500	NITE	20.20	100
LEHM	20.11	100	FACT	20.20	100
NSDQ	20.11	100	UBSW	20.21	1100
NORT	20.11	100	GSCO	20.21	1000
PIPR	20.11	100	NITE	20.21	1000
NSDQ	20.10	13500	NSDQ	20.21	500
SCHB	20.10	3500	TDCM	20.21	100
TDCM	20.10	2000	FBCO	20.21	100
PRUS	20.10	500	LEHM	20.21	100
GSCO	20.09	100	RHCO	20.21	100
NSDQ	20.09	2500	LEHM	20.22	5000
RAJA	20.09	2200	WCHV	20.22	1200
FBCO	20.09	1400	GLBT	20.22	1000
MONR	20.09	1000	NSDQ	20.22	500
NITE	20.09	1000	FBRC	20.22	500
COWN	20.09	800	DAIN	20.22	100
HDSN	20.09	400	NITE	20.22	100
UBSW	20.09	400	BEST	20.22	100

Figure 6-2: A NASDAQ TotalView quote is the most detailed available.

Type of platform

When you have an account with a brokerage firm, you have a way to get information about the markets and place your orders. The conduit is the Internet, but there has to be a way to get your orders to it. Some brokerage firms have their own software that you can use; others allow you to log in through a Web site.

Software-based platforms

With a software-based platform, you have to download and install the brokerage firm's proprietary system onto your computer. When you are ready to start your trading day, you connect to the Internet first, launch the software to see what's happening, and place your trades. Software systems generally offer more features and analytical tools, but you can trade only on a machine that has the software loaded on it.

Web-based platforms

With a Web-based trading platform, you go to the broker's Web site and log in to trade. This means you can trade from any computer that has Internet access, which is a boon if you travel or work from several different locations. In exchange, you may give up some of the analytic and backtesting tools offered through software-based platforms.

Note that Web-based platforms may be designed to work on specific Web browsers. Given the importance of having a stable connection and full functionality in a fast-moving market, if the firm recommends using, say, Internet Explorer, accept that. Don't cling to a preferred alternative.

What about mobile platforms? Some brokerage firms allow you to get price quotes and place trades through a mobile phone. This may be useful to some people, but it's a bad idea for most day traders. Day trading is a business, and that means you need some discipline about setting regular hours and working from a regular workspace. You will probably need more information to work a trade than will fit on your phone's screen. Finally, you need to take breaks from the market in order to maintain balance in your life. If you're making trades at your cousin's wedding, you're probably a little out of balance.

How to open an account

When you open a brokerage account, you have a lot of paperwork to fill out in order to comply with regulations. We explain all the laws behind these in Chapter 5. The firm needs to ensure that you are suitable for day trading;

that you understand the risks of options, futures, and margin strategies; and that your trading money did not come from ill-gotten gains.

After you fill out and sign the paperwork, you need to transfer funds. Some brokers require a minimum investment of $25,000 to open a day trading account (some set this lower and some higher). Write a cheque or set up a wire or Internet transfer from an existing bank, brokerage, or mutual fund account.

Brokers Offering Day Trading Services

Following is a list of brokerage firms with services for day traders. It's arranged by specialty (stocks and general trading, options and futures, foreign exchange) and then alphabetically within each category. It's not exhaustive. Keep in mind that every year new firms are formed and existing firms are acquired or merged away, so be sure to do your own research. Also, this list does not imply an endorsement of anyone's services.

The Globe and Mail (www.theglobeandmail.com) has an annual "online broker survey" discussing the pros and cons of a number of different discount brokerages. Although it's more geared toward the average investor, traders can find information on fees and get a better idea of which companies offer the best service. Check it out when you're ready to research.

Brokers for stocks and a bit of the rest

Day traders almost always work through online brokerage accounts. Many firms offering these accounts handle trading in almost all securities. The firms usually belong to all the exchanges, so you can trade almost anything anywhere in the world through them. They often offer a range of news and charting services to help you plan your trading. In some cases, their offerings may be overkill — you might not need all their services, and you might even find them distracting. And some may not handle your security of choice well.

Brokerage firms don't make money just on the commission charged per trade. Other sources of revenue include monthly service charges, fees for real-time quotes, interest on margin loans to customers, and, in some cases, the *spread,* which is the difference between what you pay for a security and what the firm paid to get it. Don't let the commission be the critical factor in deciding among brokerage firms. Think about the services you will need and the relative cost to you of different account offerings.

BMO InvestorLine

```
www.bmoinvestorline.com
```

The Bank of Montreal's InvestorLine is geared toward online investors but also has an active trader component. Like with most bank offerings you can trade only equities and options, and you have to make 30 or more trades per quarter to open an account. (Day traders can easily make 30 trades in a day, so qualifying won't be a problem.) View real-time level II quotes and place stop orders to help you stay in the black.

CIBC Investor's Edge

```
www.investorsedge.cibc.com
```

One benefit of trading with a bank is obtaining access to its extensive research material. CIBC Investor's Edge lets you do all the usual stuff, and also opens the doors to its CIBC Wood Gundy and CIBC World Markets reports. In addition, its "stock centre" covers more than 10,000 North American companies, and you get access to Standard & Poor's comprehensive U.S. equity reports.

Credential Direct

```
www.credentialdirect.com
```

Credential Direct gives you a wealth of information to make more informed trading decisions. Access to Morningstar's equity research and stock pick lists can take you a long way, and its 20 newswire feeds should keep you informed of the day's events. Traders can also use several technical analysis tools and take advantage of numerous alerts, including one that helps you stay on margin.

Disnat

```
www.disnat.com
```

The name might not be as familiar as some of the bank-owned trading platforms, but Disnat is no small player. It's owned by Desjardins Securities, the brokerage arm of Desjardins Group, the largest credit union in North America. If you make more than 40 trades a month, use its Disnat Direct Plus service, which gives you access to up to 600 streaming live quotes.

HSBC InvestDirect

```
www.hsbc.ca/1/2/en/personal/investdirect
```

HSBC InvestDirect offers traders access to markets in North America, Hong Kong, London, Paris, and Frankfurt. Although other services provide more research and analysis, at $6.95 trades are relatively inexpensive. (You have to have $1 million in your account or make more than 150 trades a quarter to get that price.)

Interactive Brokers

www.interactivebrokers.ca

Interactive Brokers offers software-based direct-access trading, including trading in international markets. It has options, futures, and foreign exchange trading services as well as trading in stocks. Traders can use a range of order types and order-management features to work complicated strategies.

National Bank Direct Brokerage

w3.nbdb.ca/index.jsp

Montreal's National Bank Direct Brokerage gives traders plenty of research and technical analysis tools. Use the firm's Market-Q software to track tiny fluctuations in the market and view all purchase and sell orders for any security.

Qtrade

www.qtrade.ca

Vancouver-based Qtrade may be a small, independent firm, but it offers a whole range of investment services. The firm lets you trade the basics — Canadian and U.S. stocks, bonds, T-bills, and mutual funds — but options are available as well. QTrade offers a lot of stock-related research, and the company recently began allowing traders to hold the greenback in registered accounts to avoid foreign-exchange fees.

Questrade

www.questrade.com

Toronto-based Questrade gives traders the chance to buy and sell equities, options, forex, gold, and mutual funds. Canadians can access accounts via the Web, or on their desktop by buying its pro or elite software. The latter — and most comprehensive — package is designed for people who make at least 50 trades a day.

RBC Direct Investing

www.rbcdirectinvesting.com

RBC Direct Investing offers similar options as the other banks — level II quotes, a Web-based trading dashboard, and streaming quotes for up to 15 stocks. One advantage is gaining access to RBC Capital Markets' extensive Canadian and U.S. research.

Scotia iTrade

www.scotiaitrade.com

In 2008, Scotiabank bought E*Trade Canada, renamed it Scotia iTrade, and slapped on a new logo with its red branding. It hasn't changed much from its old days; investors can trade stocks, options, and bonds, and it provides services for active traders through its Web-based trading platform. It also offers a software-based platform, Scotia iTRADE Pro, with direct-access trading and customization abilities.

TD Waterhouse

www.tdwaterhouse.ca

Although TD lets Canadians play with equities and options, its pièce de résistance is its active trading platform. The easy-to-use interface offers detailed charts and tracking data and the ability to overlay a number of analysis techniques. It's also fully customizable. Create tabs for specific sectors or companies and get level II quotes from a variety of exchanges and ECNs.

Brokers for options and futures

To effectively day trade options and futures, you need an account with a broker that has direct access to the exchanges' electronic communications networks. Several of the full-service firms we list in the previous section offer that service, as do the brokers we list here, which specialize in these markets.

JitneyTrade Inc.

www.jitneytrade.com

JitneyTrade, a Montreal-based company, allows Canadians to trade equities, options, and futures with its RealTick platform. (Its lower-level platforms don't accommodate futures trading.) Its comprehensive software allows you to place orders directly on charts and to trade multiple accounts at once.

MF Global Canada

www.mfglobal.ca

MF Global, formerly Man Financial, is a multinational company that works with hedge funds and major institutional investors, but it makes many of its services available to larger day traders. It has expertise in agricultural commodities as well as financial futures. Traders can choose from several trading platforms, with free simulated trading for those who want to check out futures trading first.

optionsXpress

www.optionsxpress.ca

OX, or optionsXpress, is designed for people who trade options and the stocks underlying them. Its customizable Xtend platform lets you trade in a variety of ways, including basket and ladder trades, and its extensive research services, market commentary, and analysis will keep you informed on what's happening outside your four walls.

thinkorswim

www.thinkorswim.ca

Providing its customers with a software-based trading platform used mostly to trade options strategies, thinkorswim — owned by TD Waterhouse — also offers a full range of products, including mutual funds. All its services can be accessed using the downloadable thinkDesktop software, but it also has an iPhone application that allows you to trade, receive alerts, use analysis tools, and more.

Brokers for foreign exchange

The foreign exchange, or forex, market is the largest trading market in the world. It has lots of opportunities for day traders to make (or lose) money. Most forex trades take place between banks, corporations, and hedge funds directly, without the use of a broker. If you want to trade directly, you need to use a trading firm that is tied in to these networks. Many of the brokers listed above offer forex, and here are a few that do little else.

CMC Markets

www.cmcmarkets.ca

CMC Markets was the first firm to allow individual investors to trade in foreign exchange and contracts for difference. The company has a software- and web-based platform that offers trading shares, commodities, indices and in 65 different currency pairs. It also has extensive technical analysis, research, and education services for its customers.

Forex.ca

www.forex.ca

Forex.ca is owned by Toronto's Cash Forex Trading, but U.S.-based Gain Capital Group provides most of the broker's back end. Users download software that lets you analyze markets and place trades. The company also offers a lot of educational programs for those interested in foreign exchange.

Friedberg Direct

www.friedbergdirect.ca

Friedberg Direct, owned by the family-run Friedberg Mercantile Group, offers margin protection, access to Thomson Reuters' IFR Markets commentary and analysis, and the ability to create detailed account statements. Before you start spending, play with $50,000 of fake money in a demo account.

Oanda

fxtrade.oanda.ca

Oanda doesn't require users to download its platform — everything can be accessed on the Web. Get real-time spreads, easily update stop loss orders, and view all open orders and open positions in its market. You can also track and execute trades on its iPad, iPhone, Android, or BlackBerry apps.

XForex

www.xforex.com

Want to learn about trading forex before spending real dough? In addition to demo accounts, XForex offers personal training, live chats, free webinars, and other educational tools. VIP users can also get a personal monthly account review, and if you refer a friend you may be able to score a $3,000 bonus.

Equipping Your Trading Laboratory

Twenty years ago, you would have had to pay millions of dollars for the equipment and telecommunications networks that you can now have in your own home for just a few thousand bucks or so.

You may be thinking, "I can do it for free! I have a PC in a corner of the family room, I have Internet access, what else do I need?" Ah, but you need plenty. Remember, successful day traders approach trading as a professional activity. That means starting off with an adequate work space and dedicated equipment. If you can't give up an entire room in your house, find a corner or hallway where you can put a desk and a computer just for day trading. It will clear your mind so that you can focus on the work at hand.

Where to sit, where to work

You need a table and a chair. Don't borrow a chair from the dining room, but instead get a good desk chair that will swivel around and adjust to you as you work. You'll need a shelf and a cabinet of some sort to hold your files and documents, too.

Want to get more comfort for the dollar in a desk chair? Consider shopping for used chairs at office equipment dealers. They may come with a few scuffs, but they will probably have more ergonomic settings than chairs at office supply superstores.

No rules apply for the layout of your equipment, but the more you can see and do without getting up from your chair, the better off you'll be. If you find yourself getting sore at the end of the day, investigate ergonomic products such as special keyboards, contoured mice, wrist pads, and foot rests, all of which are readily available at office supply stores.

Counting on your computer

You can't day trade without one computer, and you might want two or three: one to trade from, one for everything else (such as spreadsheets, e-mail, instant messaging), plus a spare in case the trading computer goes down. (See the section "The department of redundancy department" later in this chapter.) And, as Bryan learned the hard way, don't put your work computer near a child who's holding a cup of water.

Almost every personal computer on the market today has the power to handle day trading activities, so you don't need to sweat over the details. In general, faster processing speeds are better than slower ones, and more memory and storage are preferable to less.

What about the manufacturer? Well, you probably don't want an Apple Macintosh for day trading, because it's possible that not all the software packages you'll need will be Mac-compatible. If you are one of those die-hard Mac heads, though, be sure to ask brokers and software vendors about compatibility. Other than that, it doesn't matter much.

See it on the big screen

Do yourself a favour and spend money on a big flat-screen monitor, at least 19 inches on the diagonal, so that you can see what's happening in the markets. If you need to look at more than one window at once — say, to see charts and level II quotes at the same time — consider using two or more monitors hooked to the same PC. That way, you'll have a clear view of necessary data. (Most traders work with at least two monitors, because the information they need is too valuable.)

Connecting to the Internet

If you are day trading, you should hook up to the Internet with as much bandwidth as possible — at least a cable connection with download speeds of 15 megabits per second (Mbps) and upload speeds of 1 Mbps. It's probably better to get an even better package — some companies offer 50 Mbps download speeds. The extra cost is worth it. If prices are changing quickly, a delay of half a second can be costly.

Invest in a firewall and virus protection for your trading PC, but be careful how you do it. Some software will protect your system at the expense of a slow data feed, which will hurt your trading execution. When you set your virus scanner, be sure that any automatic downloads or background scans take place after market hours, so that they can't slow you down. And if you decide to *go naked* — operate without a firewall or virus scanner in order to maintain optimal speed — be sure to have a second computer at the ready.

Strangely enough, a phone is optional these days. You will rarely if ever need to place a trading-related call.

The department of redundancy department

When you're day trading, you are intentionally looking at volatile markets and fast-moving securities, because that's where you'll have the most opportunity to make money in a short time. You may very well be leveraged, either through the use of borrowed money or by trading securities with built-in leverage, such as futures. (We have a lot more to say about leverage in

Chapter 14.) If you're in a position that moves against you and you can't get out, you're sunk.

It's bad enough if you can't get out because the markets are melting down following some kind of global catastrophe. But suppose you can't get out because the batteries in your wireless mouse have died and you can't find new ones? What if you spill pop and short out your keyboard — or your entire PC? What if the developer building a McMansion next door accidentally knocks out your phone line and your DSL service? At a minimum, have a cellular phone charged and ready to go so that you can execute trades by phone or mobile app. All these little workaday calamities have happened to us — and trust us, they are downright annoying if you aren't trading. If you are, they can be ruinous. If you're serious about making money as a day trader, build in redundant systems as much as possible:

- Subscribe to two Internet service providers, one cable and one DSL. When one goes out, you can switch.
- Have two computers that are duplicates of each other, so that you can swap them out if one goes down.
- Keep extra supplies on hand: extra batteries, extra keyboard, and extra mouse. You want to be able to react quickly when things go wrong. These are all cheap to keep in inventory, too, because the computer makers give keyboards and mice away with every new PC.
- Consider investing in an uninterruptible power supply (UPS) backup for your PC, so that when the power goes down your computer will stay up. You don't need a backup generator, though — unless you think that you'd still want to trade after your town was devastated by an earthquake or a hurricane. (Of course, it's those crises that create opportunities!)
- Finally, back up your computer regularly. You can do it online through a service like Mozy (`www.mozy.com`), or through a backup drive connected to your PC. Most backup systems can be set up to work automatically, but don't schedule your backup to happen during trading hours or it will slow you down.

Taking a Trip to a Trading Arcade

Don't want to set up your own office? Not ready to commit to two Internet lines, three PCs, and four monitors? Worried you'll be bored and lonely working alone at home? Consider trying a *trading arcade*. These are offices where day traders rent desk space to trade. Some provide additional services along with the real estate, such as training, coaching, and even loans of trading capital. Some charge a flat weekly or monthly fee, some offer services on an a la carte basis, and others take a share of your trading profits.

Although trading arcades are less popular than they were a decade ago, they still exist in some major cities. To find them, do an Internet search on *trading arcade* or *trading room* and your town's name. You're more likely to find one if you live near a city with major exchanges that are phasing out floor trading — namely, Toronto or Montreal.

Before choosing an arcade, find out about its fees and services. Talk to other traders to see what they like and dislike about the operation. And keep in mind that the company may want to check *you* out.

capital. Some charge a flat weekly or monthly fee, some offer services on an a la carte basis, and others take a slice of your trading profits.

Although trading arcades are less popular than they were a decade ago, they still exist in some major cities. To find them, do an Internet search for *trading arcade* or *trading room* and your town's name. You're more likely to find one if you live in a big city with major exchanges that are phasing out floor trading — namely, Toronto or Montreal.

Before choosing an arcade, find out about its fees and services. Talk to other traders to see what they like and dislike about the operation. And keep in mind that the company may want to check you out.

Chapter 7

Research and Trading Services

In This Chapter

- Figuring out where to get a trading education
- Supplementing your trading with research
- Checking out vendors before you spend your money

Day trading is a big business with big profits, but those profits don't always accrue to the day trader. Instead, many a day trader has spent money on training services, software, newsletters, and coaching, only to find that in the real world the trader can't make enough money to make a living, let alone cover all these costs.

Why does that happen? It could very well be because the trader isn't cut out for day trading in the first place. Day trading isn't for everyone. In other cases, though, the trader failed to do good research before plunking down the cold cash for training in a system that just wasn't very good.

You've already plunked down some of your hard-earned money for *Day Trading For Canadians For Dummies*. Consider that an investment! In this chapter, we cover some of the different services that day traders might want to buy and give you advice on how to determine which ones are worthwhile and which are not.

The Trade of Trading

As much as we wish that *Day Trading For Canadians For Dummies* told you everything you need to know about trading, it's only a starting point. And let's hope that Wiley's marketing department doesn't see that, because if they do they'll be mad at us. The fact is that so many different assets exist, with so many different ways to trade them, no one resource can give you all you need. A stock trader following a news-based momentum strategy needs different services than a forex trader looking at interest rate discrepancies. That's why we don't try to teach you but rather point you to resources that can help you get started, and show you how to get the most value from the money you spend.

Day trading is a career. Every career takes time to master, and practitioners have to work to keep their skills up as the field changes. You'll find you'll need some training to get started and more training to be successful, whether you're trading futures, building bridges, or doing heart surgery.

Freebies from the exchanges

Before you spend more money, check out what several exchanges and the self-regulatory organizations offer for free to help you get started in trading. They have "webinars," online courses, and plenty of reading material. After all, the financial industry wants people to trade — that's how they make money — but they want them to be successful, because that keeps the market functioning. (Exchanges are businesses, like any other.) Going through such free material first can give you a great sense of how suitable you are for a given strategy and help you make better decisions about the other training you will need.

In this section we list a few resources that are particularly good for new day traders.

Exchanges can merge or update their Web sites, so by the time you get this book some of the links may not work. No matter what happens, though, they'll still be offering educational services so that the people participating in their markets can do so more effectively. You can find up-to-date links by doing simple Web searches using keywords such as *futures exchange* or *options exchange*.

Chicago Board Options Exchange Learning Center

`www.cboe.com/LearnCenter/default.aspx`

The Options Institute of the Chicago Board Options Exchange offers a series of online tutorials, classes, and seminars covering exchange-traded options in great depth. It also has a two-day seminar for experienced traders who want to come to Chicago. The site includes online toolboxes and calculators as well as a chance for traders to ask questions of options trading experts.

CME Group Education Center

`www.cmegroup.com/education`

Whether you're an individual who wants to learn about futures or an experienced floor trader who needs to make the transition to electronic trading, the CME Group has information for you. It has online training courses on trading in general and trading futures in particular, live online events in specific trading techniques, and papers that describe and analyze different trading strategies. The site even has links to trading simulators offered by different futures commission merchants (brokerage firms that specialize in futures), so you can apply what you learn without risking real money.

Institute for Financial Markets

www.theifm.org

The Institute for Financial Markets is a nonprofit organization that provides basic training programs for people working on the options and futures exchanges. Many of its courses are inappropriate for day traders, who aren't going to be licensed and who do not have mandatory continuing education requirements to maintain those licences. But some of them are appropriate, and low cost, as long as you can pay the airfare to Chicago or New York, where most of the classes are held. If you don't want to make the trip, you may be able to find a relevant webinar. Online training will cost you between $25 and $75 a course.

Montreal Exchange

www.m-x.ca

Traders who want to find out more about the options market should visit the Montreal Exchange's Web site and click on the education tab. You'll find webinars with titles such as "volatility trading" and "options trading using technical analysis," and new ones come out twice a month. Look for the options blog, which is updated fairly regularly, and several PDFs that provide information on different trading strategies.

NASDAQ

www.nasdaq.com/investing

Okay, let's be honest here: The stock markets want to promote investing more than trading, because they want companies to issue shares on their exchanges. The kind of high volatility that day traders love puts off some starchy corporate officers. Hence, much of the information on NASDAQ's site is about how to select stocks for the long term, though articles on options and forex trading are also included.

National Futures Association Investor Learning Center

www.nfa.futures.org/investor/investorLearningCenter.asp

The National Futures Association is the self-regulatory organization for the agricultural and financial futures exchanges. This site includes a lot of good information about trading futures as well as a tutorial on trading foreign exchange.

New York Stock Exchange

www.nyse.com/audience/individualinvestors.html

The New York Stock Exchange, like NASDAQ, wants to court investors rather than traders. Still, the exchange's site has information on trading stocks, bonds, and exchange-traded funds that can make you smarter on those topics without spending a dime.

TMX Money

www.tmxmoney.com

In 2008 the TMX Group, the company that owns the Toronto Stock Exchange and the Montreal Exchange, launched a comprehensive site that covers the Canadian and American markets and more. Learn about specific sectors — mining and energy for instance — or advance your knowledge of financial jargon by using the Stock Market Terms glossary. The site also features *The Globe and Mail*'s blogs, and a useful stock screener.

Hitting the road for conferences

Although day trading is a deskbound pursuit, you might want to get out to learn more about trading and research different companies with products for day traders. Many of the exchanges and larger day trading brokerage firms have their own seminars and conferences, but a few are open to the public.

Brokerage firms offering many seminars and training programs may have higher commissions than firms offering less service, but it may be worth it, especially as you get started. You can read more about some brokerage firms that work with day traders in Chapter 6.

The Money Show

www.moneyshow.com

The Money Show is a series of investment conferences held in different major cities around the world, including Toronto and Vancouver. Registration is free, which means that when you show up people will be trying to sell you stuff. This could be distracting to an established trader but helpful for a new trader looking to find out more about all the different software and services out there. The conferences also have high-profile speakers, so you can learn from Wall Street and Bay Street celebrities. MoneyShow.com includes articles, podcasts, and free online courses to help you learn more about trading.

TradeTech Canada

www.wbresearch.com/tradetechcanada

Find out how the big companies trade at this annual Canadian equity trading conference. Not everything will apply to day traders, but you can find some useful seminars and speakers. The attendee list includes traders from large financial institutions, and topics include regulation and trading opportunities in emerging markets.

Trading Forum

www.traderslibrary.com/tlforum/registration.asp

The Trading Forum is sponsored by Traders' Library, which sells research materials and investing books. The conference isn't cheap — and you'll have to pay your travel expenses to get to the U.S. — but it covers specific trading strategies and information. It offers a good introduction to trading, and it's all the more fun to learn when you're in Vegas or Chicago, the cities where the conference is usually held.

Taking training classes

Although it's not necessary, many day traders learn the game by enrolling in a training program. No program can guarantee success, nor is any one program right for every trader. We list a few bigger and better-known programs here, but check them out to make sure they're right for you — just as you should check out programs that aren't listed here.

The larger brokerage and research firms offer their own training courses, often at little or no cost. Consider those as a first option, but keep in mind that their introductory sessions might be sales pitches for more products and services.

Plenty of great and legitimate training firms are out there — along with a lot of scammers. Run from anyone who guarantees your success. We include some information about due diligence at the end of this chapter.

Day Trader Canada

www.daytradercanada.com

Based in Montreal, this company offers courses and education services to Quebecers. Find out how to trade stocks and options and learn (in French) about direct access platforms. If you speak French you can also get live trading advice.

Krifx Canada Ltd.

www.krifx.com

This Toronto-based company specializes in forex, futures, and commodity education for day traders, but everyone can learn something from its numerous courses. People learn, in-person, about fundamental analysis, reading charts, reward–risk ratios, and more.

Online Trading Academy

www.tradingacademy.com

This U.S.-based company has offices in Toronto and Vancouver to help Canadians learn how to trade. Topics include how to use level II quotes and direct access trading platforms, the ins and outs of fundamental and technical analysis, and how to take your emotions out of trading. You'll find courses for stock, forex, options, and futures traders — and, if you're keen to learn about something other than day trading, check out their real estate investor program.

Pristine

www.pristine.com

Pristine has a range of books and DVDs, online and in-person classes, and coaching services covering trading skills that work in most markets. Its courses operate at different levels, with some requiring extensive trading experience using specific software packages.

Trading Advantage

www.tradingadvantage.com

One thing we like about this company's Web site is that you're expected to read a disclaimer about the risks of trading before you get to the good stuff. Many of the company's programs are designed for floor traders at the exchanges who need to learn to trade futures electronically in order to stay competitive. The course includes books and DVDs.

The University of Trading

www.universityoftrading.com

If you feel like making a trip south of the border, the University of Trading offers courses in options, equities, foreign exchange, and financial and agricultural commodities at its offices in Chicago. Students have the opportunity to trade alongside experienced instructors as well as hear lectures on different aspects of the markets. The company trains professional traders, some of whom trade for themselves and some of whom take jobs with others.

Learning to play at a trading arcade

Some larger cities still have day trading arcades, also called proprietary trading firms, which are offices where traders can rent desk space and get all the quotes and analytics they need to trade. Traders pay monthly rent and may also share some of their profits with the arcade, especially if it provides any training and coaching services.

Trading arcades were the only way to day trade before the widespread availability of high-speed Internet access. Although there aren't nearly as many as there used to be, some still exist and will work with people new to trading.

The best way to find Canadian trading arcades is through an Internet search. Type "proprietary trading firm Canada" into your search engine and several relevant sites pop up.

Getting the Research You Need

Day traders need a trading system, and they often rely on subscription research services. That's fine, as long as those systems are adding value over and above their cost. Unfortunately, advising day traders is big business, and there may be more money in that than in day trading. Before you call the 800 number given in the infomercial, here's some advice to help you evaluate the service.

You'll find three main types of outside services, where

- Price data are detailed, real-time price quotes from different markets;
- Chart services help traders identify profitable trends; or
- Strategic research helps people develop a system for trading or follow a system designed by someone else.

You may need all three or none, depending on your knowledge of the financial markets and your trading style.

Many day traders find themselves subscribing to price quote and analytical services. In the following section we provide a listing of a handful of popular ones. It's not a definitive list, and this is not an endorsement. Rather, it's a guide to get you thinking about what you might need and where you might go to get it.

If you know you'll need outside pricing and data services, consider that when you are selecting a brokerage firm. Different firms have different software platforms, and some can handle outside data feeds better than others.

(Price) quote me on that

In Chapter 6, we list some of the many brokerage firms that offer day trading services. They all have services that tell you what the prices are for any security at any time, but this doesn't mean they have all the prices you need for your strategy. For example, if you're day trading common stocks, you may need a system that can signal certain price patterns in any of the thousands of stocks trading at any given day. If you're trading options based on the value of underlying stock, you may need that data as well. If you're day trading international securities, you may need real-time data, and your broker might only offer data with a ten-minute delay in some markets.

Besides needing all the prices and related volume and market-maker data, some strategies involve fast trading. *Scalping,* for example, involves making a large number of quick transactions in search of small price movements. Every second counts, and not all brokers can deliver prices fast enough to make scalping profitable. One solution is to get prices from a separate source offering faster delivery. Other trading strategies don't require real-time prices on huge numbers of securities, but they may involve a detailed analysis of end-of-day prices. To do that, you may need more information than your broker can give you.

The quote service can provide the data in real time only if you have enough bandwidth to receive it. Make sure you have the fastest Internet connection available in your area, and consider having a second way to hook up to the Internet if your primary service goes down.

CQG

www.cqg.com

CQG pulls data from more than 90 different exchanges, making it popular with people who are trading international securities. Traders can buy historical data for backtesting (see Chapter 11 for more), and they can add charting and order routing capabilities to their CQG package. Data can be linked to Microsoft Excel spreadsheets for people who want to do even more number crunching on their own.

eSignal

www.esignal.com

eSignal offers detailed prices, news, and trading alerts in most financial markets, including Canada. Its charting features are more advanced than those offered by most brokerage firms. Especially useful for traders who are looking at several different stocks, eSignal can help identify trading opportunities using a preferred strategy and scan the market for other stocks that meet specified investment criteria. The company also offers backtesting and real-time strategy testing, end-of-day analysis for traders who don't need real-time data, as well as add-on signals that support different proprietary trading strategies.

Charting your strategy

Almost all day trading strategies rely on technical analysis, which is the process of identifying buy and sell opportunities based on the supply and demand for a security. Technical analysts look at charts of price and volume changes to look for changes in the trend. (We discuss this in more detail in Chapter 12.) Some technical analysis strategies are complicated and require sophisticated charting. That's why many day traders use software that can turn price data into the information they need to make decisions.

Many users of these services get tripped up by the symbols and data displays. Take the time to learn as much as you can about how they work before you're trading in real time with real money; most of these providers offer seminars or online tutorials that will help. Yeah, many of the features are obvious, but you want to avoid costly mistakes.

MarketDelta

www.marketdelta.com

MarketDelta's software provides detailed charting services that match different strategies over several time periods, in colours that make the data stand out. The company mostly deals with professionals, but it has some products suitable for some day traders.

MetaStock

www.equis.com

MetaStock has several charting and analytical packages, including one for foreign exchange trading, another for people who day trade in stocks, and a third for stock investors who are holding for longer than a single day. Traders following specific strategies recommended by different market analysts can purchase add-ons that give them the tools needed to trade effectively.

NinjaTrader

www.ninjatrader.com

NinjaTrader is a trading platform for active traders. It can be used instead of a brokerage firm's trading software, or it can be used on its own. The service is best known for its charting capabilities in the foreign exchange and futures markets, but it can also handle market scanning, automated trade execution and backtesting, and simulation trading. Krifx Canada, a training centre we mention earlier in this chapter, gives its clients free use of the NinjaTrader platform.

OmniTrader

www.omnitrader.ca

OmniTrader is designed to automate technical analysis (read all about that in Chapter 12), especially for stock traders. The system also includes money management tools (we discuss money management in Chapter 9) as well as simulated trading and backtesting to help you find new strategies.

RealTick

www.realtick.com

RealTick combines data with charting services and market signals for stocks, options, futures, and foreign exchange, making it useful for traders who are working in several markets. The service includes direct access trading through Montreal's JitneyTrade brokerage firm.

Trade-Ideas

http://trade-ideas.com

Trade-Ideas is designed for stock traders. The software scans the incoming price data feed to find trading opportunities based on prespecified indicators, and it can also show how much the market is deviating from a trader's style. For traders watching hundreds or thousands of stocks, this can be a useful addendum to a brokerage firm's offerings. Its partners include Interactive Brokers and Day Trader Canada.

Newsletters, gurus, and strategic advice

Trading relies on information so that everyone in the market can evaluate what the right price for a security should be. Most of this information can be found from an analysis of the news and the price data, both of which are readily available from brokerage firms and quote services. But many traders follow explicit philosophies or rely on the insight of certain analysts. Here's a list of some of the bigger ones that you will come across, in case you want to find out more. We discuss many of the specific theories in more detail in Chapter 12.

Many of these market gurus have good ideas, but don't follow any of them blindly. Their techniques don't work in all markets at all times. Besides, anyone with a truly foolproof plan isn't going to give it away. These newsletters are just part of the ongoing conversation in the markets that help traders make decisions.

Elliott Wave

www.elliottwave.com

The *Elliott Wave* is a theory that markets move in grand cycles over a century or more. Within that, there are subcycles lasting years, months, weeks, days, minutes, and seconds. Given all the layers and analysis required, those who follow the theory usually subscribe to research services to help them. This site is maintained by Robert Prechter, who is one of the leading scholars of the theory.

School of Gann

www.schoolofgann.com

The Gann method of technical analysis looks at the slopes of the charts to predict changes. It's a complicated system, so traders who follow it usually rely on newsletters and research services to help them. School of Gann is one that specializes in this system.

Trending 123

www.trending123.com

Trending 123 publishes newsletters on technical analysis in the Canadian, U.S., and English stock markets and in foreign exchange. It also offers software and e-mail alerts that point out opportunities in the markets based on their analytical system. The company regularly covers psychological aspects of trading to support its customers.

Andrew Pyle

www.andrewpyle.com

Andrew Pyle is a ScotiaMcleod wealth adviser — not a guy you'd typically turn to for day trading advice. But some traders swear by his weekly newsletter. It won't give you strategic tips, but his two-page document presents an excellent overview of the economy and zeros in on specific securities such as bonds, commodities, and currencies.

The power of the printed word

Several books cover specific aspects of trading psychology, trading strategy, and research systems in much more detail than we can in the space that the good folks at Wiley have given us. If you turn to the appendix, you'll see a list of other resources that can help you in your research.

Day trading was a hot topic in the late 1990s, and you may find that a lot of the books and articles on the subject date from that era. Some are lurking in your public library; others are still available for sale or can be found on the Internet. Markets change. Don't rely on a system popularized a decade ago unless you've tested it and ensured that it still works.

Doing Your Due Diligence

Trading software, training, and research can get expensive, and some of it is an outright scam. Most of it is legitimate, but that doesn't mean it's right for you. Before you spend your money, do your research. Start with the free programs offered by the exchanges (listed in the first section of this chapter) so that you have enough knowledge to understand what a trading services purveyor is trying to do. Then, do some research and ask some questions. To find out where to go and what to ask, read on.

Where to start your research

You have a tonne of tools available to you to do your due diligence. A good first stop is the Internet. Go to your favourite search engine and enter the name of the program you're looking at plus the word *scam* or *rip-off* — and then see what you find. If nothing of much interest turns up, proceed to the regulatory agencies listed here.

It's possible that you'll learn very little about any given research firm from an Internet search or checks with the different regulatory organizations. That doesn't mean the firm in question isn't for real, just that it hasn't caused any concerns so far.

Investment Industry Regulatory Organization of Canada

www.iiroc.ca

IIROC regulates all of Canada's online brokerage firms and investment dealers. On its Web site you'll find disciplinary notices. Although many are centred around advisers or firms that aren't relevant to day traders, it's possible the broker you want to work with has gotten into some legal trouble. Check out the media releases section to get all the details.

Ontario Securities Commission

www.osc.gov.on.ca/en/Investors_check-registration_index.htm

Canada has different regulators for every province, but if a firm wants clients it'll have to be open for business in Ontario. That means it has to register with the OSC. This link will take you to a handy page that allows you to check whether a firm is registered. Be mindful of what you type in, though — for example thinkorswim doesn't come up, but its owner, TD Waterhouse, does.

Securities and Exchange Commission

www.sec.gov/investor.shtml

The Securities and Exchange Commission is, of course, U.S.-focused, but it has a tonne of great information about every aspect of stock and bond investing, with a special emphasis on problems and scams to avoid. Some of the site won't be especially useful, but it could give you ideas on what to look for when it comes to Canadian firms.

Questions to ask

After you do your basic background checks, it's time to ask some questions about the service providers you're considering. This section contains a list of questions to get you started.

Do not trust any promises of performance. Day trading is a difficult business. Many people wash out because it doesn't suit their personality. Others fail because they don't have enough startup capital, they don't take the time to figure out how to do it, or they simply have a run of bad luck. No one can promise that you will succeed.

- Can I get a free trial to check the service out?
- What training and support do you offer?
- How long will it take me to learn the system? Will I need to pay for additional training and coaching, or is your built-in support adequate?
- Who will be teaching me or advising me, and what is this person's background?
- How long have you been in business? Why was the company formed?

- What additional features are available at additional costs? How many customers subscribe to only the basic system?
- Will this support my trading style and work with the assets I prefer to trade?
- Do you screen traders for your program? Do you ask traders to leave? What are the characteristics of those who do well? Of those who don't do well?
- Can I talk to other customers?
- Is your software compatible with my broker? With other services I'm using? With my computer's operating system? With my Internet bandwidth?
- Are your performance numbers actual, or are they hypothetical and based on backtesting? How were the numbers calculated? (We talk more about performance calculation in Chapter 11.)

Hypothetical performance is based on an analysis of what would have happened had the system been in place in the past, or of what might happen if market conditions cooperate. It can be subject to data mining, which means that the system was developed to generate good performance in backtesting, not because it has any logical or theoretical basis.

Chapter 8

Managing the Stress of the Markets

In This Chapter

- Reading cautionary tales of traders gone wrong
- Finding out how to control your emotions
- Checking out the paramount trading plan
- Avoiding the dangers that lurk on the Internet

Day trading can be a ruthless business. Some days, you don't find any trades worth making. Other days, you find trades, but they don't work out the way you want them to. And some days, too many good trades come along, more than you can possibly make, and so you watch profitable opportunities slip away. When you're working with real money, it can be too much to take.

In a money management or brokerage firm, traders have tremendous camaraderie. They are working for the same employer and need to stick together to blow off the stress. What do you do at home, though? How do *you* keep from panicking, getting depressed, or otherwise letting this business hurt your profits and hurt you?

If you're going to day trade, you need to understand the very real physical and psychological stresses that the market pushes on its participants. In this chapter, we offer some information and advice that can help you avoid a crisis.

First, the Cautionary Tales

Trader lore is loaded with stories of people who flamed out in spectacular and destructive ways. People who work on trading desks or on trading floors tell tales of colleagues who went down hard, walked off the desk, broke down in the pit, or died at the trading post. They can rattle off lists of colleagues who are alcoholics, who suffered bitter divorces, who committed suicide.

Even though day traders usually work by themselves, stories of their self-destructive behaviour abound.

Sure, many day traders lead pleasant lives and suffer no more problems than any other person. That's because they have perspective, balance, and the right personality for the business. Know what can go wrong, because it can help you keep in the right.

Jesse Livermore

Jesse Livermore is sometimes considered to be the father of day trading. He's the subject of the book *Reminiscences of a Stock Operator* by Edwin LeFevre, a classic book about trading (see the Appendix for more information). Livermore was born in 1877 and started trading stocks when he was in his teens. He claimed to have made $1,000 when he was 15, which may not seem like much, except that he was very young and price levels were a little different in 1892. (That $1,000 would be worth over $20,000 in today's dollars.) He made huge fortunes betting against the market in 1907 and again in 1929, and he managed to lose it all both times. By 1934 he was broke and depressed. He attempted suicide in 1935 and succeeded in 1940.

Mark Barton

Mark Barton lost $105,000 day trading and he snapped. On July 27, 1999, he bludgeoned his wife and two children to death. Then he went to the downtown Atlanta offices of Momentum Securities, a brokerage firm that specialized in working with day traders. He had an appointment to deliver $50,000 so that he could cover his losses and start trading again. Instead, he took out a gun, opened fire, and killed four people. He then went to the offices of All-Tech Investment Group, another day trading firm where he had an account, and killed another five people. Barton killed himself before he was arrested. This case is one of the worst workplace massacres in the United States, and it did as much as the 2000 meltdown in NASDAQ technology stocks to reduce the enthusiasm for day trading.

Anecdotal suicides, divorces, alcoholism

Because not that many people day trade consistently, not a lot of good demographic studies have been conducted on just how many day traders end up abusing drugs and alcohol, getting divorced or becoming estranged from friends, and turning to suicide. The anecdotal evidence is pretty strong, though. People in the securities business face high pressure and real dollar losses every day they go to work. Their performance is constantly judged by the market, and it doesn't grade on a curve. If you spend even a few minutes talking to people in the business, you hear horror stories. Ann personally knows a trader who set fire to his house, killing his 90-year-old mother in the process, to get the insurance proceeds to cover his financial shortfalls. (He's currently doing a 190-year sentence.)

Don't be the person who finally gives researchers enough critical mass to report on day trader self-destruction. Stress is a real part of day trading, and not all day traders handle it well. If you know what you're up against and prepare for it, you'll be better off than many.

Controlling Your Emotions

The key to successful day trading is controlling your emotions. After all, the stock doesn't know that you own it, as equity traders like to say, so it isn't going to perform well just because you want it to. This can be infuriating, especially when you're going through a draw-down of your capital. Those losses look mighty personal.

Traditional financial theory is based on the idea that traders are rational. In practice, however, most of them are not. In fact, traders and investors are often irrational in completely predictable ways, which has given birth to a new area of study called *behavioural finance*. It's a hot area generating Nobel Prize winners, and it may eventually help people incorporate measures of investor behaviour into buy and sell decisions.

You have to figure out a way to manage your reactions to the market, or you shouldn't be a day trader. Day traders talk about their enemies being fear and greed. If you panic, you'll no longer be trading to win, but trading not to lose. The distinction is important: If your goal is not to lose, you won't take appropriate risk, and you won't be able to respond quickly to what the market is telling you.

This is all much easier said than done. Human beings are emotional creatures, constantly reacting (and sometimes overreacting) to everything that is happening in their lives. Knowing the emotions that affect trading and having some ways to manage them can greatly improve your overall performance.

The big five emotions

When it comes to trading, five big emotions can take over and mess up your strategy and your returns. At this point in your life, you may already know whether you have tendencies toward some of them. If so, trading can exacerbate them. If you've never experienced them, you might for the first time.

Here's a list and some descriptions so that you know what you're up against and can plan accordingly. We include some tips that can help, but if you are really in the throes of an emotional crisis that affects your trading, you should seek out professional help.

Anxiety

Anxiety is the anticipation of things going wrong, and it often includes a physical response: perspiration, clenched jaw, tense muscles, heart palpitations. Anxious people worry, agonize, overanalyze, and generally stress out. And then they avoid whatever it is that makes them upset. That means that a trader might not make an obvious trade, but instead hesitate and miss a market move. He might hold on to a losing position too long because he's worried about the effect that selling it will have on his portfolio. He becomes too nervous to trade according to his plan, and his performance suffers.

One way to fight trading anxiety is to concentrate on following the trading plan, not on making a set amount of money. That way, following the plan becomes more automatic, and you spend less time worrying about what can go wrong.

Boredom

Brace yourself for an ugly truth about day trading: It can be really dull. In an eight-hour trading session, you might spend seven and a half hours waiting for the right opening. A flurry of trades, and it's all over. To keep yourself entertained, you might start making bad trades, spending too much time in chat rooms, or letting your mind wander away from the task at hand. None of those things is conducive to profitable trading.

If you're really bored and tempted to do something stupid, close out your positions and take a break. Going for a walk or quitting early can clear your head and help you focus when you get back. Remember, day traders work for themselves, and one of the benefits of that is no boss to find out you knocked off early. Take advantage of that!

Depression

Depression is a severe downturn in your mood, especially one that causes you to feel inadequate and lose interest in things you used to like. Although everyone is susceptible to depression, the ups and downs of the market can make traders particularly vulnerable. At best, depression can make it hard for a trader to face a day with the market. At worst, it can lead to alcoholism, alienation, and even suicide.

If you think you might be depressed, check out the handy quiz at `www.depressionhurts.ca/en/symptomchecklist.aspx`. Or better yet, go to your doctor.

Fear

Fear is one of the worst emotional enemies of the day trader. Instead of trying to make money, the fearful trader is trying hard not to lose it. She is so afraid of failing that she limits herself, doesn't take appropriate risk, and questions her trading system so much that she no longer follows it, no matter how well it worked for her in the past.

By the way, it isn't just failure that traders fear. Many fear success, sometimes for deep-seated psychological reasons that we are in no position to address. A trader who fears success may think that if she succeeds, her friends will treat her differently, her relatives will try to take her money, and that she will become someone she doesn't want to be.

One way to limit fear is to have a plan for the trading business. Before you start trading, take some time — maybe half a day — to sit down and think about what you want, what will happen to you if you get it, and what will happen to you if you don't. For example, if you lose your trading capital, then you'll have to live on your walk-away fund (see later in this chapter) until you find another job. If you make a lot of money, then you can pay off your mortgage and your friends will be none the wiser.

Greed

Greed seems like a silly thing to have on this list. After all, isn't the whole purpose of day trading to make money? This isn't charity, this is capitalism at its purest. Ah, but there's a popular saying in the finance world: "Pigs get fat, but hogs get slaughtered."

Traders who get greedy start to do stupid things. They don't think through what they are doing and stop following their trading plans. They hold positions too long in the hope of eking out a return and sometimes they make rash trades that look an awful lot like gambling. The greedy trader loses all discipline and eventually loses quite a bit of money.

If your goal is simply to make more and more money, you might have a problem with greed. Sure, everyone wants to make more, but give some thought to the difference between your *need-to-make number* (enough to cover your costs and your basic living expenses) and your *want-to-make number* (enough to cover costs, basic expenses, and extras that are important to you). If you know what those numbers are, you're well on your way to preventing the problem.

Limit orders, which automatically close out positions when they hit set prices, are one way to force discipline in the face of greed. You can read more about limit orders in Chapter 2.

Having an outlet

Successful day traders have a life outside of the markets. They close out their positions, shut off their monitors, and go do something else with the rest of the day. That's the whole idea behind day trading.

The problem is that a market is always open somewhere. Traders can work overnight, after hours, and even on the weekends and sometimes move the action to exchanges in other parts of the world. Without something to mark a beginning and an end to your trading day, and without other things happening in your life, the market can consume you in a way that's simply not healthy.

So as you plan your life as a day trader, think about what else you're going to do with your days. Exercise, meditation, socializing, and having outside interests are key to maintaining balance and staying focused on the market when you have to be.

Exercise

Exercise keeps your body in fighting shape so that you can stand up to market stress and react to trends when you need to. Many times when you're trading, you have huge rushes of adrenalin that you can't do much about. You have to stay in front of your screen until the trade is over, no matter how much you want to run away screaming. But after the trading day, you can hit the track or pool or hockey rink and burn off some of that adrenalin. Figuring out a regular exercise routine can pay off for your trading.

If you aren't an exerciser now, call your local YMCA. They have introductory programs that can teach you how to use the equipment and help you design a workout that suits your current fitness levels and goals.

Meditation

You may have closed out your positions and shut down your monitors, but the day's trading may keep playing itself out over and over in your head. When you're trading, you may get upset and start thinking about everything else that has ever gone wrong in your life, instead of staying focused on the task at hand. Trading, therefore, requires mental discipline. Good traders can keep their minds clear of everything but their trading system, at least when the markets are at their hairiest.

One way to develop that discipline is to take up meditation. Yeah, it may seem goofy, being a big tough trader type doing something woo-woo like meditation, but if you have trouble keeping your focus, you really might want to take it up. An almost infinite number of meditation styles exist, many of which are associated with different religious traditions, so you can surely find something that works.

Check out the instructions for the practice at www.shambhala.org/meditationinstruction.html as a way to get started.

Friends and family

Day trading is a lonely activity. You're working by yourself all day. It's just you, your room, and your screen. It's really isolating, and if you don't get other human contact, you'll personalize the market so that you don't feel so lonely. That's bad, because the market isn't a person; it's an agglomeration of all the financial activity taking place, and it has no interest in you whatsoever.

No matter what you do in life, you want to have the support of the people you know and love. And you need to make time for them, too. Start and end your trading day at regular times, and be sure to make plans to see people who are important to you. Going to your kid's ball game, having dinner with your spouse, and seeing your buddies for a few beers on a regular basis can go a long way to keeping your life in balance — and that will keep your trading in balance.

If you like pets, consider getting one to keep you company during the day. There's nothing like a dog that needs a walk to force you to close up shop for the night.

Hobbies and other interests

A lot of people get into day trading because they have long had a fascination with the market. Trading goes from being a hobby to being a living. In many ways, that's perfect. It's so much easier to go to work if you have a job that you love.

But if the market is your only interest, then you're going to be too susceptible to its gyrations and you're going to have trouble sticking to your trading discipline. Plus, whatever upsets you during the trading day is more likely to carry over. So, find a new hobby if you don't have one. Maybe it's a TV show, a sport, or knitting, but whatever it is, you need to have something going on outside of your trading.

Trading is just one part of your life.

Support systems

Exercise and friends and family and hobbies and the like are all well and good, but they don't directly address the mindset of trading. Ah, but there's a veritable industry of support for traders, and it's easy to tap into. Many day traders find that reading books, hiring a coach, or finding other day traders helps them get through the day.

Books

A library-full of books have been written on the psychology of trading itself. In addition, many traders rely on other self-help and history books for inspiration and ideas. (Possibly every trader we've ever known owns a copy of Sun Tzu's *The Art of War,* which is about military strategies and tactics. They find that it helps them prepare their minds to face the market, or at least gives them something interesting to talk about.) We list several books in the Appendix that might help you organize your mind and keep your enthusiasm for the market.

Counselling and coaching

Because it takes a lot of mental toughness to handle big losses — and big gains — many traders find professional support. They use counsellors, psychologists, or life coaches to help them deal with the challenges of the market and understand their reactions to it. You can ask other traders or your doctor for a referral, or check the online directory at *Psychology Today*'s Web site, `http://therapists.psychologytoday.com` (you'll find many Canadian therapists there), or the International Coach Federation, `www.coachfederation.org`. When interviewing coaches or counsellors, ask whether they have experience with traders or others who work in finance.

Many day trading training and brokerage firms also offer coaching services that specialize in helping people learn and follow day trading strategies. Some day traders find these people to be invaluable, whereas others find they are just glorified salespeople.

Some day trading coaches may be more interested in selling you specific trading strategies rather than helping you manage your own system. Check references and find out what other forms of compensation the coach receives before you sign up.

Finding other traders

To offset the loneliness of trading alone, many day traders choose to work out of trading rooms operated by brokerage firms (see Chapter 6 for more on this) or join organizations where they will meet other traders. These may be formal or informal groups (we list a few in the Appendix) where traders can socialize, learn new things, or just commiserate.

Many day traders get together through social networks, which we discuss in more detail later in this chapter. These groups are less formal, more anonymous, and sometimes more destructive than supportive.

Most day traders lose money and give up their first year. You may find that spending too much time with other traders is more depressing than supportive.

Your walk-away money

A lot of traders have a secret that gets them through the worst of the markets. It's something called *walk-away money,* although traders sometimes use more colourful language to describe it. It's enough money that they can walk away from trading and do something else.

And just exactly how much is it? Well, it varies from person to person, but having enough money to pay three months' worth of expenses on hand and in cash is a good place to start. If you know that you can pay the mortgage and buy the groceries even if you don't make money trading today, you'll be better able to avoid desperate trading. You won't have to be greedy, and you won't have to live in fear.

The more money in your walk-away fund, the better. Then you have more time to investigate alternative careers should day trading prove not to be your thing, and you can relax more when you face the market every day.

Most day traders quit after a year or so. There's nothing wrong with deciding to move on and try something else. If you have some money saved, then you're in a better position to control when you stop trading and what you do next.

If all your trading capital is gone, you might be tempted to tap your walk-away fund to stay in the game. *Don't.* That's the exactly the time when you should use your walk-away money to, yes, *walk away,* if only for a short time to clear your head and rethink your strategies. Otherwise, your trading losses may become financial ruin.

Importance of a Trading Plan

You may have noticed that the idea of *trading plans* pops up several times in this book, such as in Chapters 2, 8, 12, and 13. That's because trading plans are so important to maintaining the discipline that leads to trading success. You have to know what you're doing, and how to recognize entry and exit points, and then go and do it.

In this section, we cover how you can use a trading plan to manage stress and give you a few tips for sticking to your trading plan even as the markets sometimes move against you.

Problems following direction

Was that written on all your report cards? We hope not. A good, tested trading plan sets out market patterns that work often enough that you can make good trading profits. But some people have trouble following their plan, and that leads to stressful mistakes.

Prevent choking!

In sports lingo, an athlete who *chokes* starts playing so carefully that he or she looks like a beginner. This is often caused by over-thinking — by being so afraid of failure that the mind slows and breaks down the play step by step. It's not pretty to watch a contender choke during a championship game. The fans want to see a good match.

Anyone in a high-performance situation can choke. When a trader chokes, he seems to be following the plan, but it's no longer automatic. Trading becomes so slow and deliberative that obvious trades get missed.

The more you trust your plan, the less likely you are to choke. Has it been tested? Are there parts that you can automate? In Chapter 11 we offer some ideas on how to measure a trading plan's performance before you start to trade with the plan.

Reducing panic

Panic occurs when you just stop thinking. Your most basic survival instincts take over, even when they are totally uncalled for. You're losing money? You start to trade more and more, off-plan, in a desperate gamble to win it back. You're making money? You close out all your trades right now so that you can't possibly lose, even if your plan tells you to hold your positions. When you panic, you can't think straight, and you can't follow your plan.

One problem is that when your positions are down, and you seem to be losing money, you really should be buying and sticking it out so that you can make money later. That's tough to do and requires a lot of discipline. With experience traders learn to avoid panic.

You're probably going to have more than a few losing trades when you get started. In your trading diary (see Chapter 11), keep notes about how it makes you feel to lose money. Can you handle it emotionally? If losing upsets you too much, you might not be cut out for day trading. You can't trade with a clear head when you're bogged down with negative thoughts.

Confidence versus ego

Day trading requires a lot of confidence, because you *are* going to lose money and you *are* going to get beaten up some days. You have to not only remain confident in the face of adversity, but also be careful you don't cross from confidence into an inflated ego. The more your trading success and failure become part of your personal identity, the more trouble you are going to have.

What's the difference between confidence and ego? It's "I'm smart enough to figure out what the market is telling me" vs. "I'm smarter than the market." The difference is crucial to your success.

Revising and troubleshooting your trading plan

Strong discipline is key to success in trading, but only if you're disciplined in following the right system. If your trading method is flawed, then sticking to it is going to hurt you. If something isn't working, don't get mad at the system; take some responsibility and make some changes.

How do you figure out whether your trading system is right and what changes to make? Go through your trading diary (see Chapter 11 for how to set one up) and ask yourself some questions:

- Why did you choose this system? What is the market telling you about it? Is it telling you that the system works if you follow it, or is it telling you that something is wrong with the underlying assumptions?

  What works for someone else might not work for you. There's no flaw in admitting that you made a mistake and that you need to make a change.
- Were your mistakes because you followed the plan, or because you didn't?
- What part of the system is causing the trouble? Are you having trouble identifying entry points or exit points? Or are you stuck when it comes time to enter the trade, causing you to miss a point? Or is it that the trades your system identifies never seem to work out?

  When you know where the problem is, you can change it.
- Can you improve your trade efficiency? Is there a way to reduce the number of mistakes? Would automating some or all of your trading help?

One way to get your confidence back while still staying in the market is to trade in very small amounts so that your profits and losses don't really matter. Trade 100 shares, not 1,000 shares. You give up the upside for a time, but you can also get out of the cycle of greed and fear that has destroyed many a trader.

The Follies of Chat Rooms and Social Networks

Spend any time on the Internet researching day trading and you'll come across chat rooms, message boards, and social networking groups that some traders use to exchange information. Or at least you'll come across the chat rooms and message boards that purport to be used by traders to exchange information.

Chat rooms were quite the thing during the first big wave of day trading in the late 1990s. They don't have the influence they once did, but some day traders still rely on them. Others join day trading groups on Facebook or follow day traders on Twitter. Some social network users and groups are excellent for helping people learn to trade and offer good perspectives on market action, but others are a distraction at best. At worst a user will post what you think is an interesting URL, but is really a link to a nasty virus that could destroy your computer. In this part, we cover some of the benefits and risks of online groups so you know what you are getting into before you make that first post.

Support group or groupthink?

Many day traders turn to chat rooms or social networks for the camaraderie and support they offer. It seems so great to find other people who are going through the same things that you are! They understand what's happening!

Or do they? We could make a very strong argument that traders who really know what they are doing don't want anyone else to know who they are or what their plan is. Several successful day traders that we talked to while researching this book refused to have their names in it, because they are happier staying off the radar. Meanwhile, even those day traders who make money have trouble making enough money to stick to the business for a long time.

To compound the problem, the people in a Facebook group might get so agreeable that they start reinforcing bad advice. Instead of getting support to help you through a rough time, you get dragged down.

In general, a message board that charges a subscription fee is likely to be of better quality than one that's free, just because the fee wards off the people who aren't serious. You don't have to pay to join a Facebook group, but it's a good idea to see what's being said and who is saying it before implementing someone's advice. We've listed a few good message boards and social networking groups in the Appendix. Whether membership is free or paid, spend some time lurking — watching the comments without making any yourself. Proprietors of good message boards usually offer temporary access to prospective subscribers to help them evaluate the service. Check to see how people treat each other, what experiences they have, and how their trading systems match yours. And limit your time and watch your reactions to people's postings.

Getting angry at nothing

From the very early days of newsgroups and Internet Relay Chat, people exchanging ideas on the Internet have managed to misunderstand each other and blow small things out of proportion. That's all well and good if you're talking about the latest NHL season, but it's not so good if you're day trading. The market is a tough-enough evaluator of your performance. You don't need to waste time, energy, and confidence on someone who, intentionally or not, makes a nasty comment on a message board.

At a minimum, try to limit your social networking activities to market hours. And if you're one of those people who are quick to anger (hey, we won't tell), it may be best to avoid online discussions with other day traders all together.

Sabotage

Now, consider one other nasty truth about day trader chat rooms or online groups: Sometimes the people posting are trying to manipulate the market and sabotage other traders. They plant false and misleading information, seek to undermine others' confidence, and otherwise try to seek an edge by bringing others down. In other words, there may not be much information value at all, and the value of camaraderie may be quite low, too.

The Internet is a wonderful thing, and it makes it possible for people to trade sophisticated financial instruments in real time from the comfort of home. But it has its limitations, and online interaction with other traders can actually add to the stress of day trading. Tread carefully.

Chapter 9

Managing Your Money and Positions

In This Chapter

- Calculating expected return
- Knowing your probability of ruin
- Understanding that one trade size doesn't fit all
- Mulling over the many methods of money management
- Figuring out how money management affects returns
- Deciding what to do with your profits

Much of this book is designed to give you ideas about whether to day trade at all, what you want to trade, and how you want to trade it. That leaves one remaining issue: how much of your money to put on the line each time you trade. Risk too much, and you can be put out of business when you lose your capital. Risk too little, and you can be put of out business because you can't make enough money to cover your costs and time.

Over time, many academic theorists and experienced traders have developed different systems of money management designed to help traders, investors, and even gamblers manage their money in order to maximize return while protecting capital. In this chapter, we explain how some of the better-known systems work so that you can figure out how to best apply them to your own trading.

Some of the material in this chapter is related to *leverage,* which is borrowing money to trade. Leverage can dramatically increase the money that you have available to trade as well as the risk and return profile of the trades that you make, so it affects how you manage your money. Flip to Chapter 14 for more information on leverage and why you might want to use it.

What's Your Expected Return?

Before you can figure out how to manage your money, you need to figure out how much money you can expect to make. This is your *expected return,* although some traders prefer the word *expectancy.* You start by laying out your trading system and testing it (described in Chapter 11). You're looking for four numbers:

- How many of your trades are losers?
- What's the typical percentage loss on a losing trade?
- How many of your trades are winners?
- What's the typical percentage gain on a winning trade?

Say you determine that 40 percent of the time a trade loses, and it loses 1 percent. Sixty percent of the time the trade wins, and winning trades are up 1.5 percent. With these numbers, you can calculate your per-trade expected return, like this:

```
% of losing trades × loss on losing trades + % of winning
          trades × gain on winning trades = expected
          return
```

Which in this example, works out to be:

```
.40 × -.01 + .60 × .015 = -.004 + .009 = .005
```

On average, then, you would expect to earn a half-percent on every trade you make. Make enough trades with enough money, and it adds up.

You're more likely to make more money when you have a high expectation of winning trades and when you expect those winners to perform well. As long as some probability of loss exists, you stand to lose money.

The Probability of Ruin

Expected return is the happy number. It's how much money you can expect to make if you stay in the trading game. And it has a counterpart that is not so happy but is at least as important: the *probability of ruin.*

As long as you face some probability of loss, no matter how small, some probability exists that you can lose everything when you are trading. How much you can lose depends on how large each trade is relative to your account, the likelihood of each trade having a loss, and the size of the losses as they occur.

Figure 9-1 shows the math for finding R, the probability of ruin.

$$R = \left[\frac{(1-A)}{1+A}\right]^C$$

Figure 9-1: How to calculate the probability of ruin.

A is the advantage on each trade in Figure 9-1. That's the difference between the percentage of winning trades and the percentage of losing trades. In the expected-return example we discuss earlier, trades win 60 percent of the time and lose 40 percent of the time. In that case, the trader's advantage would be:

```
60% - 40% = 20%
```

C is the number of trades in an account. Assume we're dividing the account into ten equal parts, with the plan of making ten trades today. The probability of ruin today is 1.7 percent (Figure 9-2).

$$1.7\% = \left[\frac{(1-.20)}{1+.20}\right]^{10}$$

Figure 9-2: An example of the risk of ruin calculation.

Now, 1.7 percent isn't a high likelihood of ruin, but it's not zero, either. It could happen. If your advantage is smaller, if the expected loss is larger, or if the number of trades is fewer, then the likelihood becomes even higher.

Figure 9-3 shows you the relationship between the trader's advantage, number of trades, and the corresponding probability of ruin, rounded to the nearest percentage.

Probability of Ruin

	Number of Trades									
Trader's Advantage	**1**	**2**	**3**	**4**	**5**	**6**	**7**	**8**	**9**	**10**
2%	96%	92%	89%	85%	82%	79%	76%	73%	70%	67%
4%	92%	85%	79%	73%	67%	62%	57%	53%	49%	45%
6%	89%	79%	70%	62%	55%	49%	43%	38%	34%	30%
8%	85%	73%	62%	53%	45%	38%	33%	28%	24%	20%
10%	82%	67%	55%	45%	37%	30%	25%	20%	16%	13%
12%	79%	62%	49%	38%	30%	24%	18%	15%	11%	9%
14%	75%	57%	43%	32%	24%	18%	14%	10%	8%	6%
16%	72%	52%	38%	27%	20%	14%	10%	8%	5%	4%
18%	69%	48%	34%	23%	16%	11%	8%	5%	4%	3%
20%	67%	44%	30%	20%	13%	9%	6%	4%	3%	2%

Figure 9-3: Adding trader's advantage to the mix.

The bigger the edge and the more trades you can make, the lower your probability of ruin. Now, this model is a simplification in that it assumes a losing trade goes to zero, and that's not always the case. In fact, if you use stops (automatic buy and sell orders, described in Chapter 2), you should never have a trade go to zero. But you can see steady erosion in your account that will make it harder for you to make money. Hence, probability of ruin is a useful calculation that shows whether you will lose money in the long run.

The more trades you can make with your account, the lower your probability of ruin. That's why money management is a key part of risk management.

Why Size Matters

As long as some chance of losing all your money exists, you want to avoid betting all of it on any one trade. But as long as you have a chance of making money, you want enough exposure to a winning trade so that you can post good profits. How do you figure it out?

Later in this chapter, we describe some of the different money management systems that traders use to figure out how much money to risk per trade. But first we want to explain the logic behind a money management system, so that you understand why you need one. That way, you can better manage your funds and improve the dollar returns to your trading.

Valuing volatility

Expected return gives you an idea of how much you can get from a trade on average, but it doesn't tell you how much that return might vary from trade to trade. The average of 9, 10, and 11 is 10; the average of –90, 10, and 100 is also 10. The first number series is a lot narrower than the second. The wider the range of returns a strategy has, the more *volatile* it is.

We can measure volatility in several ways. One common way is *standard deviation,* which tells you how much your actual return is likely to differ from what you expect to get. (We provide a detailed explanation of the standard deviation calculation in Chapter 11.) The higher the standard deviation, the more volatile, and riskier, the strategy.

In the derivatives markets, volatility is measured by a group of numbers known as the Greeks: delta, gamma, vega, and theta. They're based on calculus.

- **Delta** is a ratio that tells you how much the option or future changes in price when the underlying security or market index changes in price. Delta changes over time.
- **Gamma** is the rate of change on delta. That's because a derivative's delta will be higher when it is close to the expiration date, for example, than when the expiration date is farther away.
- **Vega** is the amount that the derivative would change in price if the underlying security became 1 percent more volatile.
- **Theta** is the amount that a derivative's price declines as it gets closer to the day of expiration.

Day traders seek out more volatile securities, because they offer more opportunities to make money during any given day. That means they have to have ways to minimize the damage that might occur, while being able to capitalize on the upward swings. Money management can help with that.

Staying in the market

You have only a limited amount of money to trade. Whether it's $1,000 or $1,000,000, when it's gone, you're out. The problem is that you can have a long string of losing trades before the markets go in a direction that favours you and your system.

Say you trade 100 percent of your account. If you have one trade that goes down 100 percent, then you have nothing. If you divide your account into ten parts, then you can have ten total losers before you're out. If you start with ten equal parts and double each time you lose, you can be out after four losing trades.

The riskier your trading strategy, the more thought you need to put into money management. Otherwise, you can find yourself out of the market in no time.

On the other hand, if you divide your account into 100 portions, then you can endure 100 losing trades. If you trade fractions of your account, then you can keep going infinitely, or at least until you get down to a level that's too low to place a minimum order. (That's the philosophy behind the Kelly criterion, described later in this chapter.) Money management can keep you in the game longer, and that will give you more opportunities to place winning trades.

Considering opportunity costs

Opportunity cost is the value you give up because you choose to do something else. In trading, each dollar you commit to one trade is a dollar that you cannot commit to another trade. Thus, each dollar you trade carries some opportunity cost, and good traders seek to minimize this cost. During the course of the trading day, you may see several great trades, and some opportunities will show up before you're ready to close out a different trade.

If you've committed all your capital to one trade, you will miss out on the second. That alone is a good reason to keep some money on the table each time you trade.

Money Management Styles

Over the years, traders have developed many different ways to manage their money. Some of these are rooted in superstition, but most are based on different statistical probability theories. The underlying idea is to never place all of your money in a single trade; rather, put in an amount that is appropriate given the level of volatility. Otherwise, you risk losing everything too soon.

Calculating position size under many of these formulas is tricky stuff. That's why brokerage firms and trading software packages often include money management calculators. Check Chapter 6 for more information on the brokers and Chapter 7 for more on the different software and research services.

This is only a sample of some methods. Other methods exist, and none is suitable to all markets all the time. Folks trading both options and stocks may want to use one system for option trades and another for stock trades. If that's your situation, you have one big money management decision to make before you begin: how much money to allocate to each market.

Fixed fractional

Fixed fractional trading assumes you want to limit each trade to a set portion of your total account, often between 2 and 10 percent. Within that range, you'd trade a larger percentage of money in less risky trades and stay toward the smaller end of the scale for more risky trades. (In other words, it's not all that "fixed" — but no one asked us to pick a name for the system.)

The fixed fractional equation is shown in Figure 9-4.

Figure 9-4: The equation for calculating fixed fractional trade proportions.

$$N = f\left(\frac{equity}{|trade\ risk|}\right)$$

N is the number of contracts or shares of stock you should trade, *f* is the fixed fraction of your account that you have decided to trade, *equity* is the value of your total account, and *trade risk* is the amount of money you could lose on the transaction. Because trade risk is a negative number, you need to convert it to a positive number to make the equation work. Those vertical bars in the equation (| |) are the sign for absolute value, and that means you convert the number between them to a positive number.

This means that if you've decided to limit each trade to 10 percent of your account, you have a $20,000 account, and the risk of loss is –$3,500, your trade should be what is shown in Figure 9-5.

$$0.57 = .10\left(\frac{20{,}000}{|-3500|}\right)$$

Figure 9-5: An example of a fixed fractional trade calculation.

Of course, you probably can't trade .57 of a contract, so in this case you would have to round up to one.

Fixed ratio

The *fixed ratio* money management system is used in trading options and futures. It was developed by a trader named Ryan Jones, who wrote a book about it. (Check the Appendix for more information.) In order to find the optimal number of options or futures contracts to trade, N, you use the equation shown in Figure 9-6.

$$N = 0.05\left(\sqrt{1 + 8\,(P/\Delta)} + 1\right)$$

Figure 9-6: The equation for calculating fixed ratio trading proportions.

N is the number of contracts or shares of stock that you should trade, P is your accumulated profit to date, and the triangle, delta, is the dollar amount that you would need before you could trade a second contract or another lot of stock. (This is *not* the same delta measure discussed previously, which is a measure of volatility.)

For example, the minimum margin for the Chicago Mercantile Exchange E-Mini S&P 500 futures contract, which gives you exposure to the Standard & Poor's 500 stock index, is $3,500. Until you have another $3,500 in your account, you can't trade a second contract. If you are using fixed ratio money management to trade this future, your delta will be $3,500.

If your delta is $3,500, and you have $10,000 in account profits, you should trade 1.2 contracts (see Figure 9-7). In reality, that means you can trade only one contract or two contracts, nothing in between. That's one of the imperfections of most money management systems.

$$1.2 = 0.05\left(\sqrt{1 + 8(10{,}000/3500)} + 1\right)$$

Figure 9-7: An example using the fixed ratio calculation.

The idea behind fixed ratio trading is to help you increase your exposure to the market while protecting your accumulated profits.

Gann

William Gann developed a complicated system for identifying securities trades. Part of it was a list of rules for managing money, and many traders follow that if nothing else.

The primary rule is: Divide your money into ten equal parts, and never place more than one 10 percent portion on a single trade. That helps control your risk, whether or not you use Gann. (We discuss Gann a little in Chapter 7.)

Kelly criterion

The Kelly criterion emerged from statistical work done at Bell Laboratories in the 1950s. The goal was to figure out the best ways to manage signal–noise issues in long-distance telephone communications. Very quickly the mathematicians who worked on it saw its applications to gambling, and in no time the formula took off.

To calculate the ideal percentage of your portfolio to put at risk, you need to know what percentage of your trades are expected to win as well as the return from a winning trade and the ratio performance of winning trades to losing trades. The shorthand that many traders use for the Kelly criterion is *edge divided by odds,* and in practice the formula looks like this:

```
Kelly % = W - [(1 - W) / R]
```

W is the percentage of winning trades, and R is the ratio of the average gain of the winning trades relative to the average loss of the losing trades.

In the beginning of the chapter, we had an example of a system that loses 40 percent of the time with a loss of 1 percent and that wins 60 percent of the time with a gain of 1.5 percent. Plugging that into the Kelly formula, the right percentage to trade is .60 – [(1 – .60)/(.015/.01)], or 33.3 percent.

As long as you limit your trades to no more than 33 percent of your capital, you should never run out of money. The problem, of course, is that if you have a long string of losses, you could find yourself with too little money to execute a trade. Many traders use a "half-Kelly" strategy, limiting each trade to half the amount indicated by the Kelly criterion as a way to keep the trading account from shrinking too quickly. They are especially likely to do this if the Kelly criterion generates a number greater than about 20 percent, as in this example.

Martingale

The *martingale* style of money management is common with serious casino gamblers, and many traders apply it as well. It's designed to improve the amount of money you can earn in a game that has even odds. Most casino odds favour the house (roulette wheels used to be evenly black and red, but casinos found that they could make more money if they inserted a green slice for zero, thus throwing off the odds). Day trading, on the other hand, is a zero-sum game, especially in the options and futures markets. This means that for every winner there is a loser, so the odds of any one trade being successful are even. The martingale system is designed to work in any market where the odds are even or in your favour.

Under the martingale strategy, you start with a set amount per trade, say $2,000. If your trade succeeds, you trade another $2,000. If your trade loses, you double your next order (after you close or limit the first trade) so that you can win back your loss. (You may have heard gamblers talk about *doubling down* — this is what they are doing.)

Under the martingale system, you will always come out ahead as long as you have an infinite amount of money to trade. The problem is that you can run out of money before you have a trade that works. The market, on the other hand, has almost infinite resources because of the huge volume of participants coming and going all over the world. That means you have an enormous disadvantage. As long as you have a disadvantage, thoughtful money management is critical.

Monte Carlo simulation

If you have the programming expertise or buy the right software, you can run what's called a *Monte Carlo simulation*. You enter in your risk and return parameters and your account value, let the program run, and it returns the optimal trade size. The system is not perfect — it is only a model that can't incorporate every market situation you'll face, and it has the fractional trade problem that the other systems do. But it has one big advantage: It can incorporate random changes in the markets in ways that simpler money management models cannot.

Monte Carlo simulation is not a do-it-yourself project, unless you have extensive experience creating these programs. If you're interested, you need to find a suitable program. Two options are offered by AnalyCorp (`www.analycorp.com`) and Oracle (`www.oracle.com/crystalball/index.html`). Others are out there as well.

Optimal F

The *Optimal F* system of money management was devised by Ralph Vince; he has written several books about this and other money management issues (see the Appendix for more information). The idea is that you determine the ideal fraction of your money to allocate per trade based on past performance. If your Optimal F is 18 percent, then each trade should be 18 percent of your account — no more, no less. The system is similar to the fixed fraction and fixed ratio methods discussed earlier, but with a few differences.

Figure 9-8 shows the equation for finding the number of shares of stock, N, to trade.

Figure 9-8: The equation for finding the number of shares to trade under Optimal F.

$$N = \frac{\left(F * \frac{equity}{risk}\right)}{price}$$

F is a factor based on historical data, and the risk is the biggest percentage loss that you experienced in the past. Using these numbers and the current price, you can find the contracts or shares you need to buy. If your account has $25,000, your biggest loss was 40 percent, your F is determined to be 30 percent, and you're looking at a stock trading at $25 per share, then you should buy 750 shares (Figure 9-9).

Figure 9-9: An example of the Optimal F calculation.

$$750 = \frac{\left(.30 * \frac{25,000}{.40}\right)}{25}$$

The Optimal F number itself is a mean based on historical trade results. The risk number is also based on past returns, and that's one problem with this method: it kicks in only after you have some trade data. A second problem is that you need to set up a spreadsheet to calculate it (so read Ralph Vince's book if you want to try it out; you can find more information in the Appendix.) Some traders use Optimal F only in certain market conditions, in part because the history changes each time a trade is made, and that history doesn't always lead to usable numbers.

How Money Management Affects Your Return

It's one thing to describe why you need money management, but it's more fun to show you how it works. And because Ann loves making spreadsheets (we all need a hobby, right?), she pulled one together to show you how different ways of managing your money might affect your return.

In Figure 9-2, Ann started with the expected return assumptions that she used in the earlier example: 40 percent of the time a trade loses, and it loses 1 percent. Sixty percent of the time the trade wins, and winning trades are up 1.5 percent. In Figure 9-10, she picks a hypothetical account of $20,000 and set up mock trades using these expected return numbers. Figure 9-10 compares the performance of martingale and Kelly money management to betting the whole account each time.

You may notice in Figure 9-10 that you end up with the most money from trading the entire account. That doesn't mean you always get the most money this way, just that that's how the numbers worked out in this case, given the 60/40 win ratio and a 3/2 winning size/losing size ratio. (Keep in mind that if you were using a Kelly or martingale system, you'd probably be doing something with the rest of the account rather than just letting it sit there.)

This is just an example, applying some different strategies to different hypothetical returns. We're not recommending any one system over another. The best system for you depends on what assets you are trading, your personal trading style, and how much money you have to trade.

Martingale: Starting with 10% and Doubling Losses

	Performance	Intial Account Value	% Traded	Amount Traded	Ending Account Value	% Change
Trade 1	1.5%	$ 20,000	10%	$ 2,000	$ 20,030	
Trade 2	1.5%	$ 20,030		$ 2,000	$ 20,060	
Trade 3	-1.0%	$ 20,060		$ 2,000	$ 20,040	
Trade 4	-1.0%	$ 20,040		$ 4,000	$ 20,000	
Trade 5	1.5%	$ 20,000		$ 8,000	$ 20,120	
Trade 6	1.5%	$ 20,120		$ 2,000	$ 20,150	
Trade 7	-1.0%	$ 20,150		$ 2,000	$ 20,130	
Trade 8	-1.0%	$ 20,130		$ 4,000	$ 20,090	
Trade 9	1.5%	$ 20,090		$ 8,000	$ 20,210	
Trade 10	1.5%	$ 20,210		$ 2,000	$ 20,240	1.20%

Kelly: Trading 33%

	Performance	Intial Account Value	% Traded	Amount Traded	Ending Account Value	
Trade 1	1.5%	$ 20,000	33%	$ 6,660	$ 20,100	
Trade 2	1.5%	$ 20,100	33%	$ 6,693	$ 20,200	
Trade 3	-1.0%	$ 20,200	33%	$ 6,727	$ 20,133	
Trade 4	-1.0%	$ 20,133	33%	$ 6,704	$ 20,066	
Trade 5	1.5%	$ 20,066	33%	$ 6,682	$ 20,166	
Trade 6	1.5%	$ 20,166	33%	$ 6,715	$ 20,267	
Trade 7	-1.0%	$ 20,267	33%	$ 6,749	$ 20,199	
Trade 8	-1.0%	$ 20,199	33%	$ 6,726	$ 20,132	
Trade 9	1.5%	$ 20,132	33%	$ 6,704	$ 20,233	
Trade 10	1.5%	$ 20,233	33%	$ 6,738	$ 20,334	1.67%

Betting Everything

	Performance	Intial Account Value	% Traded	Amount Traded	Ending Account Value	
Trade 1	1.5%	$ 20,000	100%	$ 20,000	$ 20,300	
Trade 2	1.5%	$ 20,300	100%	$ 20,300	$ 20,605	
Trade 3	-1.0%	$ 20,605	100%	$ 20,605	$ 20,398	
Trade 4	-1.0%	$ 20,398	100%	$ 20,398	$ 20,194	
Trade 5	1.5%	$ 20,194	100%	$ 20,194	$ 20,497	
Trade 6	1.5%	$ 20,497	100%	$ 20,497	$ 20,805	
Trade 7	-1.0%	$ 20,805	100%	$ 20,805	$ 20,597	
Trade 8	-1.0%	$ 20,597	100%	$ 20,597	$ 20,391	
Trade 9	1.5%	$ 20,391	100%	$ 20,391	$ 20,697	
Trade 10	1.5%	$ 20,697	100%	$ 20,697	$ 21,007	5.04%

Figure 9-10: How money management affects your return.

Planning for Your Profits

In addition to determining how much to trade each time you place an order, you need a plan for what to do with the profits that accumulate in your account. That's as much a part of money management as calculating your probability of ruin and determining trade size.

Are you going to add the money to your account and trade it as before? Leverage your profits by trading them more aggressively than your core account? Pull money out and put it into long-term investments? Or a combination of the three?

Compounding interest

Compound interest is a simple concept: Every time you get a return, that return goes into your account. You keep earning a return on it, which increases your account size some more. You keep earning a return on your return, and soon the numbers get to be pretty big.

In order to benefit from that compounding, many traders add their profits back into their accounts and keep trading them, in order to build account size. Although day traders earn little to no interest (which is compensation for loaning out money — say, by buying bonds), the basic principle holds: By returning profits to the trading account to generate even more profits, the account should grow over time.

This practice of keeping profits in the account to trade makes a lot of sense for smaller traders who want to build their accounts and take more significant positions over time.

Pyramiding power

Pyramiding involves taking trading profits and borrowing heavily against them to generate even more profits. Traders usually do this during the day, using unrealized profits in trades that are not yet closed as collateral for loans used to establish new positions. If the new positions are profitable, the trader can keep borrowing until it's time to close everything at the end of the day.

This works great as long as the markets are moving in the right direction. If all the positions in the pyramid remain profitable, you can make a lot of money during the course of the day. But if one of those positions turns against you, the structure collapses and you end up with a call on your margin. Figure 9-11 starts with an initial trade of $2,000 and assumes a return of 10 percent on each transaction — not realistic, necessarily, but it makes for a nice chart. If the profits from each trade are used as collateral for borrowing, and if that 10 percent return holds all day, then the trader can make 17 percent by pyramiding those gains. If a reversal hits before the end of the trading session and the positions lose 10 percent, then pyramiding magnifies the losses — assuming your broker would let you keep borrowing. After all, the borrowed money has to be repaid regardless of what happens in the market.

Pyramiding magnifies returns
Assume that you need to maintain 25% margin

	Initial Trade Equity	Amount Borrowed	Total Trade Size	Profit at 10% Return
First trade	$ 2,000	$ -	$ 2,000	$ 200
Second trade	$ 200	$ 600	$ 800	$ 80
Third trade	$ 80	$ 240	$ 320	$ 32
Fourth trade	$ 32	$ 96	$ 128	$ 13
Fifth trade	$ 13	$ 38	$ 51	$ 5
Sixth trade	$ 5	$ 15	$ 20	$ 2
Return on initial $2000 trade:	$ 332			
Percentage return:	17%			

. . . And pyramiding magnifies losses

	Initial Trade Equity	Amount Borrowed	Total Trade Size	Profit at 10% Return
First trade	$ 2,000	$ -	$ 2,000	$ (200)
Second trade	$ 200	$ 600	$ 800	$ (80)
Third trade	$ 80	$ 240	$ 320	$ (32)
Fourth trade	$ 32	$ 96	$ 128	$ (13)
Fifth trade	$ 13	$ 38	$ 51	$ (5)
Sixth trade	$ 5	$ 15	$ 20	$ (2)
Return on initial $2000 trade:	$ (332)			
Percentage return:	-17%			

Figure 9-11: Pyramiding magnifies returns and losses.

Pyramiding is not related to a *pyramid scheme*. In trading terms, pyramiding is a way to borrow against your profits to generate even bigger profits. A pyramid scheme is a fraud that requires participants to recruit new members, and fees paid by the new members go to the older ones. Eventually, the pyramid collapses because it gets too difficult to recruit new members, and those at the bottom get nothing.

Some investment frauds have been structured as pyramid schemes, so be wary of deals that sound fabulous and also require you to recruit others.

Pyramiding increases your trading risk, but also your expected return. It's a useful way to grow a portion of your trading account, especially when the market is favouring your trading system. It's a good technique for a medium-sized account that would have enough money left over to stay in the market if a pyramid were to collapse on you.

Regular withdrawals

Because day trading can be so risky, many traders look to diversify their total financial risk. One way to do this is to pull money out of the trading account to put into a less volatile long-term investment. Many traders routinely pull out a percentage of their profits and put that money into government bonds, a low-risk mutual fund, or real estate. None of these investments is as glamorous or exciting as day trading, but that's the point: Trading is hard work, and anyone can lose money any day, no matter how big their account is or how much money they have made so far. By moving some money out, a trader can build a cushion for a bad trading stretch, prepare for retirement, and have some money to walk away for a short period or even forever. That can greatly reduce the stress and the fear that go with trading.

The larger the account, the easier it is to pull money out, but even smaller traders should consider taking 5 or 10 percent of each quarter's profits and moving them into another type of investment. If you don't trust yourself to do it, many brokerage firms can set up automatic withdrawal plans that zap money from your trading account over to a stock or bond mutual fund.

Chapter 10
Taxes for Traders

In This Chapter

- Knowing the difference between trading and investing
- Hiring a savvy tax adviser
- Figuring incoming income and outgoing expenses
- Reporting to the CRA and paying estimated taxes
- Day trading inside your RRSP
- Making use of a TFSA

Think day trade returns come without a catch? Think again, because the CRA has plenty of ways to catch you come April 30. Day trading involves strategies that generate both high returns and high tax liabilities, which can eat away at your total return if you're not careful. Depending on how you file, not all of your expenses are deductible. And, even more troubling, although you might think you're day trading the CRA could have a different definition of your activities.

Taxes themselves aren't necessarily bad, because somehow we have to pay for things like roads and schools and health care. But taxes can be devastating to your personal finances if you haven't planned for them. You need to consider the tax implications of your trading strategy right from the start and keep careful records so that you're ready.

Tax issues for day traders are complex and change frequently. Check the most recent federal regulations at www.cra-arc.gc.ca and work with an accountant or tax expert who has experience in these matters. This chapter is just a guide. We're reasonably social folks and all, but we're not going on an audit with you.

Are You a Trader or an Investor?

In Chapter 4, we cover the differences between investing, trading, and gambling. Day traders aren't investing — they're looking to take advantage of short-term price movements, not to take a stake in a business for the long term. At least that's how the CRA looks at it. The taxman will brand you a trader if you meet some (not necessarily all) of the following criteria:

- You have a history of "extensive buying and selling" of securities. The CRA doesn't explain what extensive means, but if you're selling hundreds of securities a year — like most day traders do — it's likely you'll be considered a trader.
- You own securities for a short period of time. Again, no specific timeframe applies, but you can assume they're talking days, not years.
- You know a thing or two about or have experience in the securities markets.
- Trading makes up a part of your regular business activities.
- You spend a "substantial" amount of time studying markets and looking into potential purchases.
- You primarily buy on margin or use another type of debt.
- You've made it known that you're a trader, or are willing to purchase securities.
- The shares you purchase are speculative or non-dividend-paying investments.

Even if you trade part-time, have other employment, or are new to the day trading game, the CRA could define you as a trader — and therefore will be expecting a heftier tax bill at the end of the year.

Those who qualify as traders enjoy deductions that regular investors don't. You might qualify as a trader for some of your activities and as an investor for others. If this looks to be the case you need to keep detailed records to separate your trades, and you should use different brokerage accounts to make the difference clear from the day you open the position.

In political economies, taxation serves two purposes. The first is to raise money for the government. The second is to encourage people to do things that the elected officials who amend the tax code want them to do. Much of the investing tax code is intended to promote the formation and growth of wealth and savings. The intention of short-term day trading isn't to do that — it's so people can make heaps of money in an exciting, high-pressure environment (often from the comfort of home), instead of toiling at a nine-to-five job. So, if you qualify as a trader, the CRA will tax you as though it's your job. Instead of paying the financially preferable capital gains tax, you'll be paying tax on your total income earned.

Legally, if you day trade you have to file income tax as though it's your full time job. Capital gains taxes will not apply. However, lots of traders try to push the boundaries and file capital gains taxes rather than income tax until they're told otherwise, an approach we don't advocate. Talk to your tax adviser about how you should file and the consequences of filing incorrectly.

Hiring a Tax Adviser

You don't have to hire someone to do your taxes, but you probably should. If you're claiming capital gains, day trading will generate a lot of separate transactions to track, and the tax laws are tricky. Mistakes can end up costing you your entire trading profit.

Do yourself a favour and find a tax expert. You can talk to other traders, get references from the attorneys and accountants you work with now, or even do Internet searches to find people who understand both CRA regulations and the unique needs of people who frequently buy and sell securities, whether or not the CRA calls them traders.

Anyone can represent clients before the CRA in audits, collections, or appeals, but it's a good idea to hire an accountant, or someone who knows a lot about tax and, preferably, investing.

The many flavours of tax experts

Okay, you're waiting for us to say there's only one flavour, and it's vanilla, right? Wrong. Tax experts fall into several different categories, and knowing which is which can help you determine who is best for you.

Chartered accountants

Chartered accountants are the most educated of the bunch. Although many great accountants exist across all designations, if you want to hire the one whose name is followed by the most prestigious letters, the CA tops the list. CAs need to have a university degree with specific business-related credits before they can take on the Chartered Accountants of Canada's extensive course load.

Certified management accountants

A CMA can do almost everything a CA can (at least for your purposes), but it's an easier designation to obtain. Generally, CMAs focus on managerial accounting and hold jobs in industry and government. But they can help prepare your taxes too.

Certified general accountants

It's the easiest designation to get, but that doesn't mean CGAs are less qualified to help you prepare returns and calculate gains, losses, or income. CGAs often specialize in taxation, accounting, and business consulting, whereas the other designations work in a variety of finance-related jobs.

Tax lawyers

Tax lawyers often work with accountants; they are called in to study the legality of proposed strategies or to represent a client in tax litigation. They aren't appropriate for most traders, but there may be situations that call for one.

Canada Revenue Agency

The CRA might be a bureaucratic machine, but get them on the phone and they're quite helpful. Their reps have the tax code at their fingertips, so if you're unsure of whether to check a box, or what you can or can't deduct, call them up.

Questions to ask a prospective adviser

After you identify a few prospective candidates to prepare your taxes, talk to them and ask them questions about their experience. Because you're supposed to claim your day trading profits as earned income, there really isn't anything special your tax expert needs to do beyond knowing what to deduct. The main goal is to find someone who can help you determine what you owe in taxes and not one penny more.

You'll feel more comfortable with your tax preparer if *you* have an understanding of the issues at stake. Even if you are hiring someone — and you should — keep reading this chapter and check the Appendix for more in-depth references on taxes and trading.

Some things you should ask a potential tax preparer include the following:

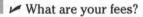

- What investors and traders have you worked with? For how long?
- Who will be preparing my return? How involved will you be?
- What's your audit record? Why have your clients been audited? What happened on the audit?
- What are your fees?

It is illegal for tax preparers to base their fees on the size of your tax refund.

You still want to do it yourself?

It's possible for traders to do their own taxes, especially if they're claiming earned income. If you are comfortable with tax forms, you might be able to do this yourself. You need a few things: the proper CRA forms and, if you're not classifying yourself as a full-time trader, tax preparation software that can handle investment income.

Everything you want to know about taxes is at www.cra-arc.gc.ca

The CRA Web site, `www.cra-arc.gc.ca`, is a treasure trove of tax information. All the regulations, publications, forms, and explanations are there, and some of it is even in plain English. It's so vast and detailed that you will probably be overwhelmed; get back at the CRA by calling them up and asking them to explain it all to you.

The primary section that covers the tax implications of trading and other investing activities is the Income Tax Interpretation Bulletin IT-479R, "Transactions in Securities." To find this document, go to the CRA's Web site and type IT-479R into the search bar. Click on the first result, and voilà.

Tax preparation software

Those who do their own taxes know that tax prep software is a godsend, and it's even more valuable for those do-it-yourselfers who trade a lot. The software fills out the forms, automatically adds and subtracts, and even catches typographical errors. In many cases, it can download data straight from your brokerage account, making data entry really simple.

Some of the big brands, such as TurboTax, are set up to import and manage investment data, but if you're making regular and frequent trades you may want to shell out the close to $1,000 it costs to purchase something like TJPS Software, which offers a range of trading-related functions.

What Is Income, Anyway?

Income seems like a straightforward concept, but not much about taxation is straightforward. To the CRA, income falls into different categories, with different tax rates, different allowed deductions, and different forms to fill out. In this section we cover income definitions you'll run into as a day trader.

Earned income

Earned income includes wages, salaries, bonuses, and tips. It's money that you make on the job. If day trading is your only occupation — and even if it isn't — your earnings could be considered earned income. This means that day traders will have to pay tax based on their current marginal tax rate (also known as personal income tax rate).

Canada has both federal and provincial tax rates — the latter varies by province, but the former is consistent for all Canadians. In the federal system, you're taxed:

- 15 percent on the first $40,970 of taxable income
- 22 percent on the next $40,971 of taxable income
- 26 percent on the next $45,080 of taxable income
- 29 percent of taxable income over $127,021

Got that? To put it another way, if you fall into the highest tax bracket, about 46 percent of your yearly earnings will go to the government. (***Note:*** these numbers are 2010 amounts — the rates can change from year to year.)

Provincial tax rates vary from province to province. To find out how much you'll be taxed, go to `www.cra-arc.gc.ca/tx/ndvdls/fq/txrts-eng.html`, scroll halfway down the page, and find your province.

Most traders are self-employed, which means you can deduct expenses and reduce your income's dollar figure. That could bump you into a lower bracket and therefore you'll pay less tax.

The big benefit of claiming your gains as income is that, if you lose money, you can apply those losses against all sources of income or any profits down the road. So, if you have a part-time job, those losses will help bring down your tax bill leaving more money in your pocket. The CRA allows you to apply losses against income earned for the last three years, or carry them forward indefinitely.

Keep your long-term investments separate from your day trading income — if you don't, the CRA could assume all your investing is related to trading. And that is bad news. The tax treatment for investments is different than work income, so if the CRA thinks all your investing, including that mutual fund you've held for 20 years, is related to day trading, all your gains will be taxed at the marginal tax rate.

Being a day trader once meant you didn't have access to employment insurance benefits. That's not the case anymore. Starting January 31, 2010 traders who pay income tax can apply for maternity, parental, sickness, and compassionate care benefits. You have to opt in to this yourself — and decide whether you want to send even more money to the taxman. Visit CRA's Web site to find out more.

Capital gains and losses

A *capital gain* is the profit you make when you buy low and sell high, and that's the aim of day trading. The opposite of a capital gain is a *capital loss,* which happens when you sell an asset for less than you paid for it. Investors can offset some of their capital gains with some of their capital losses to reduce their tax burden.

Those who trade frequently and can avoid having their gains classified as earned income will have many capital gains and losses. Day traders get tripped up by capital gain and loss problems all the time, so when designing your trading strategy think long and hard about how to ease the pain taxes might cause.

The financial world is filled with horror stories of people who thought they found a clever angle on making big profits, only to discover at tax time that their tax liability was greater than their profit. That's why properly tracking gains and losses is a must. It's not easy. The price difference of every trade you make needs to be accounted for, so create an Excel spreadsheet or use Write-Up, a comprehensive computer program offered by TJPS Software (`www.tjpssoftware.com`).

Tax treatment

Day traders want to pay taxes on capital gains, rather than earned income, because only half of a capital gain is taxed. If you make $1,000 on a trade, and it's being taxed as income, the entire gain will be subject to tax. If you're paying capital gains you'd pay only tax — at your marginal tax rate — on $500. See why the CRA wants day trading profits to be taxed as income?

If you lose money on a trade you can claim capital losses. It's similar to applying losses against earned income, but you can only use half of the amount you lose, rather than the entire price tag of the loss. Capital losses would be applied against gains, which can reduce your total tax bill. Capital losses can be carried back three years or used indefinitely in the future.

Now's a good time to remind you, again, that the CRA frowns upon traders who claim capital gains instead of earned income. If you meet the criteria of a trader, which we list earlier in the chapter, you're supposed to claim your earnings as income — just as you would if you worked in a cubicle shuffling papers.

Covering your basis

Capital gains and losses are calculated using a security's *basis,* which may or may not be the same as the price that you paid for it or sold it at. Some expenses, such as commissions, are added to the cost of the security, and that can reduce the amount of your taxable gain or increase the amount of your deductible loss.

For example, if you bought 100 shares of stock at $50 per share and a $0.03 per share commission, your basis would be $5,003 — the $5,000 you paid for the stock and the $3.00 you paid in commission.

The superficial loss problem

Say you love LMNO Company, but the price of the shares is down from what it was when you purchased them. You'd like to get that loss on your taxes, so you sell the stock, and then you buy it back at the lower price. You get your tax deduction and still keep the stock. How excellent is that?

It's too excellent to be true. The CRA does not count the loss. This trick is called a *superficial loss*. The rule was designed to keep long-term investors from playing cute with their taxes, but it has the effect of creating a ruinous tax situation for naïve day traders.

Under the superficial loss rule, you cannot deduct a loss if you have both a gain and a loss in the same security within a 30-day period. (That's calendar days, not trading days, so weekends and holidays count.) However, you *can* add the disallowed loss to the basis of your security.

Consider this example to understand what we mean. On Tuesday, you bought 100 shares of LMNO at $100. LMNO announced terrible earnings, the stock promptly dropped to $80, and you sold all 100 shares for a loss of $2,000. Later in the afternoon, you noticed that the stock had bottomed and looked like it might trend up, so you bought another 100 shares at $60 and resold them an hour later at $70, closing out your position for the day. The second trade had a profit of $1,000. You had a net loss of $1,000 (the $2,000 loss plus the $1,000 profit), but the CRA will disallow the $2,000 loss and let you show only a profit of $1,000. However, the CRA will let you add the $2,000 loss to the basis of your replacement shares, meaning that instead of spending $6,000 (100 shares times $60), for tax purposes, you spent $8,000 ($6,000 plus $2,000; you've essentially bought the stock back at $80 per share). If the price rises back to $100 a share, you only make a profit of $2,000 instead of the $4,000 your buddy made by buying 100 shares at the $60 price.

Day traders likely won't have to worry about this rule. Technically, the superficial loss rule applies only when you own the share 30 days after the original sale's settlement date. (The settlement date is usually three days after you sell a stock.) Because you're buying and selling shares quickly, it's unlikely you'll own the stock at the end of the month. But keep track. If you sell it and then 30 days later you buy it again for some reason, the rule will kick in.

Tracking Your Investment Expenses

Day traders have expenses. They buy computer equipment, subscribe to research services, pay trading commissions, and hire accountants to prepare their taxes. It adds up, and the tax code recognizes that. That's why day traders who pay personal income tax can deduct many of their costs from their income taxes. In this section, we go through some of what you can deduct.

You'll make your life much easier if you keep track of your expenses as you incur them. You can do this in a notebook, in a spreadsheet, or through personal finance software such as Quicken or UFile.

Day traders who try to get around paying personal income tax don't have nearly as many expensing opportunities. That's one of the benefits of treating your day trading activities as a regular job.

Qualified and deductible expenses

You can deduct expenses as long as they are considered to be ordinary, necessary, and used to produce or collect income, manage property held for producing income, and directly related to the taxable income produced.

Clerical, legal, and accounting fees

You might use the services of a lawyer to help you get set up, and you will almost definitely want to use an accountant who understands investment expenses to prepare your income tax returns each year. The good news is you can deduct attorney and accounting fees related to your income. If your trading operation gets big enough that you hire clerical help to keep track of all those trade confirmations, you can deduct that cost, too.

Office expenses

If you do your day trading from an outside office, you can deduct the rent and related expenses. You can deduct the expenses of a home office, too, as long as you use it regularly and for business. Your trading room can be used as the guest room, but you need to figure out how many hours you use it for business. According to the CRA, calculate how many hours in a day you use the room and divide that by 24. Multiply the number by your business-related home expenses. Deduct that number.

You can also deduct certain office expenses for equipment and supplies used in your business; just use the same formula above to determine how much of your computers, desks, chairs, and the like you can write off. (If it's an office chair that's used only for work, you can write off the entire amount. If it's a love seat that doubles as a work chair, you can claim only part of it).

To get the deduction you have to spend the money first, and your expenses don't reduce your taxes dollar-for-dollar. If you're in the 46 percent tax bracket, then each dollar you spend on qualified expenses reduces your taxes by $0.46. In other words, don't go crazy at the office supply store just because you get a tax deduction. It may be helpful to think of deductible expenses as discounts, because in the end that's more or less what they are.

Investment counsel and advice

The CRA allows you to deduct fees paid for counsel and advice about investments that produce taxable income. This includes books, magazines, newspapers, and research services that help you refine your trading strategy. It also includes anything you might pay for investment advisory services, such as trade coaching or analysis.

Safe deposit box rent

Have a safe deposit box down at the bank? You can deduct the rent on it if you store any investment-related documents. If you also keep jewellery that you inherited and never wear or other personal items in the same box, you can deduct only part of the rent.

Investment interest

If you borrow money as part of your strategy, and most day traders do, you can deduct the interest paid on those loans. In most cases this is *margin interest* (see Chapter 8 for more information on margin), and for most day traders it is relatively small because few day traders borrow money for more than a few hours at a time.

If you borrow money against your account for anything other than income-producing activities, you can't deduct the interest. And yes, most brokerage firms let you take out margin for your own general spending, as a way to let you stay in the market and still get cash.

You can deduct expenses only if day trading is your day job and you're getting taxed on earned income. Again, paying income tax, rather than capital gains tax, will allow you to claim all that good stuff we mentioned. Sure, you may have to pay more in tax than if you just paid gains, but, as a consolation, you can write off a lot more — and you don't have to worry about being reprimanded by the CRA!

Commissions

If you're a day trader paying income, you can deduct commissions come tax time. However, if you're paying capital gains, you're out of luck. We know, it's disappointing, but that's life. (Well, at least the way CRA wants life to be.) Again, if you really want to deduct those extra fees, claim your profits as income.

Paying Taxes All Year

If you have been an employee for years and years, all of your tax liabilities would have been covered by your payroll tax deductions. The CRA likes it best that way, because then it gets money all year 'round. And really, the easier it is to pay, the more likely you are to do it.

People who are self-employed don't get the luxury of having their tax bill taken care of by someone else. To ensure you have squirrelled away enough for the CRA, estimate your tax liability for the year, divide it by 12, and put aside a portion of your profits every month. Nothing's worse than having to pay tax and not having the money at the end of the year. (It's tempting, but don't buy a new plasma TV with what's supposed to be the government's money.)

In your first two years as a day trader you won't be forced to pay in installments, but after that, and if you're making over $30,000 annually, the government will require you to send in a cheque four times a year. The CRA bases the amount on what you've made the prior two years; if you end up owing less you'll get money back, and if you owe more your final cheque will make up the difference.

Estimated taxes are paid via Form INNS3, also known as the Installment Remittance Voucher. Fortunately, they're due on a nice, even, quarterly schedule: the 15th of March, June, September, and December.

Using Your RRSP

Much of the tax hassle associated with day trading is eliminated if you trade through a self-directed *Registered Retirement Savings Plan,* or RRSP. Most brokerage firms can set them up for you and handle the necessary paperwork. You're allowed to contribute 18 percent of your previous year's earned income up to a maximum of $22,000. If you didn't use up all your room the year before, you can carry it forward indefinitely. That means if you haven't used an RRSP before you could deposit a lot of cash.

When you put money into the registered account you'll get a tax break, which can be nice if you've made a lot of money that year. However, if you want to take cash out you'll be taxed at your marginal rate (refer to the section, "What Is Income, Anyway?" in this chapter for more). That's why most people wait until they're 71 to withdraw — the older you are, the lower your earned income is likely to be. So it's not a good idea to use an RRSP if you need immediate access to your money.

What's different about day trading in an RRSP is that capital gains and losses don't apply. You don't have to pay any tax on the investments. You're asked to pay the taxman only on the amount you remove from the account. Again, if you can hang on to the money until you retire (though day trading is not a good retirement strategy) then you'll pay a lot less tax. You're also not allowed to trade on margin in an RRSP (see Chapter 14 for more on leverage), and you can't participate in *naked call options* (when an investor sells a call option without owning the security) or *short selling* (selling a security you don't own and buying the stock back at a lower price). The CRA considers it carrying on a business activity inside an RRSP, which is a no-no.

Do your bulk of trading in an unregistered account so you can have quick access to money without incurring the withdrawal taxes that come with investing in an RRSP.

Trading within a Tax-Free Savings Account

On January 1, 2009, the federal government introduced a new savings vehicle for Canadians called the *tax-free savings account* (TFSA). The idea is to get more people saving money. You're allowed to put $5,000 into the account each year and remove it tax free at any time. The room also accumulates by $5,000 each year, so if you didn't deposit anything in 2009 you could put in $10,000 in 2010, and so on. The TFSA is meant for long-term investors — you'd put your cash in a mutual fund, in the TFSA account, and let it grow. You might withdraw it if you wanted to buy a car or house, because you can take it out without incurring a tax penalty.

The TFSA is similar to an RRSP, except you don't get a tax break when you deposit money into the account and you don't get taxed when you remove it.

The best part is that neither capital gains nor earned income is taxed on profits made in a TFSA. That's good news for traders who claim gains or income. However, you can't claim losses — not so good if you're losing money. Your initial deposit also can't exceed your contribution room, so this is not the place to make a $100,000 trade. If you do put more in the account than your allotted amount — $5,000 per year — 100 percent of the profits from the extra cash will go to the taxman.

Like an RRSP, you can't participate in naked call options or short selling and you can't take advantage of margin in a TFSA. Use this as a secondary account, not your primary one.

Chapter 11

But Did You Make Money? Evaluating Performance

In This Chapter

- Testing before you trade
- Tracking while you trade
- Evaluating performance after the trade

Any one trade involves a lot of variables: price bought, price sold, commissions charged, volume traded, and amount of leverage used. And each of these affects your overall performance. In the heat of a trading day, it can be hard to juggle all these factors and determine just how well you did — or did not do.

Performance calculation starts before you trade. You want to test your strategies to see whether they work for you, which requires backtesting and paper trading. You want to keep track of your trades in real time with the help of a trading diary. And then, on a periodic basis (at least monthly), you should review your progress to see how much money you are making and whether you need to change your strategy.

Before You Trade: Testing Your System

Performance measurement starts before the trading does. That's because you want to figure out how you will trade before you start betting real money. Chapter 3 describes some of the different securities that can be traded on a daily basis, and Chapters 12–15 cover some of the strategies that day traders use. After you figure out the combinations of securities and strategies you want to use, you'll want to see whether they would have made you money in the past. Then you should try them out to see whether they still work now.

The happy news? All this is possible without risking a dime, except of course for the money you might spend on backtesting and simulation software. You knew there had to be a catch, right? Consider it an investment in the success of your business.

Backtesting

In *backtesting*, a trader specifies the strategy that he or she would use and then runs it through a database of historical securities prices to see whether the strategy would have made money. The test includes assumptions about commissions, leverage, and position size. The results give information on returns, volatility, and win-loss ratios that can be used to refine a trading strategy and implement it well.

Starting with a hypothesis

What trades do you want to do? After you figure out what and how to trade, you can start setting forth what your strategy will be. Will you look for high-momentum, small-cap stocks? Seek out price changes related to news events in agricultural commodities? Ride large-cap stocks within their ranges? Arbitrage — simultaneously buying and selling similar financial instruments on different markets — stock index futures and their options?

After you have done your research, you can lay out your strategy as a hypothesis. It might be something like this: "High-momentum, small-cap stocks tend to close up for the day, so you can buy them in the morning and make money selling them in the afternoon." Or: "News events take at least half an hour to affect pork belly prices, so you can buy or sell on the news and make a profit." With this statement, you can move on to the test to see whether it holds.

One of the most valuable parts about backtesting is that you have to be very specific about what your trading rule is. Computers cannot understand vague instructions, and if you find that your trading strategy is too complicated to write out and set into a backtesting program, it's probably too complicated for you to follow.

Running the test

Say you start with something simple: Maybe you have reason to think that pharmaceutical companies moving down in price on decreasing volume will turn and close up for the day. The first thing you do is enter into the software the industry group and the buy pattern you're looking for. The results will show whether your hunch is correct, and how often and for what time periods.

If you like what you see, you can add more variables. What happens when you add *leverage* (use borrowed money) in your trades? That increases your risk of loss, but it also increases your potential return. How does that affect your trade? Suppose you increase the size of your trades. Would that help you make more money or less? By playing around with the system, you can get a good sense of the best way to make money with your trade ideas. You can also get a sense of when your rule *won't* work, to help you avoid problems.

Most backtesting software allows for optimization, which means that it can come up with the leverage, position, holding period, and other parameters that will generate the best risk-adjusted return. You can then compare this to your trading style and your capital position to see if it works.

Backtesting is subject to something that traders call *over-optimization,* mathematicians call *curve-fitting,* and analysts call *data mining.* This means that the person performing the test looks at a past time where the market performed well, then identifies all the variables and specifications that generated that performance. Although it sounds great, what often happens is that the test generates a model that includes unnecessary variables — which makes no logical sense in practice. If you find a strategy that works when the stock closes up one day, down two days, then up a third day, followed by four down days when it hits an intra-day high, you probably haven't made an amazing discovery — you've just fit the curve.

People who use iPhones and MP3 players have elaborate ideas about how the "random shuffle" feature on these devices works. Ask, and they'll explain at length their theory that certain types of songs show up more often than others, songs with similar titles are played together, and other patterns they're convinced are there. Why? Because human beings have evolved to see patterns, even when none *is* there. It's the same with the market. It's entirely possible that although the results of your test look great, they show a random event that only happened to work out once. That's why you need to keep testing, even after you start trading.

Comparing the results with market cycles

The markets change every day in response to new regulations, interest rate fluctuations, economic conditions, nasty world events, and run-of-the-mill news stories. (It's like the joke about the weather: If you don't like it now, wait a minute and it will change.) Different securities and strategies do better in some market climates than in others.

When you're backtesting, do it for enough time that you can see how your strategy would work over different market conditions. Some things to check include the following:

- How did the strategy do in periods of inflation? Economic growth? High interest rates? Low interest rates?
- What was happening in the markets during the time that the strategy worked best? What was happening when it worked worst? How likely is either of those to happen again?
- How does market volatility affect the strategy? Is the security more volatile than the market, less volatile, or does it seem to be removed from the market?
- Have there been major changes in the industry over the period of the test? Does this mean that past performance still applies?
- Have there been changes in the way that the security trades? For example, the bulk of trading in most commodities used to take place in open-outcry trading pits. Now, it's mostly electronic. Does that change affect your test results?

In the capital assets pricing model, which is a key part of academic finance theory, the market risk is known as *beta*. The value that a portfolio manager adds to investment performance is known as *alpha*. In the long run, conventional finance theory says that the return on a diversified portfolio comes from beta; alpha does not exist. In the short run, where day traders play, this relationship might not be so strong.

Past performance is not indicative of future results. A strategy may test perfectly, but that doesn't mean it will continue to work. Backtesting is an important step to successful day trading, but it is only one step.

Simulation trading

With a backtested strategy in hand, you might be tempted to start putting real money on the line. Don't, just yet. Start with what is known variously as *ghost trading, paper trading,* and *simulation trading*. Sit down in front of your computer screen and start watching the price quotes. When you see your ideal entry poi`nt, write it down. When you see your exit point, write it down. Do exactly what you plan to do with real money, just don't use the money. Then, figure out what your performance would have been.

If your strategy does not generate a lot of trades, you can probably keep track with a pen and paper and then enter the data into a spreadsheet to calculate the effects of commissions and leverage and to analyze the performance on both a percentage and a win-loss basis. For more complex strategies that involve a large number of trades on a large number of securities, you might want to use simulation software. These are trading simulation software packages that mimic trading software (and are usually added features to trading software packages; see Chapters 6 and 7 for more information). They let you enter the size of your order, let you use leverage, and tell you whether your trade can be executed given current market conditions.

Markets are affected by supply and demand, and your trade can affect that. And that's the biggest drawback of simulation trading: It's difficult to take the market effects of your trade into account in any reliable way.

The results of your trading simulation can help you refine your trading strategy further. Does it work in current market conditions? Are you able to identify entry and exit points? Can you make enough trades to make money to make your day trading efforts worthwhile? Do you want to refine your strategy some more, or are you ready to go with it?

It may take a long time to find a suitable strategy. Some traders report spending months finding a strategy they felt comfortable using. Day trading is a business like any other. Consider this part of the market research and education process that you need to go through, just as you would have to spend time doing research before opening a store or training for a new career. Stay patient. It's better to do good simulation for months than to lose thousands of real dollars in hours.

Backtesting and simulation software

Several vendors have risen to meet the challenge of backtesting. The list in this section is by no means exhaustive, nor is it an endorsement of their services. It's just a good place for you to start your research.

If you are just getting started with trading, you may want to work with a cheaper package just to see how it works. If you already have an account with a brokerage firm, check to see whether backtesting and simulation are among the services offered. You can always move up as your needs change or if you start pursuing exotic strategies with unusual securities.

If you have the programming expertise, or if your strategy is not well represented in current backtesting programs, you might want to create your own system. Many software-savvy day traders write programs using Excel's Visual Basic functions, allowing them to create custom tests that they then run against price databases.

AmiBroker

AmiBroker (`www.amibroker.com`) offers a robust backtesting service at a relatively low price. This makes it a popular choice with people who are getting started in day trading and who don't have more expensive services. It also allows users to make sophisticated technical charts that they can use to monitor the markets. One drawback is that you might have to pay extra for the market price quote data, depending on what securities and time periods you want to test.

MetaStock Pro

Owned by Thomson Reuters, this powerful trading software (www.equis.com) offers plenty of backtesting data including historical numbers for the TSX. Users can test stocks, bonds, mutual funds, futures, currencies, and more. But it'll cost you — you have to buy the entire program at $1,395 and pay $1,300 a year for data to use the backtesting component.

Tradecision

Tradecision's (www.tradecision.com) trade analysis software package is a little pricier than most retail trading alternatives, but it offers more advanced capabilities, including an analysis of the strengths and weaknesses of different trading rules. It can incorporate advanced money management techniques and artificial intelligence to develop more predictions about performance in different market conditions. The system may be overkill for most new day traders, but it could come in handy for some.

TradeStation

TradeStation (www.tradestation.com) is an online broker that specializes in services for day traders. Its strategy testing service lets you specify different trading parameters and then it shows you where these trades would have taken place in the past using price charts. That way, you can see what would have happened, which is helpful if you are good at technical analysis. It also generates a report of the strategy, showing dollar, percentage, and win-loss performance over different time periods. Unfortunately, it doesn't carry Canadian data, and doesn't have a trade simulation feature, but if you're just looking to backtest U.S. securities, this is all you'll need.

During the Day: Tracking Your Trades

After you put your strategy to work during the trading day, it's easy to let the energy and emotion overtake you. You get sloppy and you stop keeping track of what's happening. And that's not good. Day trading is not a video game, it's a job. Keeping careful records helps you identify how well you follow your strategy and helps you identify ways to refine it. It can also show you how successful your trading is, and it makes your life a lot easier when it's time to do your taxes. (See Chapter 10 for more information on what the friendly folks at the CRA expect from traders, besides a cut of their profits.)

Setting up your spreadsheet

The easiest way to get started is with a spreadsheet software program such as Microsoft Excel. Set up columns for the asset being purchased, the time of the trade, the price, the quantity purchased, and the commission. Then set up similar columns to show what happens when the position is closed out. Finally, calculate your performance based on the change in the security's price and the dollars and percentage return on your trade. Figure 11-1 gives you an example.

Trade Tracker
2/1/11

POSITIONS Symbol	Description	Purchase Date	Purchase Time	Purchase Price	Lot Attempted	Lot Filled	Comm.	Total Cost	Sale Time	Sale Price	Sale Quantity	Comm.	Total Proceeds	Gain/Loss in Points	Gain/Loss in Dollars	Gain/Loss in Percent
INTC	Intel	2/1/11	9:31	20.98	1000	1,000	6.00	(20,986.00)	9:52	21.10	1000	6.00	21,094.00	12	108.00	0.51%
NVDA	Nvidia	2/1/11	9:33	30.38	1000	1,000	6.00	(30,374.00)	9:58	30.87	1000	6.00	30,864.00	49	490.00	1.61%
AKAM	Akamai	2/1/11	9:46	57.44	500	500	3.00	(28,717.00)	10:36	56.60	500	3.00	28,297.00	-84	(420.00)	-1.46%
INTC	Intel	2/1/11	10:18	21.08	1000	1,000	6.00	(21,074.00)	10:40	20.95	1000	6.00	20,944.00	-13	(130.00)	-0.62%
AKAM	Akamai	2/1/11	11:08	55.09	500	200	1.20	(11,016.80)	12:08	55.39	200	1.20	11,076.80	30	60.00	0.54%
NVDA	Nvidia	2/1/11	11:08	30.38	1000	1,000	6.00	(30,374.00)	11:28	30.31	1000	6.00	30,304.00	-7	(70.00)	-0.23%
INTC	Intel	2/1/11	11:11	20.91	1000	1,000	6.00	(20,904.00)	11:45	21.03	1000	6.00	21,024.00	12	120.00	0.57%
NVDA	Nvidia	2/1/11	11:55	30.38	1000	1,000	6.00	(30,374.00)	12:15	30.72	1000	6.00	30,714.00	34	340.00	1.12%
INTC	Intel	2/1/11	12:23	20.93	1000	1,000	6.00	(20,924.00)	12:56	21.07	1000	6.00	21,064.00	14	140.00	0.67%
INTC	Intel	2/1/11	13:08	21.05	1000	1,000	6.00	(21,044.00)	13:52	21.04	1000	6.00	21,034.00	-1	(10.00)	-0.05%
AKAM	Akamai	2/1/11	13:22	55.43	500	500	3.00	(27,712.00)	13:41	55.48	500	3.00	27,737.00	5	25.00	0.09%
INTC	Intel	2/1/11	14:05	21.03	1000	1,000	6.00	(21,024.00)	14:26	21.09	1000	6.00	21,084.00	6	60.00	0.29%
NVDA	Nvidia	2/1/11	14:09	30.52	1000	1,000	6.00	(30,514.00)	15:09	30.54	1000	6.00	30,534.00	2	20.00	0.07%
INTC	Intel	2/1/11	15:05	21.10	1000	1,000	6.00	(21,094.00)	15:59	21.11	1000	6.00	21,104.00	1	10.00	0.05%
Starting Capital:															$ 165,239.00	
Day's Profit:															$ 743.00	
Percent Change:															0.45%	
Ending Capital:															$ 165,982.00	
Ratio of winning to losing trades:															10 : 4	
Hourly Wage:															$ 92.88	
Total commissions paid:															$ 146.40	

Figure 11-1: You can use this sample to make your own trade-tracking spreadsheet.

Some brokerage firms and trading platforms automatically store your trade data for analysis. You can then download the data into your own spreadsheet or work with it in your trading software. If you make too many trades to keep track of manually, then this feature will be especially important to you.

Profit and loss statements

If you look at the bottom of Figure 11-1, you'll see some quick summary statistics on how the day's trading went: trading profits net of commissions, trading profits as a percentage of trading capital, and the ratio of winning to losing transactions. Transfer this information into another spreadsheet so that you can track your ongoing success.

Figure 11-2 shows an example of a profit and loss spreadsheet.

Calculate your hourly wage for each day that you trade. Simply take each day's profit and divide it by the number of hours that you worked. That number, more than any other, will help you see whether it makes sense for you to keep trading or if you'd be better off pursuing a different line of work. If you find that calculating the number daily is too stressful, try doing it monthly.

Profit and Loss

	Initial Capital	Net Profit (Loss)	Ending Capital	Percentage Change	Hourly Wage
1/3/11	$ 161,298	$ 134	$ 161,432	0.08%	$ 16.75
1/4/11	$ 161,432	$ (268)	$ 161,164	-0.17%	$ (33.50)
1/5/11	$ 161,164	$ 450	$ 161,614	0.28%	$ 56.25
1/8/11	$ 161,614	$ (183)	$ 161,431	-0.1 1%	$ (22.88)
1/9/11	$ 161,431	$ 192	$ 161,623	0.12%	$ 24.00
1/10/11	$ 161,623	$ 598	$ 162,221	0.37%	$ 74.75
1/11/11	$ 162,221	$ (168)	$ 162,053	-0.10%	$ (21.00)
1/12/11	$ 162,053	$ 987	$ 163,040	0.61%	$ 123.38
1/16/11	$ 163,040	$ (196)	$ 162,844	-0.12%	$ (24.50)
1/17/11	$ 162,844	$ 59	$ 162,903	0.04%	$ 7.38
1/18/11	$ 162,903	$ (273)	$ 162,630	-0.17%	$ (34.13)
1/19/11	$ 162,630	$ (124)	$ 162,506	-0.08%	$ (15.50)
1/22/11	$ 162,506	$ 689	$ 163,195	0.42%	$ 86.13
1/23/11	$ 163,195	$ (397)	$ 162,798	-0.24%	$ (49.63)
1/24/11	$ 162,798	$ 967	$ 163,765	0.59%	$ 120.88
1/25/11	$ 163,765	$ (387)	$ 163,378	-0.24%	$ (48.38)
1/26/11	$ 163,378	$ 469	$ 163,847	0.29%	$ 58.63
1/29/11	$ 163,847	$ 798	$ 164,645	0.49%	$ 99.75
1/30/11	$ 164,645	$ (129)	$ 164,516	-0.08%	$ (16.13)
1/31/11	$ 164,516	$ 723	$ 165,239	0.44%	$ 90.38
January:	$ 161,298	$ 3,941	$ 165,239	2.44%	$ 24.63
2/1/11	$ 165,239	$ 743	$ 165,982	0.45%	$ 92.88

Figure 11-2: A sample profit and loss spreadsheet.

The trading diary

As part of your trading spreadsheet, or in addition to it, you should track the reasons for making every trade. Was it because of a signal from your system? Because of a hunch? Because you saw an opportunity that was too good to pass up? Then you can keep track of how the trade worked out. Is your trading system giving off good signals? Are you following them? Are your hunches so good that maybe your system needs to be refined? Are you missing good trades because you are following your gut and not the data in front of you?

A *trading diary* gives you information to systematically assess your trading. Start by writing down why you are making a particular trade, and do it when you make the trade. Trust us, if you wait until later, you'll forget and you'll change your logic to suit your needs. You can enter the information in a spreadsheet, jot something quick on a piece of scratch paper, or keep a notebook dedicated to your trading. It doesn't have to be fancy, as long as you take the time to make the note so that you can refer back to it.

Some traders create a form, make copies of it, and keep a stack on hand so they can easily fill out the form during the day. They even create predetermined indicators that match their strategies and that they can check off or circle. At the end of the day they collect their diary sheets into a three-ring binder, and they refer back to the data when it's time to evaluate their trading strategy and their performance.

Figure 11-3 offers an example of a trading diary. You can customize it for your own trading strategy, including those indicators that matter most to you.

Trading Diary

Date: ______________
Time: ______________
Security Name: ______________ **Symbol:** ________ **Market:** ______________

Price entered: ______________ **Long/short?** long short
Quantity: ______________ **Leverage used?** yes no

Indicators:

Price trend is	rising	falling	rangebound
Volume is	rising	falling	steady
Sector is	rising	falling	rangebound
Market is	rising	falling	rangebound

Technical Pattern: ______________

Price closed: ______________
Quantity: ______________
Time: ______________

Indicators:

Price trend is	rising	falling	rangebound
Volume is	rising	falling	steady
Sector is	rising	falling	rangebound
Market is	rising	falling	rangebound

Technical Pattern: ______________

I initiated this trade because (check one):

______ The trading system signalled it
______ I had a hunch (explain below)
______ The market looked right, even though the signal didn't go of f (explain below)
______ Other (explain below)

I closed out this trade because (check one):

______ The trading system signalled it
______ I needed to cut my losses
______ I had a hunch (explain below)
______ The market looked right, even though the signal didn't go of f (explain below)
______ Other (explain below)

Explanation and lessons learned:

____
____
____
____
____
____
____

Figure 11-3: A trading diary should be customized to your own preferences.

The trading diary form in Figure 11-3 is just an example. If your trading style is so fast that you don't have time to fill it out, don't fret — come up with some kind of shorthand so that you can keep a running tally of trades based on a signal from your system, trades based on your own hunches, and trades based on other interpretations of market conditions. Then match your notes against the trader confirmations from your broker to see how you did.

After You Trade: Calculating Overall Performance

Calculating performance seems easy: Simply use the balance at the end of the year and the balance at the start of the year to find the percentage change. But what if you added to your investment in the middle of the year? What if you took cash out in the middle of the year to buy a new computer? Quickly you're left with algebra unlike any you've seen since high school, but you need to solve it to see how you are doing.

In addition to the increase in your assets you want to track your *volatility,* which is how much your gains and losses can fluctuate. It's an important measure of risk, especially if your trading strategy relies on leverage (see Chapter 14 for more information on that).

Types of return

The investment performance calculation starts by dividing returns into different categories: income and capital gains. Although almost all a day trader's gains will come from capital gains, we go over the definitions of each so that you know the differences.

Income

When investors talk about *income returns,* they mean regular payments from their investments, usually in the form of dividends from stocks or interest payments on bonds. As a day trader, you may earn income on the cash balance in your brokerage account, but probably not from your trading activities.

Capital gains

A *capital gain* is the price appreciation in an asset — a stock, a bond, a house, whatever it is that you're investing in. You buy it at one price, sell it at another, and the difference is a capital gain. (Unless, of course, you sell the asset for less than you paid, and then you have a capital loss.)

Income in tax terms is different from income in financial terms. Much of what an investor would consider to be a capital gain, the CRA considers to be income.

Calculating returns

Give someone with a numerical bent a list of numbers and a calculator, and she can some up with several different relationships among the numbers. When the asset values for each time period have been determined, rates of return can be calculated. But how? And over how long a time period? The process gets a little more complicated.

Percentage change

The most common way to calculate investment returns is to use a time-weighted average. It's perfect for traders who start with one pool of money and do not add to it or take money out. This is also called the *compound average rate of return* (CAGR). If you're looking at only one month or one year, it's a simple percentage, as shown in Figure 11-4.

Figure 11-4: Calculating performance on a percentage basis.

$$\frac{EOY - BOY}{BOY}$$

EOY stands for *end of year asset value* and BOY is *beginning of year value.* The result is the percentage return for one year, and it's simple arithmetic.

Now, if you want to look at your return over a period of several years, you need to look at the *compound* return rather than the simple return for each year. The compound return shows you how your investment is growing. You are getting returns on top of returns, and that is a good thing. But the math gets a little complicated, because now you have to use the root function on your calculator. The equation looks like Figure 11-5.

EOP stands for *end of the total time period*; BOP stands for *beginning of the total time period*; and that N is the *number of years* we're looking at.

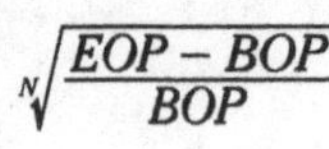

Figure 11-5: The equation for compound annual growth rate.

The basic percentage rate of return is great; it's an accurate, intuitive measure of how much gain you're generating from your trading activities. As long as you don't take any money out of your trading account or put any money into it, you're set.

However, you may be putting money into your account. Maybe you have a salaried job and are day trading on the side, or maybe your spouse gives you a percentage of his income to add to your trading account. You might also be taking money out of your day trading account to cover your living expenses or to put into other investment opportunities. All that money flowing into and out of your account can really screw up your performance calculation. You need a way to calculate the performance of your trading system without considering the deposits and withdrawals to your trading account.

Consider this example: You start day trading on January 1 with $100,000 in your account. On June 1 your income tax refund from last year arrives, and you add $1,000 of the money to your account and start trading with it. On December 1, you take out $5,000 to buy holiday presents. At the end of the year, your account is worth $115,000. How did you do?

As a day trader, you have a few methods at your disposal for calculating your performance when you make withdrawals and deposits:

- **The modified Dietz method** loses a little accuracy but makes up for it with simplicity.
- **The time-weighted rate of return** isolates investment and trading performance from the rest of the account.
- **The dollar-weighted rate of return** has many flaws but gives a sense of what the account holder has.

Read on to see the return that would be calculated using each of these methods.

Modified Dietz method

The *modified Dietz method* is related to the simple percentage change formula, but it adjusts the beginning and ending period amounts for the cash inflows and cash outflows. The equation is shown in Figure 11-6.

$$\frac{EOY - BOY - deposits + withdrawals}{BOY + deposits - withdrawals}$$

Figure 11-6: The equation for the modified Dietz method.

So with the numbers in our example, it would look like Figure 11-7.

$$\frac{115{,}000 - 100{,}000 - 1{,}000 + 5{,}000}{100{,}000 + 1{,}000 - 5{,}000}$$

Figure 11-7: Calculating using the modified Dietz method.

And that equals 19.8 percent.

The advantage of the modified Dietz method is that it is so easy to do. You can calculate it to give you a rough idea of how you're doing with your trading when you don't have the time to run a more detailed analysis. The key disadvantage is that it doesn't consider the timing of the deposits and withdrawals. It would generate the same answer if you took out $5,000 in June and put in $1,000 in December, even though the amount of money you would have to trade between June 1 and December 1 would be very different.

Time-weighted rate of return

The *time-weighted rate of return* shows the investment performance as a percentage of the assets at hand to trade. It's the standard of trader evaluation, but the math is much more complicated than with the basic percentage change or the modified Dietz method. You need to calculate the CAGR for each time period and then do a second calculation to incorporate each of those over a longer period. Using our example, you'd calculate one return for the first four months of the year, another for the next seven months, and then a third return for the month of December. These three returns would be then be multiplied to generate a return for the year.

The general equation looks like Figure 11-8.

$$\sqrt[N]{(1+r_{p1})(1+r_{p2})(1+r_{p3})\ldots(1+r_{pn})}-1$$

Figure 11-8: Figuring the time-weighted rate of return.

N is the total number of time periods that you are looking at, and r_{pn} is the return for that particular time period. To make it easy, you can do the calculation in a spreadsheet. Figure 11-9 shows the time-weighted return for this example.

	January	May	December
Beginning of Period Account Value	$ 100,000	$ 109,000	$ 123,000
Deposit/(Withdrawal)	$ -	$ 1,000	$ (5,000)
Adjusted Beginning Account Value	$ 100,000	$ 110,000	$ 118,000
Trading Earnings	$ 9,000	$ 13,000	$ (3,000)
End-of-Period Account Value	$ 109,000	$ 123,000	$ 115,000
Period Percentage Return:	9.00%	11.82%	-2.54%
Annual Return:			18.78%

Figure 11-9: An example of the time-weighted rate of return calculation.

The result is 18.78 percent, a little below the modified Dietz return.

If you plan on adding to or taking money out of your account, you can make your return calculations much easier by setting a regular schedule and sticking to it. Otherwise, you'll have to do calculations for fractional time periods. It's not impossible, but it's kind of a hassle.

The time-weighted rate of return gives you the best sense of your trading performance, and its precision for this use more than offsets the complexity of the calculation. You want to look at this number when you're deciding whether to change or refine your strategy.

Dollar-weighted returns

The *dollar-weighted return,* also called the *money-weighted return,* is the rate that makes the net present value of a stream of numbers equal to zero. That calculation is also called the *internal rate of return* or *IRR,* and it is used for other things than just return calculations. It's a way of determining what the return is for a stream of numbers over time, and it's useful for calculating returns when you're putting money into or taking money out of your trading account. And if you have a financial calculator, such as the Hewlett-Packard HP12C or the Texas Instruments BA2+, it's pretty easy to calculate.

Ah, but there's a catch! Although it's useful, the dollar-weighted method can misstate returns and can occasionally show nonsensical results if too many negative returns occur in a series. And yes, day traders often have negative returns. Figure 11-10 shows the dollar-weighted rate of return using the same data used in the two examples.

	January	May	December
Beginning of Period Account Value	$ 100,000	$ 109,000	$ 123,000
Deposit/(Withdrawal)	$ -	$ 1,000	$ (5,000)
Adjusted Beginning Account Value	$ 100,000	$ 110,000	$ 118,000
Trading Earnings	$ 9,000	$ 13,000	$ (3,000)
End-of-Period Account Value	$ 109,000	$ 123,000	$ 115,000
Period Percentage Return:	9.00%	11.82%	-2.54%
Annual Return:			12.10%

Figure 11-10: Calculating the dollar-weighted rate of return.

The result is 12.1 percent, lower than the other two examples because the dollar-weighted return overstates the withdrawal and the loss in the last month of the year. The withdrawals affect the account's spending power, offsetting the investment performance. But the overall account balance is up more than 12.1 percent, even considering the deposit at the beginning of June — the weight of the cash flows threw off this calculation.

Because of the problems with dollar-weighted returns, professional investors who analyze investment returns usually prefer the time-weighted, compound-average approach. Still, the dollar-weighted return has some value, especially for an investor who wants to know how the asset value has changed over time. Because a day trader is usually both an investor and an account owner, the dollar-weighted rate of return can show whether the investment performance is affecting spending power. This measure is particularly useful when you are trying to decide whether to continue day trading.

Just as you have alternatives in calculating your performance, so too does anyone trying to sell you a trading system or training course. Ask questions about the performance calculation method and how cash flows and expenses are handled. The numbers might not look so great after you grade the math behind them.

The risk to your return

Now that you have return numbers from your profit and loss statements and your return calculations, it's time to perform black-belt-performance jujitsu and determine your risk levels. We're not going to go into all of the many risk and volatility measures out there, because believe us when we say that the good editors of the *...For Dummies* books don't want to proofread all the math.

Batting average

Baseball players are judged by how often they hit the ball. After all, they can't score until they get on base, and they can't get on base without a hit or a walk. The number of hits relative to the number of times at bat is the batting average. It's a simple, beautiful number.

Day traders often calculate their batting average, too, although they might call it their *win-loss percentage* or *win ratio*. It's the same: the number of successful trades to the total number of trades. Not all trades have to work out for you to make money, but the more often the trades work for you, the better your overall performance is likely to be. If you have both good performance and a high batting average, then your strategy may have less risk than one that relies on just a handful of home run trades amidst a bunch of strikeouts.

Standard deviation

Want something harder than your batting average? Turn to *standard deviation,* which is tricky to calculate without a spreadsheet but forms the core of many risk measures out there.

The standard deviation calculation starts with the average return over a given time period. This is the *expected* return, the return that, on average, you get if you stick with your trading strategy. But any given week, month, or year, the return might be very different from what you expect. The more likely you are to get what you expect, the less risk you take. Insured bank savings accounts pay a low interest rate, but the rate is guaranteed. Day trading offers the potential for much higher returns, but also the possibility that you could lose everything in any one month — especially if you can't stick to your trading discipline.

The explanation is a lot easier to understand when you take a gander at Figure 11-11.

In Step One, you take every return over the time period and then find the average. A simple mean will do. Here, there are 12 months, so we added all 12 returns and then divided by 12.

Calculating Standard Deviation

	Step One: Find the expected return	**Step Two: Subtract expected return from each reported return**		**Step Three: Calculate the square of each difference**
	Percentage Return	**R-E(R)**		**(R-E(R))^2**
January	(0.02)	(0.0211)		0.0004
February	0.01	0.0079		0.0001
March	(0.00)	(0.0040)		0.0000
April	0.09	0.0849		0.0072
May	0.01	0.0082		0.0001
June	0.01	0.0082		0.0001
July	(0.08)	(0.0818)		0.0067
August	0.02	0.0182		0.0003
September	0.03	0.0282		0.0008
October	(0.04)	(0.0418)		0.0017
November	(0.01)	(0.0118)		0.0001
December	0.01	0.0049		0.0000
Total	0.02		Sum of the squares:	0.0176
E(R)	0.0018	**Step Four:**	Average of the sum of the squares	0.0015
		Step Five:	Square root of the average of the sum of the squares, also known as standard deviation	0.0383

Figure 11-11: Calculating standard deviation.

In Step Two, you take each of the 12 returns and then subtract the average from it. This shows how much any one return differs from the average, to give you a sense of how much the returns can go back and forth.

In Step Three, you take each of those differences and then square them (multiply them by themselves). This gets rid of the negative numbers. When you add those up, you get a number known in statistics as the *sum of the squares.*

Now you have enough for Step Four: taking the average of the sum of the squares.

And for Step Five: the square root of the average of the sum of the squares. That square root from Step Five is the *standard deviation,* the magic number we're looking for.

Of course, you don't have to do all this math. Almost all trading software calculates standard deviation automatically, but at least you now know where the calculation comes from.

The higher the standard deviation, the riskier the strategy. This number can help you determine how comfortable you are with different trading techniques you might be backtesting, as well as whether you want to stick with your current strategy.

In academic terms, *risk* is the likelihood of getting any return other than the return you expect. To most normal human beings, no risk exists in getting more than you expect — the problem is in getting less of a return than you were counting on. This is a key limitation of risk evaluation.

Past performance is no indicator of future results. That truism applies to risk as well as to return.

Using benchmarks to evaluate your performance

To understand your performance numbers, you need one more step: what your performance is relative to what else you could be doing with your money.

Performance relative to an index

The most common way to think about investment performance is relative to a *market index*. These are the measures of the overall market you hear quoted all the time in the news, such as the S&P/TSX Composite Index and S&P 500. Not only are these widely watched, but many mutual funds and futures contracts are designed to mimic their performance. That means investors can always do at least as well as the index itself, if their investment objectives call for exposure to that part of the broad investment market.

Indexes aren't perfect. One big problem is that day traders often look at the wrong index for the type of investment that they have. They'll compare the performance of trading in agricultural commodities to the S&P/TSX Composite Index when a commodities index would be a better measure.

If you aren't sure what to use, visit the Bloomberg Web site (`www.bloomberg.com`). The site has long list of stocks, bonds, and commodity indexes, covering many world markets including Canada and the United States. You can find the one that best matches your strategy and use it to compare your performance.

In some cases, your trading practices may overlap more than one index. If so, pick the indexes that are appropriate and compare them only to those trades that match. If you trade 40 percent currencies and 60 percent metals, then you should create your own hybrid index that's 40 percent currencies and 60 percent metals.

Performance relative to your time

A few pages back when we talk about tracking your trades and doing a profit and loss statement, we say that you should calculate your hourly wage. There's a reason for that. Instead of day trading, you could put your money in a nice, simple, index mutual fund and take a regular job. If your hourly wage is less than what you can earn elsewhere, you might want to consider doing just that.

Of course, some of the benefits to working on your own don't often show up in your bank account. If you enjoy day trading and you make enough money to suit your lifestyle, by all means, don't let the relative numbers stop you.

Part III
Day Trading Strategies

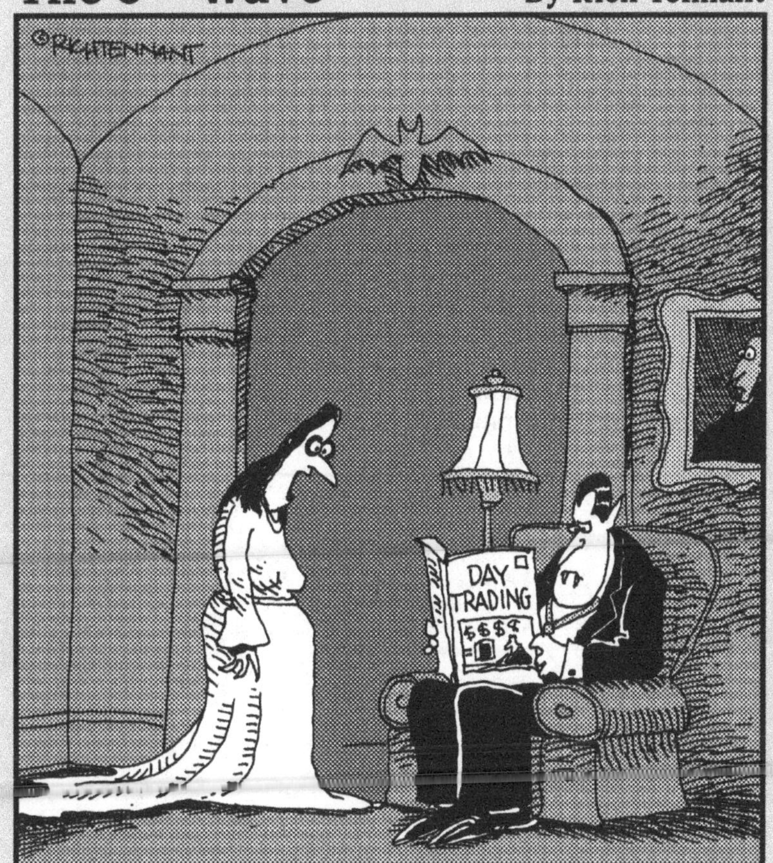

"Oh, it's just what they call it. I'm sure you can do it at night, too."

In this part . . .

Good day traders don't just rush in and buy and sell willy-nilly. They use research and follow strategies to help them determine where and when to buy and sell their positions. Some of the strategies and tools include selling short to profit from securities that are declining in price and using leverage to make bigger trades in hopes of bigger returns. This part includes information that can help you make better portfolio decisions, even if you decide not to become a day trader. Of course, the markets are the best teacher — and the harshest. The more you understand the information that traders want to see, the better you'll understand what the markets are telling you.

Chapter 12

Using Fundamental and Technical Analysis

In This Chapter

- Researching markets and trades
- Using technical analysis to forecast prices
- Gleaning information from the charts
- Reviewing schools of thought in technical analysis
- Avoiding the traps that technical analysts can fall into

In some ways, day trading is easy. Open up an account with a brokerage firm and off you go, buying and selling securities! But how are you going to know when to buy and when to sell? That's not a simple matter. Most day traders fail because it's easy to place the order, but hard to know if the order is the right one.

Traders use different research systems to evaluate the market. They have access to tools that can help them figure out when a security is likely to go up in price and when it is likely to go down.

Research systems fall into two categories: fundamental and technical. *Fundamental* research looks at the specific factors that affect a security's value. What's the relationship between the trade deficit and futures on two-year Treasury notes? What's the prediction for summer rainfall in Saskatchewan, and how will that affect December wheat futures? How dependent is a company on new products to generate earnings growth?

Technical research, on the other hand, looks at the supply and demand for the security itself. Are people buying more and more shares? Is the price going up as they buy more, or does the price go up just a little bit? Does it seem like everyone who is likely to buy has already bought, and what does that mean for the future price?

Anyone with a surefire system has already made a fortune and retired to a private island in a tropical climate. He or she is too busy enjoying drinks with umbrellas in them to share that surefire trading system with you.

Research Techniques Used in Day Trading

Day traders need to make decisions fast, and they need to have a framework for doing so. That's why they rely on research. But what kind? Most day traders rely heavily on *technical* research, which is an analysis of charts formed by price patterns to measure the relative supply and demand for the security. But some use fundamental analysis to help inform their decisions, too.

What direction is your research?

Securities are affected by matters specific to each type and by huge global macroeconomic factors that affect every security in different ways. Some traders prefer to think of the big picture first, whereas others start small. And some use a combination of the two approaches. Neither is better; each is simply a different perspective on what's happening in the markets.

Top-down research

With a *top-down* approach, the trader looks at the big economic factors: interest rates, exchange rates, government policies, and the like. How will these things affect a particular sector or security? Is this a good time to buy stocks or short interest rate futures? The top-down approach can help evaluate the prices in big market sectors, and it can also help determine what factors are affecting trading in a subsector. You don't have to trade stock market index futures to know that the outlook for the overall stock market will have an effect on the trading of any specific company's stock.

Bottom-up research

Bottom-up analysis looks at the specific performance of the asset. It looks at the company's prospects and then works backward to figure out how it will get there. What has to happen for a company's stock price to go up 20 percent? What earnings does it have to report, what types of buyers have to materialize, and what else has to happen in the economy?

Fundamental research

Day traders do very little fundamental research. Sure, they know that demand for ethanol affects corn prices, but they really want to know what the price will do right now relative to where the price was a few minutes ago. How a proposed farm bill might affect ethanol prices in six years doesn't figure into day trade, though. Knowing a little bit about the fundamentals — those basic facts that affect the supply and demand for a security in all markets — can help the day trader respond better to news events. It can also give you a better feel for when *swing trading* (holding a position for several days) will generate a better profit than closing out every night. But knowing a lot can drag a day trader down.

Fundamental analysis can actually *hurt* you in day trading, because you may start making decisions for the wrong reasons. If you know too much about the fundamentals, you might start considering long-term outlooks instead of short-term activity. For example, someone may buy a Standard & Poor's (S&P)/TSX Composite Index ETF for their RRSP because they believe that in the long run, the market will go up. That doesn't mean people should trade S&P/TSX Composite Index Mini Futures today, because there can be a lot of zigzagging between right now and the arrival of the long-run price appreciation.

Fundamental research falls into two main categories: top-down and bottom-up. As we mention earlier, top-down starts with broad economic considerations and then looks at how those will affect a specific security. Bottom-up looks at specific securities and then determines whether those are good buys or sells right now.

If you love the very idea of fundamental research, then day trading is probably not for you. Day trading requires quick responses to price changes, not a careful understanding of accounting methods and business trends. A little fundamental analysis can be helpful in day trading, but a lot can slow you down.

Technical analysis

Information about the price, time, and volume of a security's trading can be plotted on a chart. The plots form patterns that can be analyzed to show what happened. How did the supply and demand for a security change, and why? And what does that mean for future supply and demand? Technical analysis is based on the premise that securities prices move in trends, and that those trends repeat themselves over time. Therefore, a trader who can recognize a trend on the charts can determine where prices are most likely to go until some unforeseen event comes along that creates a new trend.

The basic element of technical analysis is a *bar*, which shows you the high, low, open, and closing price of a security for a given day. It looks like Figure 12-1.

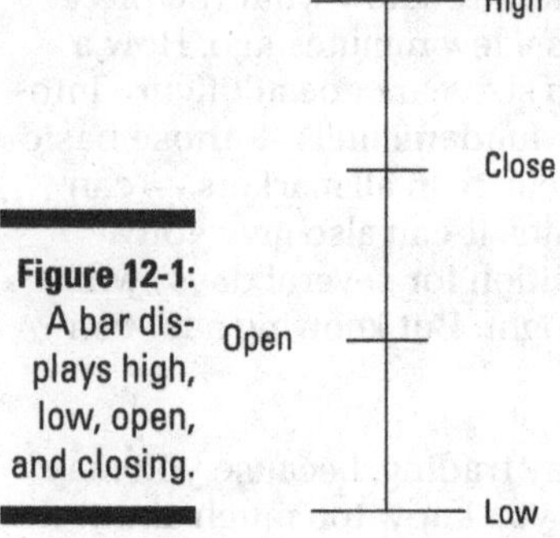

Figure 12-1: A bar displays high, low, open, and closing.

In most markets, every day generates a new *bar* (many traders talk about bars instead of days, and they aren't talking about where they go after work). A collection of bars, with all their different high, low, open, and close points, is put together into a larger *chart*. Often, a plot of the volume for each bar runs underneath, with the result looking like Figure 12-2.

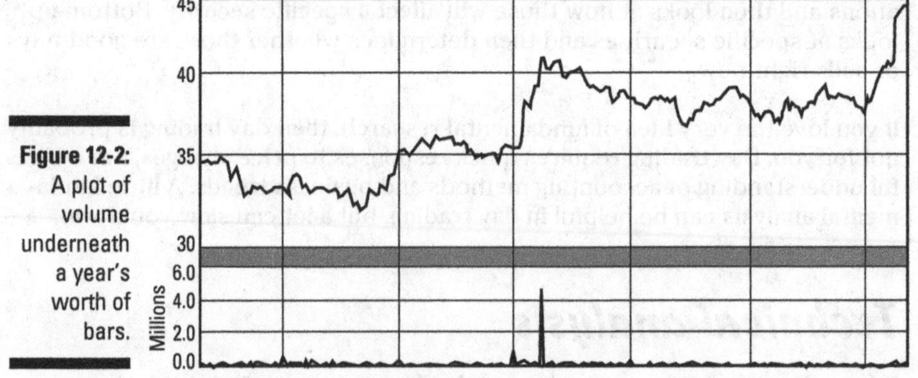

Figure 12-2: A plot of volume underneath a year's worth of bars.

Many patterns formed in the charts are associated with future price moves. Technical analysts thus spend a lot of time looking at the charts to see whether they can predict what will happen. Many software packages (some of which we discuss in Chapter 7) send traders signals when certain technical patterns occur, so that the traders can place orders accordingly.

Bulls and bears and pork bellies, oh my!

Traders work cattle and hogs at the Chicago Mercantile Exchange, but bulls and bears are in every market. What do those mythical animals symbolize?

Bulls believe that the market is going up, and bullish news and bullish patterns are good.

Bears believe that the market is going down, so bearish news and bearish patterns are bad.

No one is exactly sure why the words came into use, but the best guess for the symbolism is that when attacked, bulls charge and bears retreat.

Technical analysis is a way to measure the supply and demand in the market. It's a tool for analyzing the markets, not predicting them. If it were that easy, everyone would be able to make money in the markets.

Price changes

Market observers debate *market efficiency* all the time. In an efficient market, all information about a security is already included in the security's price, so no point exists to doing any research at all. Few market participants are willing to go that far, but they concede the point that the price is the single most important summary of information about a company. That means that technical analysis, looking at how the price changes over time, is a way of learning about whether a security's prospects are improving or getting worse.

Volume changes

The basic bar shows how price changed during the day, but adding *volume* information tells the other part of the story: how much of a security was demanded at that price. If demand is going up, then more people want the security, so they are willing to pay more for it. The price tells traders what the market knows; the volume tells them how many people in the market know it.

How to Use Technical Analysis

Technical analysis helps day traders identify changes in the supply and demand for a security that may lead to profitable price changes ahead. It gives traders a way to talk about and think about the market so that they can be more effective.

Charts are generated by most brokerage firm quote systems, sometimes with the help of additional software that automatically marks the chart with trendlines. That's because a technical trader is looking for those trendlines. Is the security going up in price, and is that trend going to continue? That's the information that a trader needs before placing an order to buy or sell.

One interesting aspect of technical analysis is that the basics hold no matter what market you are looking at. Technical analysis can help you monitor trends in the stock market, the bond market, the commodity market, and the currency market. Anywhere people try to match their supply and their demand to make a market, technical analysis can be used to show how well they're doing it.

Finding trends

A technical analyst usually starts off by looking at a chart and drawing lines that show the overall direction of the price bars for the period in question. Rather than plot the graph on paper or print out the screen, she probably uses software to draw the lines. Figure 12-3 shows what this basic analysis looks like.

With the basic trendlines in place, the trader can start thinking about how the trends have played out so far and what might happen next.

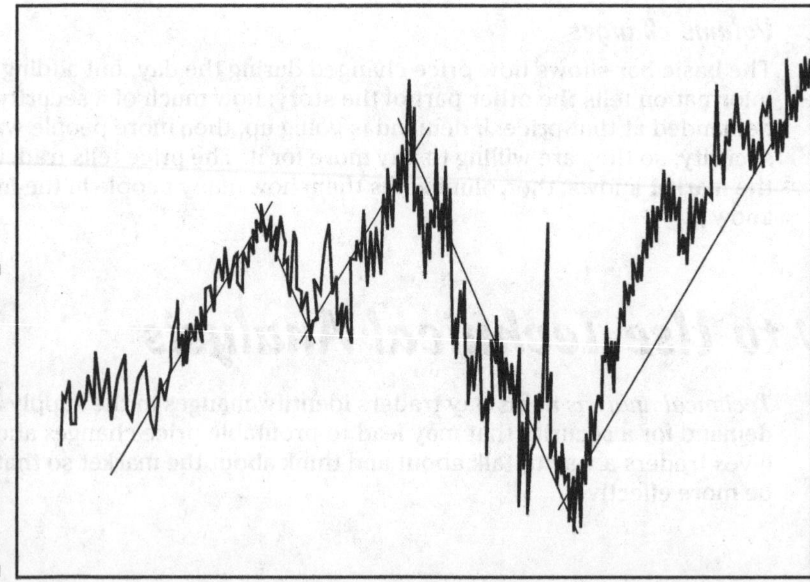

Figure 12-3: Basic analysis of trends in price bar changes draws lines showing the general movement.

Here's the thing about trends: Sometimes it's good to follow, and sometimes it's good to deviate. Remember when you were a kid, and you wanted to do something that all your friends were doing? And your mother would invariably say, "If all your friends jumped off of a bridge, would you have to jump off, too?"

Well, Mom, guess what? If the bridge was on fire, if the escape routes were blocked by angry mobs, if the water were just a few metres down, yes, we just might jump off the bridge like everyone else. Likewise, if someone was paying us good money to jump, and we knew we weren't likely to get hurt on the way down, we'd be over the railing in a flash. Sometimes it's good to be a follower.

But if our friends were idiots, if there were no fire and no angry mob, and if we couldn't swim, we might not be so hasty.

Trend following is like those mythical childhood friends on that mythical hometown bridge. Sometimes, you should join the crowd. Other times, it's best to deviate.

Draw those trendlines!

The most basic *trendline* is a line that shows the general direction of the trend. And that's a good start, but it doesn't tell you all you need to know. The next step is to take out your ruler, or set your software, to find the trendlines that connect the highs and the lows. That will create a channel that tells you the *support level* — the trendline for the lows — and the *resistance level* — the trendline for the highs. Unless something happens to change the trend, securities tend to move within the channel, so extending the line into the future can give you a sense of where the security is likely to trade. Figure 12-4 shows you an example.

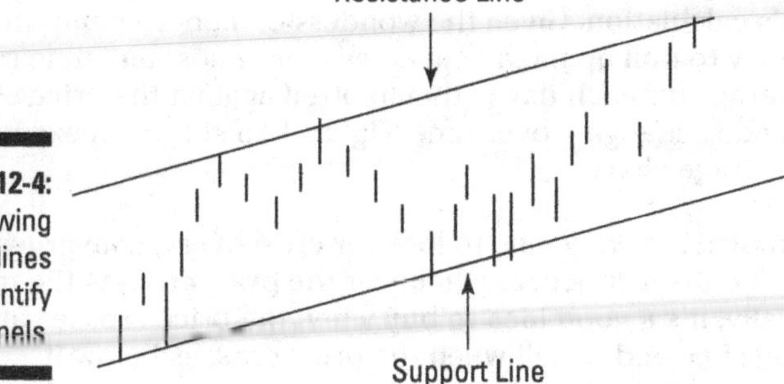

Figure 12-4: Drawing trendlines to identify channels

When a security hits its support level, it is usually seen as relatively cheap — so that's a good time to buy. When a security hits its resistance level, it is usually seen as relatively expensive, so that's a good time to sell. Some day traders find that simply moving between buying at the support and selling at the resistance can be a profitable strategy, at least until something happens that changes those two levels.

Calculating indicators

In addition to drawing lines, technical analysts use their calculators — or have their software make calculations — to come up with different *indicators*. These are numbers that are used to gauge performance. The following is a list of some common indicators, with definitions.

Pivot points

A *pivot point* is the average of the high, low, and close price for the day. If the next day's price closes above the pivot point, that sets a new support level, and if the next day's price is below the pivot point, that sets a new resistance level. Hence, calculating pivot points and how they change might indicate new upper and lower stops for your trading. (You can read more about using stops in Chapter 2.)

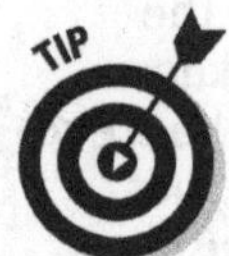

For markets that are open more or less continuously, such as foreign exchange, the close price is set arbitrarily. The usual custom in Canada and the United States is to use the price at 4:00 p.m. Eastern time, which is the closing time for the Toronto Stock Exchange and the New York Stock Exchange.

Moving averages

Looking at all those little high-low-open-close lines on a chart will give your bifocals a workout. To make the trend easier to spot, traders calculate a *moving average*. It's calculated by averaging the closing prices for a given time period. Some traders prefer to look at the last 5 days, some at the last 60 days. Every day, the latest price is added, and the oldest price is dropped to make that day's calculation. Given the wonders of modern computing technology, it's easy to pull up moving averages for almost any time period you want. The average for each day is then plotted against the price chart to show how the trend is changing over time. Figure 12-5 shows an example of a ten-day moving average chart.

Traders use the moving average line to look for crossovers, convergences, and divergences. A *crossover* occurs whenever the price crosses the moving average line. Usually, it's a good idea to buy when the price crosses above the moving average line and to sell when the price crosses below it.

To use *convergence* and *divergence* in analysis, the trader looks at moving averages from different time periods, such as 5 days, 10 days, and 20 days. Figure 12-6 shows what it looks like.

Figure 12-5: This price chart shows a ten-day moving average.

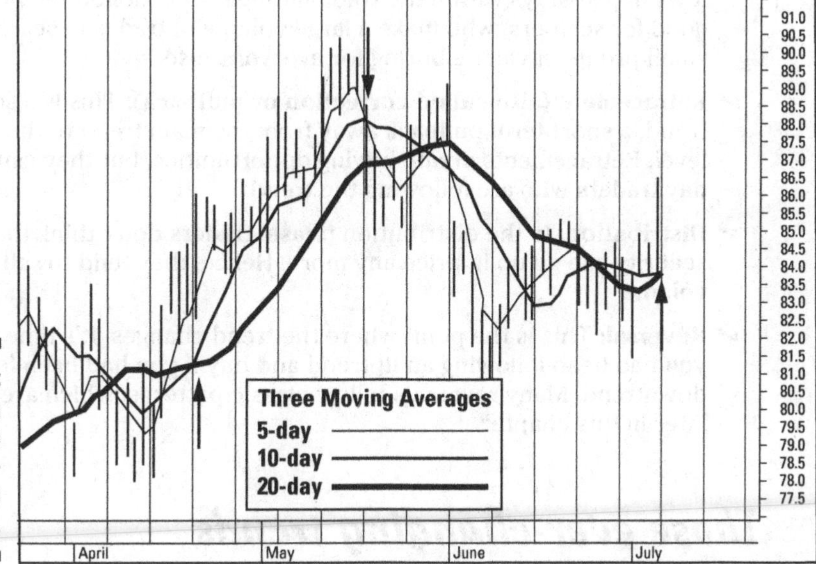

Figure 12-6: Moving average convergence and divergence.

When two or three of the moving average lines converge (come together), it means the trend may be ending. That often makes it a good time to buy if the trend has been down — and a good time to sell if the trend has been up. If two or three of the moving average lines split up and diverge, that means the trend is likely to continue. It's probably a good time to buy if the trend is up and sell if the trend is down.

A moving average is a lagging indicator. It sums up trading activity in the last 5, 10, 30, or 60 days. That means that the line will smooth out changes in the trend that may affect future prices.

Trends move in phases

Price trends tend to move in cycles that can be seen on the charts or observed in market behaviour. Knowing the phases of a trend can help you better evaluate what's happening. Here is a summary of some phases of a trend:

- **Accumulation:** This is the first part of the trend, where traders get excited about a security and its prospects. They start new positions or add to existing ones.
- **Main phase (also called continuation):** Here, the trend moves along nicely, with no unusual price action. The highs get higher on an uptrend, and the lows get lower on a downtrend. A trader might make money, but not big money, following the trend here.
- **Consolidation (also called congestion):** This is a sideways market. The security stays within the trend, but without hitting higher highs or lower lows. It just stays within the trading range. A consolidation phase is good for scalpers, who make a large volume of trades in search of very small profits. It can be boring for everyone else.
- **Retracement (also called correction or pullback):** This is a secondary trend, a short-term pullback away from the main trend to the support level. Retracements create buying opportunities, but they can also kill day traders who are following the trend.
- **Distribution:** In the distribution phase, traders don't think that the security can go up in price any more. Hence, they tend to sell in large volume.
- **Reversal:** This is the point where the trend changes. It's time to sell if you had been following an uptrend and buy if you had been following a downtrend. Many reversals follow classic patterns, which are discussed later in this chapter.

Those ever-changing trends

Although technical traders look to follow trends, they also look for situations where the trend changes so that they can find new profit opportunities. In general, day traders are going to follow trends, and swing traders — those who hold securities for a few days or even weeks — are going to be more interested in identifying changes that may play out over time.

Momentum

Following the trend is great, but if the trend is moving quickly you want to know so that you can get ahead of it. If the rate of change on the trend is going up, then rising prices are likely to occur.

To calculate *momentum*, take today's closing price for a security, divide that by the closing price ten days ago, and then multiply by 100. This gives you a *momentum indicator*. If the price didn't go anywhere, the momentum indicator will be 100. If the price went up, the indicator will be greater than 100. And if it went down, it will be less than 100. In technical analysis, trends are usually expected to continue, so a security with a momentum indicator above 100 is expected to keep going up, all else being equal.

But it's that "all else being equal" that's the sticky part. Technical analysts usually track momentum indicators over time to see if the positive momentum is, itself, a trend. In fact, momentum indicators are a good confirmation of the underlying trend.

Momentum is a leading technical indicator. It tells you what is likely to happen in the future, not what has happened in the past.

Momentum trading is usually done with some attention to the fundamentals. When key business fundamentals such as sales or profits are accelerating at the same time that the security is going up in price, the momentum is likely to continue for some time. You can read more about momentum trading and investing in Chapter 16.

Finding breakouts

A *breakout* occurs when a security price passes through and stays above — or below — the resistance or support line, which creates a new trend with new support and resistance levels. A one-time breakout may just be an anomaly, what technicians sometimes call a *false breakout*, but pay attention to two or more breakouts. Figure 12-7 shows what breakouts look like.

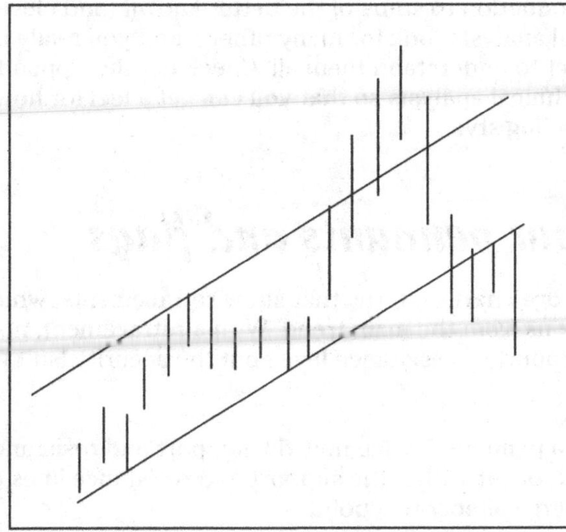

Figure 12-7: A breakout indicates a new trend.

When a true breakout occurs, a new trend starts. That means an upward breakout will be accompanied by rising prices, and a downward breakout will be accompanied by falling prices.

With a false breakout, some traders buy or sell thinking that the trend will continue, see that it doesn't, and then turn around and reverse their positions at a loss.

A false breakout can cause those misled traders to wreak havoc for a day or two of trading. This is where the ability to size up the intelligence of the other traders in the market can come in handy.

Good technical analysts look at several different indicators in order to see whether a change in trend is real or just one of those things that goes away quickly as the old trend resumes.

Reading the Charts

How long does it take to find the trend? How long does it take for the trend to play out? When do you act on it? Do you have minutes, hours, or days to act?

Because markets tend to move in cycles, technical analysts look for patterns in the price charts that give them an indication of how long any particular trend may last. In this section, we show you some of the common patterns that day traders look for when they do technical analysis. Alas, some are obvious only in hindsight, but knowing what the patterns mean can help you make better forecasts of where a security price should go.

This is just an introduction to some of the better-known (and cleverly named) patterns. Technical analysts look for many others, and you really need a book on the subject to understand them all. Check out the Appendix for more information on technical analysis so that you can get a feel for how you can apply it to your trading style.

Waving your pennants and flags

Pennants and *flags* are chart patterns that show retracements, which are short-term deviations from the main trend. With a retracement, no breakout comes from the support or resistance level, but the security isn't following the trend, either.

Figure 12-8 shows a pennant. Notice how the support and resistance lines of the pennant (which occur within the support and resistance lines of a much larger trend) converge almost to a point.

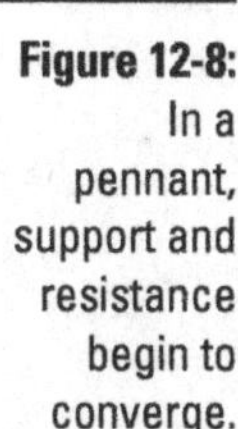
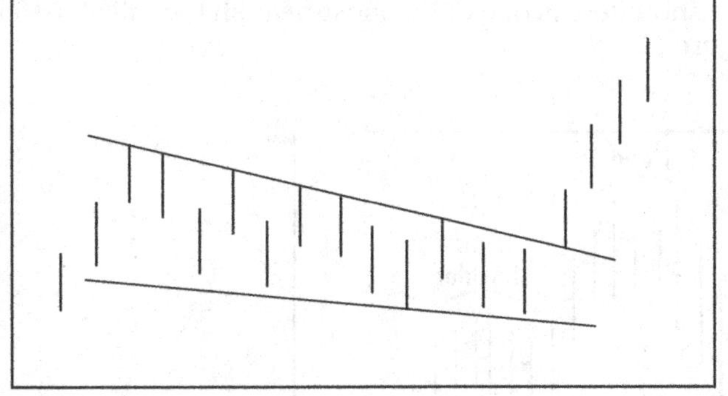

Figure 12-8: In a pennant, support and resistance begin to converge.

Figure 12-9, by contrast, is a flag. The main difference between a flag and a pennant is that the flag's support and resistance lines are parallel.

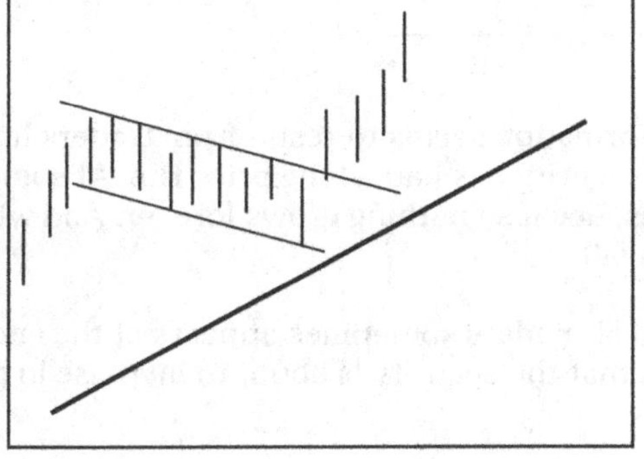

Figure 12-9: A flag, like a pennant, usually indicates falling volume.

Pennants and flags are usually found in the middle of the main phase of a trend, and they seem to last for two weeks before going back to the trendline. They are almost always accompanied by falling volume. In fact, if the trading volume isn't falling, you're probably looking at a *reversal* — a change in trend — rather than a retracement.

Not just for the shower: Head and shoulders

The *head and shoulders* formation is a series of three peaks within a price chart. The peaks on the left and right (the shoulders) should be relatively smaller than the peak in the centre (the head). The shoulders connect at a price known as the neckline, and when the right shoulder formation is reached, the price plunges down.

The head and shoulders is one of the most bearish technical patterns, and it looks like Figure 12-10.

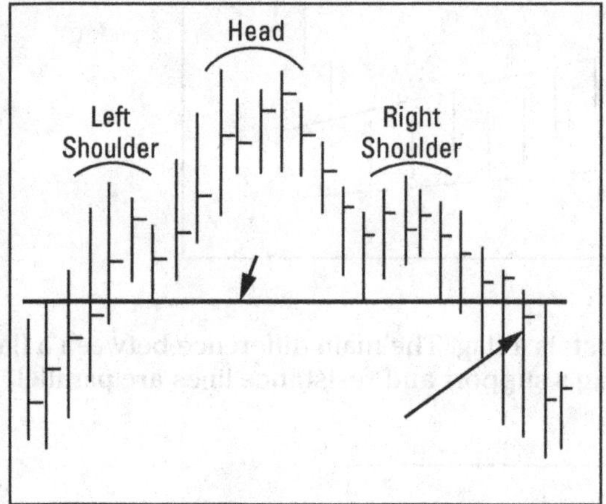

Figure 12-10: In a head and shoulders formation, the price goes down after the right shoulder formation.

The head and shoulders formation seems to result from traders holding out for a last high after a security has had a long price run. At some point, though, the trend changes, because nothing grows forever. And when the trend changes, the prices fall.

An upside-down head and shoulders sometimes appears at the end of a downtrend, and it signals that the security is about to increase in price.

Drinking from a cup and handle

When a security hits a peak in price and falls, sometimes because of bad news, it can stay low for a while. But eventually, the bad news works itself out, the underlying fundamentals improve, and it becomes time to buy again. The technical analyst sees this play out in a *cup and handle* formation, and Figure 12-11 shows you what it looks like.

The handle forms as those who bought at the old high and who felt burned by the decline take their money and get out. But other traders, who do not have the same history with the security, recognize that the price will probably resume going up now that those old sellers are out of the market.

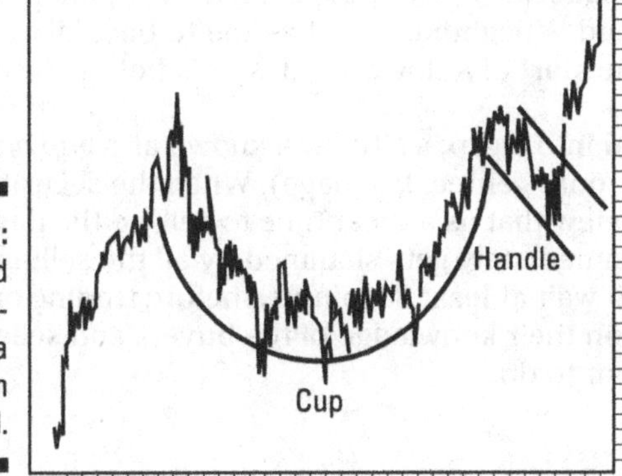

Figure 12-11: A cup and handle formation is a long-term trend.

A cup and handle formation generally shows up over a long period of trading — sometimes as long as a year — so many subtrends will occur during that time. A day trader will likely care more about those day-to-day changes than the underlying trend taking place. Still, if you see that cup formation and the hint of a handle, it's a sign that the security will probably start to rise in price.

Mind the gap

Gaps are breaks in prices that show up all the time, usually when some news event takes place between trading sessions that causes an adjustment in prices and volume. Whether it's an acquisition, a product line disappointment, or a war that broke out overnight, the news is significant enough to change the trend, and that's why traders pay attention when they see gaps.

A gap is a break between two bars, and Figure 12-12 shows what one looks like:

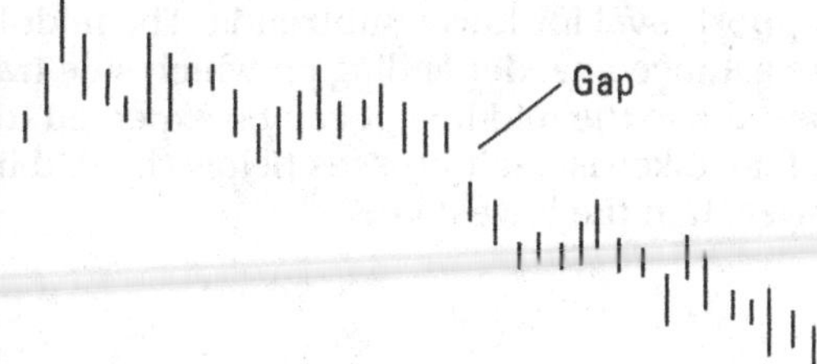

Figure 12-12: A gap down often means it's time to sell.

Gaps are usually great signals. If a security gaps up at the open, that usually means that a strong uptrend is beginning, so it's time to buy. Likewise, if it gaps down, that's often the start of a downtrend, so it's better to sell.

Day traders can get sucked into a gap, a situation known as a *gap and crap* (or *gap and trap*, if you prefer more genteel language). When the security goes up in price, many traders view that as a great time to sell, so the day trader who buys on the gap up immediately gets slammed by all the selling pressure. Some day traders prefer to wait at least 30 minutes before trading on an opening gap, while others rely on their knowledge of the buyers and sellers in a given market to decide what to do.

Grab your pitchforks!

A *pitchfork* is sometimes called an *Andrews pitchfork* after Alan Andrews, the technical analyst who popularized it. It identifies long-run support and resistance levels for subtrends by creating a channel around the main trendline. Figure 12-13 shows what it looks like.

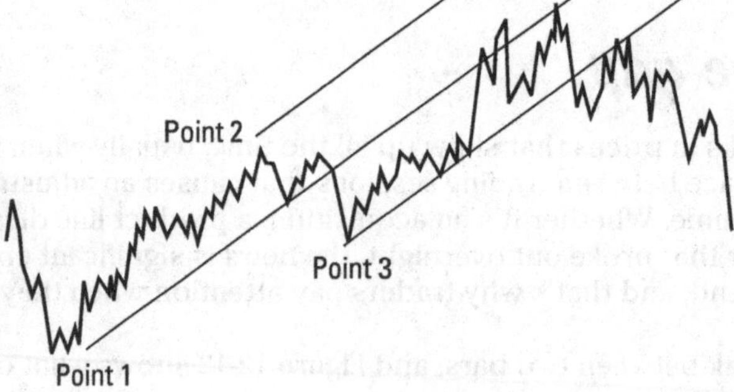

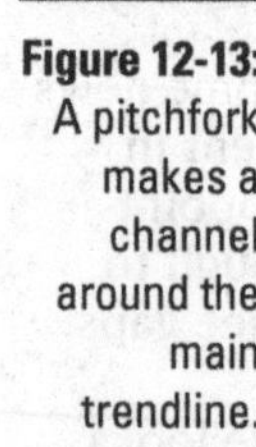
Figure 12-13: A pitchfork makes a channel around the main trendline.

The upper fork shows the resistance level for upward subtrends, and the lower fork shows the support level for lower subtrends. The middle line forms a support and a resistance line, depending on which side trading takes place. If the price crosses above the mid-line, it can be expected to go no higher than the highest line. Likewise, if it crosses below the mid-line, it can be expected to go no lower than the lowest line.

Different Approaches to Technical Analysis

Technical analysts tend to group themselves under different schools of thought. Each approaches the charts differently and uses them to glean different information about how securities prices are likely to perform. In this section, we offer an introduction to a few of these approaches. If one strikes your fancy, you can look in the Appendix for resources to find out more.

Dow Theory

The *Dow Theory* was developed by Charles Dow, the founder of *The Wall Street Journal.* The theory and the market indexes that are part of it helped sell newspapers; they also helped people make money in the markets. It's the basis for the traditional technical analysis described in this chapter. Dow believed that securities move in trends; that the trends form patterns that traders can identify; and that those trends remain in place until some major event takes place that changes them. Further, trends in the Dow Jones Industrial Average and the Dow Jones Transportation Average can predict overall market performance.

Not all technicians believe that the Dow Jones Industrial Average and Dow Jones Transportation Average are primary indicators in the modern economy, but they rely on the Dow Theory for their analysis, and they still read the *Journal.*

Fibonacci numbers and the Elliott Wave

Remember back when you had to take standardized tests, you'd often have to figure the next number in a series? Well, here's such a test. What's the next number in this series? (***Hint:*** This is not a phone number in Chad.)

```
0, 1, 1, 2, 3, 5, 8, 13, 21
```

If you answered 34, you're right! The series is known as the *Fibonacci numbers*, sometimes called the Fibonacci series or just the Fibs. It's found by adding together the preceding two numbers in the series, starting with the first two digits on the number line. 0 + 1 = 1; 1 + 1 = 2; 1 + 2 = 3; and so on into infinity. Furthermore, when the series gets well into the double digits, the ratio of one number to the one next to it settles at .618, a number known as the *golden proportion*; this means that the ratio of the smaller and the larger of two numbers is the same as the ratio of the larger number to the sum of the two numbers. In nature, this is the proportion of a perfect spiral, like that found on a pinecone or a pineapple.

Ralph Elliott was a trader who believed that over the long run, the market moved in waves described by the Fibonacci series. For example, Elliott believed that a bull market would be characterized by three down waves and five up waves. Furthermore, he believed that support and resistance levels would be found 61.8 percent above lows and below highs. If a security falls 61.8 percent from a high, that would be good time to buy, under the Elliott Wave system.

Elliott believed that these waves ranged from centuries to minutes, so traders and investors both use the system to identify the market trends that suit their timeframes. Others think it's highly unlikely that the human activity in the stock market would follow the same natural order as the ratio of the spiral on a mollusk shell.

Japanese candlestick charting

Candlestick charts were developed by traders in the Japanese rice futures markets in the 18th century, and they've carried through into the present. The basic charts are similar to the high-low-close-open bars that we talk about earlier in this chapter, but they are shaped a little differently to carry more information. Figure 12-14 shows an example:

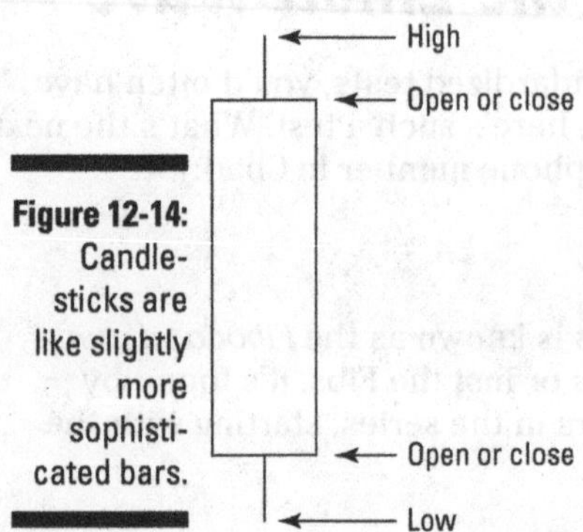

Figure 12-14: Candlesticks are like slightly more sophisticated bars.

The length of the rectangle (the so-called *candle*, also known as the body) between the open and the close price gives a sense of how much volatility the security has, especially relative to the high and low prices above and below the rectangle (the so-called *wick*, also known as the shadow). The shapes and colours create different patterns that traders can use to discern the direction of future prices. (Most technical analysis packages will colour the candlesticks green on up days and red on down days, to make finding trends even easier.)

The Gann system

William Gann supposedly made $50 million in the stock and commodities markets in the first half of the 20th century using a system that he may or may not have taught to others before his death. A lot of mystery and mythology surrounds the Gann system; some traders rely on what they perceive to be his method, whereas others dismiss it, in part because Gann relied on astrology to build his forecasts.

The *Gann system,* as it is defined nowadays, looks at the relationship between price and time. If a security moves one point in one day, that's a 1 x 1 Gann angle, and that's normal trading. If a security moves two points in one day, it would be said to create a 2 x 1 Gann angle, which is bullish. An angle of less than 1 x 1 would be bearish.

Furthermore, Gann recognized that the market would move back and forth while in a general upward or downward cycle, but some of those fluctuations were more positive than others. Just as the system looks for price movements over time with even proportions (1 × 1, 2 × 1, and so on), it also looks for orderly retracements. When a security moves back 50 percent, say from a low of $20 to a high of $40 and then back to $30, it would be a good time to buy under the Gann system.

Many traders swear by the 50-percent retracement guide — even those who think that Gann is otherwise a crazy system. This may be the origin of one hoary trading chestnut: buy whenever a price dips, because it's likely to be heading on its way back up.

Pitfalls of Technical Analysis

As discussed in Chapter 7, a lot of people make a lot of money selling services to day traders. They produce videos, organize seminars, and (ahem) write books to tell you how to be a success. But in the financial world, success is a combination of luck, skill, and smarts.

Before you commit wholeheartedly to any particular school of research, and before you plunk down a lot of money for some "proven" system demonstrated on an infomercial, think about who are you are and what you're trying to do. Despite all the books and all the seminars and all the business-school debates, every form of research has its drawbacks. Keep them in mind as you develop your day trading business plan.

If it's obvious, no opportunity exists

Many day trading systems work much of the time. For example, a security gaps up, meaning that due to positive news or high demand, the price jumps from one trade to the next (refer to Figure 12-12 for a gap formation). This is good, and the security is likely to keep going up. So you buy the security, you make money. Bingo! But here's the thing: Everyone is looking at that gap, everyone is assuming that the stock will go up, so everyone will buy and that will bid up the security. Double bingo! The profit opportunity is gone. So maybe you're better off going short? Or avoiding the situation entirely? Who knows! And that's the problem. Looking for obvious patterns like gaps tells you a lot about what is happening in the market, but only your own judgment and experience can tell you what the next move should be.

Reverse-reverse psychology

Sitcoms always revert to tired formulas. The smart kid brags about how he or she will dominate a talent or quiz show and then panics on the big day. The two people who can't stand each other will get a horrible sickness that requires them to be quarantined — in the same hospital ward. The teenage son can't believe what fabulous soup his mother made, and it turns out she was brewing a homemade cleaning solution.

Or how about this one: The kids want to do something that the parents don't approve of. The parents try reverse psychology. "Go to the party, kids, have fun!" they say, thinking that the kids will not want to do anything their parents approve of. The kids, knowing that the parents are trying to pull the reverse psychology, decide to play along with reverse-reverse psychology. "Don't worry, we'll stay home!" they say — and then sneak out. Hilarity ensues.

Technical analysis is a useful way to gauge market psychology. But when trying to determine the mood of the market, it's really easy to start overanalyzing and working yourself into a knot. Should you follow the trend or trade against it? But if everyone trades against it, would you be better off following it?

Instead of puzzling over what's really going on, develop a system that you trust. Do that through backtesting, simulation, and performance analysis. Chapter 11 has plenty of advice on how to do this. The more confident you feel in how you should react given a market situation, the better your trading will be.

The random walk with an upward bias

Under the efficient markets theory, all information is already included in a security's price. Until new information comes into the market, the prices move in a random pattern, so any security is as likely to do as well as any other. In some markets, like the stock market, this random path has an upward bias, meaning that as long as the economy is growing, companies should perform well, too; therefore, the movement is more likely to be upward than downward, but the magnitude of the movement is random.

If price movements are random, some people are going to win and some are going to lose, no matter what systems they use to pick securities. If price movements are random with an upward bias, then more people are going to win than lose, no matter what systems they use to pick securities. Some of those who win are going to tout their system, even though it was really random chance that led to their success.

Technical analysis is a useful way to measure the relative supply and demand in the market, and that in turn is a way to gauge the psychology of those who are trading. But it's not perfect. Before you plunk down a lot of money to learn a complex trading system or to subscribe to a newsletter offering a can't-miss method of trading, ask yourself whether the person selling it is smart or just lucky. A good system gives you discipline and a way to think about the market relative to your trading style. A bad system costs a lot of money and may have worked for a brief moment in the past, with no relevance to current conditions.

Chapter 13

Market Indicators and Day Trading Strategies

In This Chapter

- Studying the psychology and moods of the market
- Following the flow of funds
- Knowing what to look for during the trading day
- Avoiding dangerous traps and weird anomalies

Day traders put their research to work through a range of different strategies. All strategies have two things in common: They are designed to make money, and they are designed to work in a single day. And the best ones help traders cut through the psychology of the market.

Although some trading is handled through automatic algorithms and other programs that place orders whenever certain conditions occur, the vast majority of trading takes place between human beings who want to make money, in markets where short-term profit potentials can be very small. As much as they want to be dispassionate, traders are going to get sucked into hope, fear, and greed: the three emotions that ruin people every day. To complicate matters, many markets, such as options and futures, are zero-sum markets, meaning that there is a loser for every winner. Some markets, such as the stock market, have a positive bias, meaning that there are more winners than losers in the long run — but that doesn't mean that will be the case today.

With thin profit potential and so much emotional upheaval, it can be tough to make money in the long run. This chapter might help. In it, we cover some common day trading strategies, and we discuss some of the cold analysis that goes into figuring out the psychology of the markets.

The Psychology of the Markets

For every buyer, there is a seller. There has to be, or no transaction will take place. The price changes to reach the point where the buyer is willing to buy the security and the seller is willing to part with it. This is basic supply and demand. The financial markets are more efficient at matching supply and demand than almost any other market out there. There are no racks of unsold sweaters at the end of the season, no hot model cars that can't be purchased at any price, no long lines to get a table. The prices change to match the demand, and those who want to pay the price — or receive the price — are going to make a trade.

Despite this ruthless capitalistic efficiency underlying trading, the markets are also dominated by human emotion and psychology. All the buyers and all the sellers are looking at the same information, but reaching different conclusions. A seller exists for every buyer, so the trader looking to buy needs to know why the seller is willing to make a deal.

And why would someone be on the other side of your trade?

- **The other person may have a different time horizon.**

  For example, long-term investors might sell on bad news that changes a security's outlook. A short-term trader might not care about the long-term outlet, if the selling in the morning is overdone, creating an opportunity to buy now and sell at a higher price in the afternoon.

- **The other person may have a different risk profile.**

  A conservative investor might not want to own shares in a company that's being acquired by a high-flying technology company. That investor will sell, and someone with more interest in growth will be buying.

- **The other person may be engaging in wishful thinking, or acting out of fear, or trading from sheer greed.**
- **You may be engaging in wishful thinking, acting out of fear, or trading from sheer greed.**

It's highly unlikely that you're smarter than everyone else trading, but you might be more rational and disciplined. In the long run, controlling your emotions and sticking to your limits will make you more money than if you are smart but can't control your trading. And if you happen to be both disciplined and smart, you might do very well.

Betting on the buy side

Every market participant has his or her own set of reasons and rationales for placing an order today. In general, though, it's safe to say that although many reasons exist to sell — to pay taxes, generate cash for university tuition, or meet a pension obligation, among many others — there's only one reason to buy: You think the security is going up in price.

For that reason alone, traders often pay more attention to what is happening to buy orders than to sell orders. They look at the number of buy orders coming in, how large they are, and at what price to get a sense of who out there is projecting a profit. We cover volume and price indicators in more detail later in the chapter.

Because there are so many good reasons to sell but only one good reason to buy, it can take a long time for the market to recognize bearish (pessimistic) sentiment indicators. Even if you see that prices should start to go down in the near future, you have to consider that the market today can be very different from what you see coming up. And day traders only have today.

The projection trap

If you took a peek at some of the technical analysis charts in Chapter 12, you may have noticed that it's possible to see what you want to see in some price charts. And if you thought a little about fundamental analysis, you might have realized that it's just as easy to interpret information the way you want to, too. Instead of looking objectively at what the market is telling them, some traders see what they want to see. That's one reason why it's so important to know your system and use your limits. Information in Chapters 2 and 11 can help you with both.

The best traders are able to figure out the psychology of the market almost by instinct. They can't necessarily explain what they do — which makes it hard for someone trying to learn from them. But they can tell you this much: If you can rationally determine why the person on the other side of the trade is trading, you can be in a better position to make money and avoid the big mistakes brought on by hope, fear, and greed.

Measuring the Mood of the Market

For decades, most traders were rooted on the floors of the exchanges. They had a good sense of the mood of the market because they could pick up the mood of the people in the pits with them. They often knew their fellow traders well enough to know how good they were or the needs of the people they were working for. It made for a clubby atmosphere, despite all the shouting and arm waving. It wasn't the most efficient way to trade big volume, but it allowed traders to read the minds of those around them.

And now, almost all trading is electronic, and not all those old floor traders have been able to make the transition. Some find that unless they can watch the behaviour of other traders and hear the emotions in their voices, they can't gauge what's happening in the markets.

Other professional traders, who work for brokerage firms or fund companies, trade electronically, but along long tables (known as trading desks) where they sit next to colleagues trading similar securities. Even though everyone is trading off a screen, they share a mood and thus a sense of what's happening out there. Some day traders can replicate this by setting up shop at a trading arcade, a business that operates trading desks for day traders (you can read more about them in Chapter 6), but most traders are working alone at home, with nothing but the information on their screens to tell them what's happening in the market.

There are ways to figure out what's happening, even just looking at the screen, and some of these may work for you. These include price, volume, and volatility indicators, and you're in the right place to find out more about them.

Some traders rely on Internet chat rooms or social media networks to help them measure market sentiment. This can be risky. Some Internet users are smart people who are willing to share their perspectives on the market, but many are novice traders who have no good information to share, or they're people who are trying to manipulate the market in their favour. Do your due diligence when it comes to online sources before you start participating.

Pinpointing with price indicators

In an efficient market, all information about a security is included in its price. If the price is high and going up, then the fundamentals are doing well. If the price is low and going lower, then something's not good. And everything in between means something else.

The change in a security's price gives you a first cut of information. Price changes can be analyzed in other ways to help you know when to buy or when to sell.

Momentum

Momentum, which we also discuss in Chapter 12, is the rate at which a security's price is increasing (or decreasing). If momentum is strong and positive, then the security will show both higher highs and higher lows. People want to buy it for whatever reason, and the price reflects that. Likewise, momentum can be strong and negative, and negative momentum is marked with lower highs and lower lows. No one seems interested in buying, and that keeps dragging the price down.

The exact amount of momentum that a security has can be measured with indicators known as *momentum oscillators*. A classic momentum oscillator starts with the moving average, which is the average of the closing prices for a past time period, say the last ten trading days. Then the change in each day's moving average is plotted below the price line. When the oscillator is positive, traders say that the security is *overbought*; when it is negative, they say that the security is oversold. Figure 13-1 shows a momentum oscillator plotted below a price line.

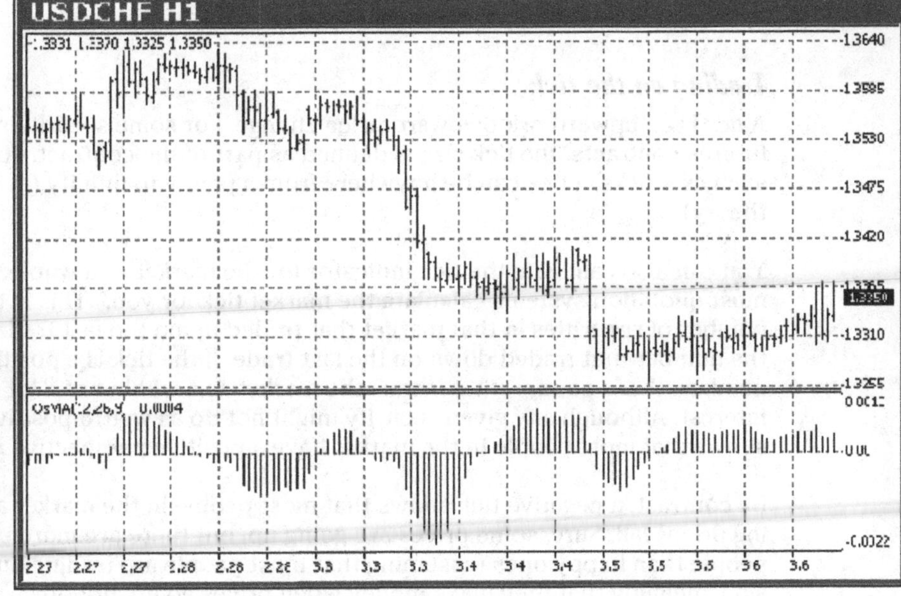

Figure 13-1: A momentum oscillator indicates (no surprise here) momentum.

If a momentum oscillator shows that a security is overbought (when it's above the centre line), that means that too many people own it relative to the remaining demand in the market, and some of them will start selling. Remember, some of these people have perfectly good reasons for selling that may have nothing to do with the underlying fundamentals of the security, but they are going to sell anyway, and that will bring the price down. Traders who see that a security is overbought will want to sell in advance of those people.

If a momentum oscillator shows that a security is oversold (when the line is below the centre line), it means the security is probably too cheap. Everyone who wanted to get out has gotten out, and now it may be a bargain. When the buyers who see the profit opportunity jump in, the price will go up.

The trend is your friend . . . until the end. Although great reasons exist to follow price trends, remember that they all end, so you still need to pay attention to your money management and your stops, no matter how strong a trend seems to be.

Given that most trends end, or at least zig and zag along the way, some traders look for securities that fit what they call the *1-2-3-4 criterion*. If a security goes up in price for three consecutive days, then it's likely to go down on the fourth day. Likewise, if a security has fallen in price for three days in a row, it's likely to be up on day four. Be sure to run some simulations (see Chapter 11) to see if this works for a market that interests you.

Trading on the tick

A *tick* is an upward or downward price change. For some securities, such as futures contracts, the tick size is defined as part of the contract. For others, such as stocks, a tick can be anywhere from a penny to infinity (at least in theory).

You can also calculate the tick indicator for the market as a whole. (In fact, most quotation systems calculate the market tick for you.) This is the total number of securities in that market that traded up on the last trade, minus the number that traded down on the last trade. If the tick is a positive number, that's good — that means the market as a whole has a lot of buying interest. Although any given security might not do as well, a positive tick shows that most people in the market have a positive perspective right now.

By contrast, a negative tick shows that most people in the market are watching prices fall. Sure, some prices are going up, but there are more unhappy people than happy ones (assuming that most people are trading on the long side, meaning that they make money when prices go up, not down). This shows negative sentiment in the market right now.

Tracking the trin

Trin is short for *trading indicator,* and it's another measure of market sentiment based on how many prices have gone up relative to how many have gone down. Most quotation systems will pull up the trin for a given market, but you can also calculate it on your own. The math looks like Figure 13-2.

$$\frac{\frac{advances}{declines}}{\frac{advance\ volume}{decline\ volume}}$$

Figure 13-2: Calculating the trading indicator (the trin) can give you a measure of market sentiment.

The numerator is based on the tick: the number of securities that went up divided by (not less) the number that went down. The denominator includes the volume: the number of shares or contracts that traded for those securities that went up, divided by the number of securities traded for those that went down in price. This tells you just how strongly buyers supported the securities that were going up and just how much selling pressure faced those securities that went down.

If the trin is less than 1.00, that usually means a lot of buyers are taking securities up in price, and that's positive. If the trin is above 1.00, then the sellers are acting more strongly, and that indicates a lot of negative sentiment in the market.

Volume

The trin indicator looks at price in conjunction with volume. That makes this a good time to introduce volume indicators.

Volume tells you how much trading is taking place in the market. How excited are people about the current price? Do they see this as a great opportunity to buy or to sell? Are they selling fast, to get out now, or are they taking a more leisurely approach to the market these days? This information is carried in the volume of the trading, and it's an important adjunct to the information you see in the prices. Volume tells you whether enough support exists to maintain price trends, or if price trends are likely to change soon.

Force index

The *force index* gives you a sense of the strength of a trend. It starts with information from prices — namely, if the closing price today is higher than the closing price yesterday that's positive for the security. And that means that if today's closing price is lower than yesterday's, the force is generally negative. Then that price information is combined with volume information. The more volume that goes with that price change, the stronger that positive or negative force.

Although many quotation systems will calculate force for you, you can do it yourself, too. For each trading day,

```
Force index = volume × (today's moving average -
           yesterday's moving average)
```

In other words, the force index simply scales the moving average momentum oscillator (discussed above) for the amount of volume that accompanies that price change. That way, the trader has a sense of just how overbought or oversold the security is any particular day.

On-balance volume

The *on-balance volume* is a running total of the amount of trading in a security. To calculate it, first look at today's closing price relative to yesterday's. If today's close is higher than yesterday's, then add today's volume to yesterday's on-balance volume. If today's closing price is less than yesterday's, then subtract today's volume from yesterday's total. And if today's close is the same as yesterday's, don't do anything: Today's balance is the same as yesterday's.

Many traders track on-balance volume over time, and here's why: A change in volume signals a change in demand. That might not show up in price right away if there are enough buyers to absorb volume from sellers. But if still more buyers are out there, then the price is going to go up. Hence, the volume from even small day-to-day increases in price needs to be added up over time. If the volume keeps going up, then at some point prices are going to have to go up to meet the demand.

On the downside, the volume from small price declines will add up, too. Over time, it may show very little pent-up interest, indicating that prices could languish for some time.

Many traders look to on-balance volume to gauge the behaviour of so-called *smart money,* such as pension funds, hedge funds, and mutual fund companies. Unlike individual investors, these big institutional accounts tend to trade on fundamentals rather than emotion. They tend to start buying a security at the point where the dumb money is tired of owning it, so their early buying may show big volume with little price change. But as the institutions keep buying, the price will have to go up to get the smarter individuals and the early institutions to part with their shares.

Open interest

Open interest has a different meaning in the stock market than in the options and futures markets, but in both cases it gives traders useful information about demand.

In the stock market, open interest is the number of buy orders submitted before the market opens. If the open interest is high, people are ready to add shares to their positions or initiate new positions, and that in turn means the stock is likely to go up in price on the demand.

In the options and futures markets, open interest is the number of contracts at the end of every day that have not been exercised, closed out, or allowed to expire. Day traders won't have open interest, because by definition, day traders close out at the end of every day. But some traders will keep open interest, either because they think that their position has the ability to increase in profitability or because they are hedging another transaction and need to keep that options or futures position in place. If open interest in a contract is increasing, then new money is coming into the market and prices are likely to continue to go up. This is especially true if volume is increasing at about the same rate as open interest. On the other hand, if open interest is falling, then people are closing out their positions because they no longer see a profit potential, and prices are likely to fall.

Volatility

The *volatility* of a security is a measure of how much it tends to go up or down in a given time period. The more volatile the security, the more the price will fluctuate. Most day traders prefer volatile securities, because that creates more opportunities to make a profit in a short amount of time. But volatility can make it tougher to gauge market sentiment. If a security is volatile, the mood can change quickly. What looked like a profit opportunity at the market open might be gone by lunchtime — and back again before the close.

Average true range

The *average true range* is a measure of volatility that's commonly used in commodity markets, but some stock traders use it, too. Many quotation systems calculate it automatically, but if you want to do it yourself, start with finding each day's *true range*. This is the greatest of

- The current high less the current low.
- The absolute value of the current high less the previous close.
- The absolute value of the current low less the previous close.

Calculate those three numbers, then take the highest of them and average it with the true range for the past 14 days.

Each day's true range number shows you just how much the security swung between the high and the low, or how much the high or the low that day varied from the previous day's close. It's a measure of how much volatility occurred each day. When averaged over time, it shows how much volatility takes place over time. The higher the average true range, the more volatile a security is.

Beta

Beta is the *covariance* (that is, the statistical measure of how much two variables move together) of a stock relative to the rest of the market. The number comes from the capital assets pricing model, which is an equation used in academic circles to model the performance of securities. Traders don't use the capital assets pricing model, but they often talk about beta to evaluate the volatility of stocks and options.

What does beta mean?

- A beta of one means that the security moves at a faster rate than the market. You would buy high betas if you think the market is going up, but not if the market is going down.
- A beta of less than one means that the security moves more slowly than the market. This is good if you want less risk than the market.
- A beta of exactly one means that the security moves at the same rate as the market.
- A negative beta means that the security moves in the opposite direction of the market. The easiest way to get a negative beta security is to *short* (borrow and then sell) a positive beta security.

MVX

MVX is short for the Montreal Exchange's Implied Volatility Index. The calculation of it is complex, but it is available on quotation systems and on the exchange's Web site at `http://www.m-x.ca/indicesmx_mvx_en.php`.

The MVX is based on the implied volatility of options on the iShares of the Canadian S&P/TSX 60 Fund (XIU), which are traded on the Montreal Exchange. Because the XIU's value is based on Canada's equity benchmark — S&P/TSX

60 Index — the MVX is a good way to determine investor sentiment for the entire Canadian equity market. The greater the volatility, the more uncertainty investors have, and the more options that show great volatility, the more widespread the concern is within the market. Some would consider the MVX to be a gauge of market fear. The greater the MVX, the more bearish the outlook for the markets in general.

Traders can use the MVX to help them value options and futures on the market indexes. The MVX can also be used to help confirm bullish or bearish sentiment that shows up in other market signals, such as the tick or the on-balance volume measures described earlier.

VIX

VIX stands for the Chicago Board Options Exchange Volatility Index. It works the same way as the MVX, but it gauges sentiment in the American markets. It's available on many quotation systems and on the exchange's Web site at `www.cboe.com/micro/vix/introduction.aspx`.

The VIX is based on the implied volatility of options on stocks included in the S&P 500 Index and, like the MVX, if the index is high that means more risk exists in the market.

In addition to the VIX, the exchange also tracks the *VXN* (volatility on the NASDAQ 100 Index) and the *VXD* (volatility on the Dow Jones Industrial Average).

Volatility ratio

The *volatility ratio* tells traders what the implied volatility of a security is relative to the recent historical volatility. It shows whether the security is expected to be more or less volatile right now than it has been in the past, and it's widely used in option markets. The first calculation required is the *implied volatility,* which is backed out using the Black-Scholes model, an academic model for valuing options. When you plug in time until expiration, interest rates, dividends, stock price, and strike price to the model, the implied volatility is the volatility number that then generates the current option price. (You don't have to do this yourself, because most quotation systems generate implied volatility for you.)

After you have the implied volatility, you can compare it to the historical volatility of the option, which tells you just how much the price changed over the last 20 or 90 days. If the implied volatility is greater than the statistical volatility, the market may be overestimating the uncertainty in the prices, and the options may be overvalued. And, if the implied volatility is much less than the statistical volatility, the market may be underestimating uncertainty, so the options may be undervalued.

Measuring Money Flows

Money flows tell you how much money is going into or out of a market. They are another set of indicators that tell you where the market sentiment is right now and where it might be going soon. They combine features of price and volume indicators to help traders gauge the market. Although amounts spent to buy and sell have to match — otherwise, no market would exist — the enthusiasm of the buyers and the anxiousness of the sellers shows up in the volume traded and the direction of the price change. Just how hard was it for the buyers to get the sellers to part with their positions? And, how hard will it be to get them to part with their positions tomorrow? That's the information contained in money flow indicators.

The most basic money flow indicator is closing price multiplied by the number of shares traded. If the closing price was higher than the closing price yesterday, then the number is positive; if the closing price today was lower than the price yesterday, then the number is negative.

Accumulation/distribution index

In trading terms, *accumulation* is controlled buying, and *distribution* is controlled selling. This is the kind of buying and selling that doesn't lead to big changes in securities prices, and it's usually because the action was planned. No one accumulates or distributes a security in a state of panic.

But even if the buying and selling activity isn't driven by madcap rushes in and out of positions, it's still important to know whether, on balance, the buyers or the sellers have the slight predominance in the market, because that may affect the direction of the price in the near future. For example, if a security has been in an upward trend, but more and more down days are occurring with increasing volume, that means that the sellers are starting to dominate the trading and that the price trend is likely to go down.

Here's the equation:

```
Accumulation/distribution = ((Close - Low) - (High -
          Close)) / (High - Low) × Period's volume
```

Some traders look at accumulation/distribution from day to day, whereas others prefer to look at it for a week or even a month's worth of trading.

Money flow ratio and money flow index

Money flow is closing price multiplied by the number of shares traded. That basic statistic can be manipulated in strange and wonderful ways to generate new statistics carrying even more information about whether the markets are likely to have more buying pressure or more selling pressure in the future.

The first is the *money flow ratio.* This is simply the total money flow for those days where prices were up from the prior day (days with positive money flow), divided by the total money flow for those days where prices were down from the prior day (days with negative money flow). Day traders tend to calculate money flow ratios for short time periods, such as a week or ten days, while swing traders and investors tend to care about longer time periods, like a month or even four months of trading.

The money flow ratio is sometimes converted into the *money flow index,* which can be used as a single indicator or tracked relative to prices for a given period of time. This equation looks like Figure 13-3.

Figure 13-3: This equation figures out the money flow index.

$$MFI = 100 - \frac{100}{1 + money\ ratio}$$

If the money flow index is more than 80, the security is usually considered to be overbought — meaning that the buyers are done buying, and the sellers will put downward pressure on prices. If the money flow index is less than 20, then the security is usually considered to be oversold, and the buyers will soon take over and drive prices up. In between, the money flow index can help clarify information from other market indicators.

Short interest ratios

Short selling is a way to make money if a security falls in price. In the options and futures markets, one simply agrees to sell a contract to someone else. In the stock and bond markets, it's a little more complicated. The short seller borrows stocks or bonds through the brokerage firm, and then sells them.

Ideally, the price will fall, and then the trader can buy back the stocks or bonds at the lower price to repay the loan. The trader keeps the difference between the price where the security was sold and the price where the security was repurchased. (The process is described in more detail in Chapter 14.)

People take the short side of a position for only one reason: They think that prices are going to go down. They may want to hedge against this, or they may want to make a big profit if it happens. In the stock market in particular, monitoring the rate of short selling can give clues to investor expectations and future market direction.

The New York Stock Exchange and NASDAQ report the short interest in stocks listed with them. The data are updated monthly, as it can take a while for brokerage firms to sort out exactly how many shares have been shorted and then report those data to the exchanges. The resulting number, the *short interest ratio,* tells the number of shares that have been shorted, the percentage change from the month before, the average daily trading volume in the same month, and the number of days of trading at the average volume that it would take to cover the short positions.

Traders can get similar data for the Toronto Stock Exchange. Twice a month the exchange generates a Short Position Report for the top 20 largest consolidated short positions. The PDF document includes the total number of shares shorted and the net change from previous report. You can get to these reports from the Stock Market News section on the TMX's Web site (`www.tmx.com`).

The loans that enable short selling have to be repaid. If the lender asks for them back, or if prices go up so that the position starts to lose money, the trader is going to have to buy shares in order to make repayment. The harder it is to get the right number of shares in the market, the more desperate the trader will become, and the higher prices will go.

An increase in short interest shows that investors are becoming nervous about a stock. However, given that short interest is not calculated frequently, the number would probably not give a trader a lot of information about the prospects for the company itself. This doesn't mean short interest doesn't carry a lot of useful information for traders. It does. If the short interest is high, then the security price is likely to go up when all the people who are short need to buy back stock. Likewise, if short interest is low, little buying pressure will occur in the near future.

High short interest, along with other bullish indicators, is a sign that prices are more likely to go up than down in the near future.

Information Cropping Up During the Trading Day

Technical analysis (refer to Chapter 12) and all the indicators discussed in this chapter offer useful information about what's happening in the markets, but there's one problem: Because so many of those indicators are based on closing prices and closing volume, they aren't much use during the trading day. And, in fact, many traders read through the information in the morning before the open to sort out what is likely to happen and what the mood of the market is likely to be, but then they have to recalibrate their gauge of the market as information comes to them during the trading day. That information doesn't show up on charts or in neat numerical indicators until the day ends. But several sources of information are updated while the market is open to give a trader a sense of what's happening at any given time.

Price, time, and sales

The most important information for a trader is the current price of the security, how often and in what volume it has been trading, and how much the price has moved from the last trade. This is the most basic real-time information out there, and it's readily available through a brokerage firm's quotation screens.

In Chapter 6 we discuss the different quotation services that traders can obtain from their brokerage firms. Although your broker may charge you more to get more detailed quotes, it's worth it for most trading strategies. Knowing how the price is moving can give you a sense of whether the general mood of the market is being confirmed or contradicted. That can help you place more profitable trades.

Order book

High-level price quote data, such as that available through TMX Datalinx, NASDAQ Level II, or NASDAQ TotalView, include information on who is placing orders and just how large those orders are. (Refer to Chapter 6 to see what this looks like.) The book gives you key data, because it gives you a sense of how smart the other buyers and sellers are. Are they day traders just trying not to be killed? Or are they institutions that have done a lot of research and are under a lot of performance pressure? Sure, day traders are often very right and institutions are often very wrong, but the information you see in the order book can help you sense whether people are trading on information or on emotion.

An additional piece of information from the order book can help you figure out what's happening in the market now — namely, the presence of an *order imbalance*. An order imbalance means that the number of buyers and sellers don't match. This often happens during the open, because some traders prefer to place orders before the market opens, whereas others prefer to wait until after the open. These imbalances tend to be small and clear up quickly. However, if a major news event takes place, or there's a great deal of fear in the market, large imbalances can occur during the trading day. These can be disruptive, and in some cases the exchange stops trading until news is disseminated and enough new orders are placed to balance out the orders.

News flows

Although much of the discussion in this chapter has been about the information contained in price, volume, and other trade data, the actual information that comes from news releases is at least as important.

Much of the news is regularly scheduled and much predicted: corporate earnings, Bank of Canada rate announcements, unemployment rates, housing starts, and the like. When this information comes in, traders want to know how the actual results compare with what was expected, and how this fits with the overall bullish or bearish sentiment of the market.

The second type of news is the unscheduled breaking event, such as corporate takeovers, horrible storms, political assassinations, or other happenings that were not expected and that take more time for the market to digest. That's in part because these events have the ability to change trends rather than play out against them. In some cases, the markets will halt trading to allow this information to disseminate; in others, traders have to react quickly based on what they know now and what they suspect will happen in the near future.

What's the difference between risk and uncertainty? *Risk* is something that happens often enough that people can quantify the damage. *Uncertainty* is something that might happen, but no one can figure out the likelihood. A fire that knocks out power to downtown Vancouver sometime in the next ten years is a risk; the invasion of the planet by aliens from outer space is uncertainty.

News can happen at any time. It can change a trend and throw all your careful analysis into disarray. That's why careful analysis is no substitute for risk management. Watch your position sizes and have stops in place so that you exit when you need to. Chapter 2 has a lot of information on these topics.

Anomalies and Traps

Traders can be superstitious, and that shows up in different anomalies and traps that affect the mood of the market even if no logical reason can explain their existence. You want to be aware of them, because they can affect trading, even if there doesn't seem to be a justification for them.

An *anomaly* is a market condition that occurs regularly, but for no good reason. It can be related to the month of the year, the day of the week, or the size of the company involved.

A *trap* is a situation where the market doesn't perform the way you expect it to given the indicators that you are looking at. You have a choice: Go with what the market is telling you, or go with what your indicators are telling you.

To a long-term investor, perception is perception. When it's different from reality, there's an opportunity to make money. To a short-term trader, perception is reality, because that affects what happens before everyone figures out what's real.

Bear traps and bull traps

Traders talk about getting caught in traps, which neatly fits the language of bulls and bears. When this happens, they are stuck moving against the market, and that causes them big trouble. After all, day trading is about identifying trends and moving with them, because you have only a few hours to work before it's time to close out. In this section, we list a few common traps to help you identify them and, hopefully, avoid them.

The best antidote for a trap is to take your loss and move on to the next trade.

Chart traps

If you go back to Chapter 12 and look at some of the sample charts, and if you look at actual price charts created in the market every day, you might notice that sometimes, it's really hard to tell whether a breakout is false or real, whether a trend is changing or just playing out with a smaller subtrend. A ton of subjectivity goes into reading charts, and some days you'll read them wrong. You'll be thinking that you are ahead of the market when you've actually just traded against it. Ouch!

Some traders try to work around this by automating their trading. Several different software packages will scan the market and identify potential trading opportunities (see Chapter 7 for more information). But even the best software will misread the market on some occasions. That's why you need to monitor your positions and make sure you stick to your loss limits.

Contrarian traps

In Chapter 1, we note that about 80 percent of day traders lose money. So maybe you're thinking that the way to make money is to just do the opposite of what everyone else is doing. But the reason why they lose money isn't so much that they're wrong about the trend, it's that they're sloppy in their trading and don't limit their losses. (That's why so much of this book is about the business of trading, rather than the actual mechanics of placing buy and sell orders.)

In a *contrarian trap,* the trader has made the decision to trade against the market, and that's exactly what happens: He or she loses money because the market is moving in the opposite direction. Taking a contrary position doesn't work too well in day trading. In most cases, you have to go with the flow, not against it, to make money in a single day's session. The market is always right in the short term.

Calendar effects

Many trading anomalies follow time periods. That's not completely unexpected, as many economic and business trends follow the calendar. Companies report their results quarterly. Most close their books for tax purposes at the end of the year. Investors are also evaluated quarterly. Retail sales follow holiday seasons, demand for commodities follows the growing season, and fuel demand varies with the weather. Whatever you decided to trade, you need to do enough fundamental research (the study of the business and economic factors that affect the security, described in Chapter 12) so that you know how your chosen securities move over time.

But some of the calendar effects make little logical sense, yet they influence trading. Hence, this explanation of the January effect, the Monday effect, and the October effect.

The January effect

Many years, the stock market goes up in the early part of January. Why? No one is entirely sure, but the guess is that people tend to sell at the end of December for tax reasons, and then buy back those securities in January. It may also be that in the new year, everyone is flush with excitement and ready to see the market go up, so they put money to work and start buying.

If stocks go up in January, then you can get a jump on the market by buying in December, right? And that would make prices go up in December. To get a jump on the December rally, you could buy in November. And that's exactly what people started to do, and the once-pronounced January effect is now weak to non-existent. (People still talk about it, though.) In an efficient market, people will eventually figure out these unexplained phenomena, then trade on them until they disappear. Use these anomalies as a way to gauge psychology, not as hard and fast trading rules.

The Monday effect

The market seems to do more poorly on Monday than on the other days of the week. And no matter what the evidence shows (and the research is ambiguous and the findings vary greatly based on the time period and the markets examined), many traders believe this, so it has an effect. Why? There are two thoughts. The first is that everyone is in a bad mood on Monday because they have to go back to work after the weekend. The second is that people spend all weekend analyzing any bad news from the end of the prior week, then sell as soon as they get back to the office.

The October effect

The stock market has had three grand crashes, all in October. On October 29, 1929, a day known as Black Tuesday, the Dow Jones Industrial Average declined 12 percent in one day as market speculators caught up with the less rosy reality of the economy. This crash kicked off a general decline that contributed to the Great Depression of the 1930s. On October 19, 1987, known as Black Monday, the Dow Jones Industrial Average declined 23 percent. No one is really sure why it happened, but it did. And starting October 6, 2008, and continuing for five days, the Dow Jones Industrial Average fell 18 percent. Many call it the Black Week, but you could probably call it the Black Year — those five days kicked off what would become the worst financial crisis since the Great Depression.

The TSX usually reacts in similar fashion to the American exchanges, so if the U.S. market falls, so does the Canadian one. For example, between October 6 and 10 in 2008, the S&P/TSX Composite Index dropped about 13 percent. However, it's interesting to note that the S&P/TSX Composite Index actually started falling on September 25. Between that Thursday and October 10 the Canadian stock market plunged just over 27 percent.

Because of these crashes, many traders believe that bad things happen in October, and they act accordingly. Of course, bad things happen in other months. The crash in the NASDAQ market that marked the end of the 1990s tech bubble took place in March 2000. In May 2010 a bizarre trader error caused the Dow Jones Industrial Average to drop 1,000 points in 16 minutes. No one talks about a March or May effect, however.

Chapter 14

Short Selling and Leverage

In This Chapter

- Making money with other people's money
- Garnering tall profits from short sales
- Using leverage in every market you can imagine
- Borrowing for business and personal needs
- Considering the consequences of leverage

In a certain sense, day trading isn't risky at all. Day traders close out their positions overnight to minimize the possibility of something going wrong while the trader isn't paying attention. Each trade is based on finding a small price change in the market over a short period of time, so it's unlikely that anything is going to change dramatically. But here's the thing: Trading this way leads to small returns. It's hard to justify trading full time if you aren't making a lot of money when you do it, no matter how low your risk is.

And, of course, some days there aren't many good trades to make. You can be looking for securities to go up, and they're not. Zero trades lead to zero risk, and zero return.

That's why savvy traders think about other ways to make money on their trades, even if it involves taking on more risk. It's that risk that generates the return many traders crave. In this chapter, we cover two techniques for finding trades and increasing returns: *short selling* and *leverage*. Both involve borrowing, also known as leverage, and both increase risk.

Taking Other People's Money to Make Money

The dollars you make from trading depend on two things: your percentage return on your trades and the dollars you have to start out with. If you double your money but only have a $1,000 account, then you are left with

$2,000. If you get a 10 percent return but have a $1,000,000 account, then you make $100,000. Which would you rather have? (Yes, we know, you'd rather double your money with the $1,000,000 account. But we didn't give you that choice, alas.)

The point is that the more money you have to trade, the more dollars you can generate, even if the return on the trade itself is small. If you have $500,000 and borrow $500,000 more, then your 10 percent return will give you $100,000 to take home, not $50,000. You have doubled the dollars returned to you by doubling the money you used to place the trades, not by doubling the performance of the trade itself. Clever, huh?

Leverage gives you more money to trade. That helps you generate more dollars for your account — or lose more dollars, if you aren't careful or have a string of reversals.

When you borrow money or shares of stock, you have to pay it back, no matter what happens. That's why borrowing can be risky.

Why leverage is important in short-term trading

Day traders and other short-term traders aren't looking to make big money on any single trade. Instead, the goal is to make small money on a whole bunch of trades. Unfortunately, it can be hard for all those little trades to add up to something big. That's why many day traders turn to leverage. They either borrow money or stock from their brokerage firm, or they trade securities that have built-in leverage, such as futures and foreign exchange.

The fine print on margin agreements

Leverage adds risk not only to your own account, but also to the entire financial system. If everyone borrowed money and then some big market catastrophe happened no one would be able to repay their loans, and those who lent the money would go bust, too.

As a result, there's an incredible amount of oversight that goes with leverage strategies. The Investment Industry Regulatory Organization of Canada (IIROC) regulates how much money a trader can borrow. Many brokerage firms have even stricter rules in place as part of their risk management.

This means you have about as much flexibility when you borrow from your broker in order to buy and sell securities as you would have if you borrowed from your friendly neighbourhood loan shark to play a high-stakes poker game. Meaning: not much. Margin loans are highly regulated, and you must meet the broker's terms. If you fail to repay the loan, your positions will be sold from underneath you. If you try to borrow too much, you will be cut off. No amount of begging and pleading will help you.

Your brokerage firm makes you sign a margin agreement, which says that you understand the risks and limits of your activities. You probably can't have a margin account unless you meet a minimum account size, usually between $5,000 and $10,000, and the amount you can borrow depends on the size of your account. Generally, a large-cap stock account must hold 30 percent of the purchase price of securities when you borrow the money. A mid-cap stock requires minimum margin of 50 percent; you have to have 75 percent of the purchase price to borrow money for small-cap or penny stocks. The price of those securities can go down, but if they go down below the value of the loan, you'll get a margin call. (Some brokers will call in loans faster than others; their policies are disclosed in their margin agreements.)

Brokerage firms handle margin trades all the time. You do the paperwork once, when you sign a margin agreement. Each time you place an order, you're asked if you are making the trade with cash or on margin. Click the "Margin" box, and you've just borrowed money. It's that easy.

Managing margin calls

If the value of your account starts falling, and it looks like it is falling below the 30 percent minimum margin requirement (this depends on the security you're trading), you'll get a *margin call.* Your broker will call you and ask you to deposit more money in your account. If you can't do that, the broker will start selling your securities to close out the loan. And if you don't have enough to pay off the loan, the broker will close your account and put a lien, which is a claim on your assets, against you.

Most brokerage firms have risk-management limits in place, so you'll probably get plenty of warning before you get a margin call or see your account closed out. After all, neither you nor your brokerage firm wants to lose money. Just keep in mind that it's a possibility.

Some brokerage firms advertise that, as a service to you, they will close out your account as soon as you lose the amount in it, to keep you from losing more money. It's as much a service to the brokerage as it is to you, but it's an example of the built-in risk management that firms have to limit risks to everyone.

The dangers of risk: Long-Term Capital Management

Leverage adds risk to low-risk strategies, which increases returns as long as nothing goes wrong. But sometimes things go horribly wrong, even for the big guys. In 1998, Long-Term Capital Management — a hedge fund formed by several leading traders and academics, including a few Nobel Prize winners — failed.

The fund's basic trading style had very little risk. Its traders looked for small price differences between bonds that were expected to go away. (This is known as *arbitrage* and is discussed in Chapter 15.) To generate big money, the fund borrowed tonnes of money, which turned that low-risk strategy into a risky one. In the summer of 1998, the Russian government defaulted on its bonds. Investors panicked and traded their European and Japanese bonds for U.S. government bonds.

Long-Term Capital Management had bet that small differences in price between the U.S. bonds and the overseas ones would disappear; instead, the concern over Russia's problems caused the small price differences to get bigger. Much bigger. This made it difficult for Long-Term Capital Management's managers to repay the money that the fund had borrowed, which put pressure on the banks and brokerage firms that had given the loans. The Federal Reserve Bank organized a restructuring plan with the banks that were owed money by Long-Term Capital Management in order to prevent a massive financial catastrophe. In total, Long-Term Capital Management lost US$4.6 billion.

Margin bargains for day traders only

Day traders are often able to avoid margin calls because they borrow money for such short periods of time. Good day traders look for small market moves and cut their losses early on, which minimizes the risk of using other people's money. And, by definition, day traders close out their positions every night.

Short Selling

Traditionally, investors and traders want to buy low and sell high. They buy a position in a security and then wait for the price to go up. It's not a bad way to make money, especially because if the country's economy continues to grow even a little bit, then businesses are going to grow and so are their stocks.

But even in a good economy, some securities go down. The company may be mismanaged, it may sell a product that's out of favour, or maybe it's just having a string of bad days. For that matter, maybe it went up a little too much in price, and now investors are coming to their senses. In these situations, you can't make money buying low and selling high. If only there were a way to reverse the situation.

Well, there is a way — selling short. And, in short (hah!), *selling short* means that you borrow a security and then sell it in hopes of repaying the loan of the shares by buying back cheaper shares later on.

In trading lingo, when you own something, you are considered to be *long*. When you sell it, you are considered to be *short*. You don't have to be long before you go short.

How to sell short

Most brokerage firms make it easy to sell short. You simply place an order to sell the stock, and the broker asks whether you're selling shares that you own or selling short. After you place the order, the brokerage firm goes about borrowing shares for you to sell. It loans the shares to your account and executes the sell order.

You can't sell short unless the brokerage firm is able to borrow the shares. Sometimes, so many people have sold a stock short that no shares are there to borrow. It's also possible that even after you sell a stock short, the stock could be come hard to borrow and you may be forced to buy back the shares sooner than you'd like. If any of these cases arise, you'll probably have to find another stock or another strategy to use this time.

After the shares are sold, you wait until the security goes down in price, then you buy the shares in the market at a bargain. These purchased shares are returned to the broker to pay the loan, and you keep the difference between where you sold and where you bought — less interest, of course.

The stock exchanges are in the business of helping companies raise money, so they have rules in place to help maintain an upward bias in the stock market. That can work against the short seller. The key regulation is what's called the *uptick rule,* which means you can sell a stock short only when the last trade was a move up. You can't short a stock that's moving down.

Figure 14-1 shows how short selling works. The trader borrows 400 shares selling at $25 each and then sells them. If the stock goes down, she can buy back the shares at the lower price, making a tidy profit. If the stock stays flat, she loses money because the broker will charge her interest based on the value of the shares she borrowed. And if the stock price goes up, she not only loses money on the interest expense, but also is out on her investment.

Figure 14-1: Looking at short selling in the equities market.

The trader borrows 400 shares of SuperCorp shares to sell. The shares are trading at $25 each. She sells them for $10,000. The brokerage firm charges 10% interest

Beginning Price	Shares Borrowed	Proceeds from Sale	Repurchase Price	Repurchase Cost	Loan Value	Net Profit	Interest Expense	Rate of Return	% Change in Stock Price
$ 25	400	$ 10,000	$ 40	$ (16,000)	10,000	$ (6,000)	$ 1,000	-70%	60%
$ 25	400	$ 10,000	$ 25	$ (10,000)	10,000	$ -	$ 1,000	-10%	0%
$ 25	400	$ 10,000	$ 15	$ (6,000)	10,000	$ 4,000	$ 1,000	30%	-40%

The interest and fees that the broker charges those who borrow stock accrue to the broker, not to the person who actually owns the stock. In fact, the stock's owner will probably never know that his shares were loaned out.

Choosing shorts

Investors — those people who do careful research and expect to be in their positions for months or even years — look for companies that have inflated expectations and are possibly fraudulent. Investors who work the short side of the market spend hours, usually doing careful accounting research, looking for companies that are likely to go down in price some day.

Day traders don't care about accounting. They don't have the time to wait for a short to work out. Instead, they're looking for stocks that go down in price for more mundane reasons, like more sellers than buyers in the next ten minutes. Most day traders who sell short simply reverse their long strategy. For example, some day traders like to buy stocks that have gone down for three days in a row, figuring that they'll go up on the fourth day. They'll also short stocks that have gone up three days in a row, figuring that they'll go down on the fourth day. You don't need a CA to do that!

We cover trading strategies in more detail in Chapters 12 and 13, if you're looking for some ideas.

Short squeezes and other risks

Shorting stocks carries certain risks, because a short sale is a bet on things going wrong. In theory, no limit exists on how much a stock can go up, so no limit exists on how much money a short seller can lose. Two traps in particular can get a short seller. The first is a short squeeze due to good news, the second is a concerted effort to hurt those who are short.

Squeeze my shorts

With a *short squeeze,* a company that has been popular with a lot of short sellers has some good news that drives the stock price up. When the price goes up, short sellers lose money, and some may even have margin problems. And the original reason for going short may be proven to be wrong. Those who are short start buying the stock back in order to reduce their losses, but their increased demand drives the stock price even higher, causing even bigger losses for those who are still short. Ouch!

Calling back the stock

All is not sweetness and light in the world of short selling. Many market participants distrust those folks who are doing all the careful research, in part because they are often right. Company executives are frequently optimists who don't like to hear bad news, and they'll blame short sellers for all that is wrong with their stock price.

Meanwhile, some short sellers have been known to get impatient if their sale isn't making money and start spreading ugly rumours. Many companies, brokers, and investors hate short sellers and try tactics to bust them. Sometimes they issue good news or spread rumours of good news to create a squeeze. Other times, they collectively ask holders of the stock to request that their brokerage firm not loan out their shares. This means that those who shorted it have to buy back and return the shares even if it makes no sense to do so.

Lots to Discover about Leverage

Leverage is the use of borrowed money to increase returns. Day traders use it a lot to get bigger returns from relatively small price changes in the underlying securities. And as long as they consistently close out their positions at the end of the day, day traders can borrow more money and pay less interest than people who hold securities for a longer term.

The process of borrowing works differently in different markets. In the stock and bond markets, it's straightforward: You just tell your broker you're borrowing when you place the order. In the options and futures markets, you're buying and selling contracts that have leverage built into them. You don't borrow money outright, but you can control a lot of value in your account for relatively little money down.

In stock and bond markets

Leverage is straightforward for buyers of stocks and bonds: You simply click the box marked "Margin" when you place your order, and the brokerage firm loans you money. (The margin process is defined in more detail earlier in the chapter.) Then, when the security goes up in price, you get a greater percentage return because you've been able to buy more for your money. Of course, that also increases your potential losses.

Figure 14-2 shows how it works. The trader borrows money to buy 400 shares of SuperCorp. If the stock goes up 4 percent, she makes 8 percent. Whoo-hooo! But if the stock goes down 4 percent, she still has to repay the loan at full dollar value, so she ends up losing 8 percent. That's not so good.

A trader buys $10,000 of SuperCorp with $5,000 of her own cash and a $5,000 loan
SuperCorp trades at $25/share, so the trader purchases a total of 400 shares.
The trader closes out at the end of the day, so no interest is charged.
What happens as the stock price changes?

Ending Price	Ending Value	Loan Value	Net Equity	Trader's Rate of Return	% Change in Stock Price
$ 26.00	$ 10,400	$ 5,000	$ 5,400	8%	4%
$ 25.50	$ 10,200	$ 5,000	$ 5,200	4%	2%
$ 25.00	$ 10,000	$ 5,000	$ 5,000	0%	0%
$ 24.50	$ 9,800	$ 5,000	$ 4,800	-4%	-2%
$ 24.00	$ 9,600	$ 5,000	$ 4,600	-8%	-4%

Figure 14-2: An example of trading stocks on margin.

If you hold your margin position overnight or longer, you'll have to start paying interest. That will cut into your returns or increase your losses.

In options markets

An *option* gives you the right, but not the obligation, to buy or sell a stock or other item at a set price when the contract expires. A *call option* gives you the right to buy, so you would buy a call when you think the underlying asset is going up. A *put option* gives you the right to sell, so you would buy a put when you think the underlying asset is going down. (You can read more about options in Chapter 3, if you are so inspired.) By trading an option, you get exposure to changes in the price of the underlying security without actually buying the security itself. That's the source of the leverage in the market.

A day trader might use options to get an exposure to price changes in a stock for a lot less money than it would cost to buy the stock itself. Suppose a call option is *deeply in-the-money*. That means that its *strike price,* the price that you would be able to buy the stock at if you exercised the option, is far below the current stock price. If this happens, the obvious thing is for the option price to be set at the difference between the current stock price and the strike price, and that's more or less what happens (more in theory, less in practice). When the stock price changes, the option price changes at almost exactly the same amount. This means that you can buy the price performance of the stock at a discount, the discount being the strike price of the stock.

Figure 14-3 shows the performance-boosting leverage from this strategy. The trader buys call options with an exercise price of $10 on a stock trading at $25. The option price changes the same amount that the stock price does, but the call holder gets a greater percentage return than the stock holder.

Figure 14-3: What happens to the option value when the stock price changes?

A trader buys deep in-the-money call options on SuperCorp. The exercise price is $10, and the stock is trading at $25.

Stock Price	Initial Option Price	Exercise (Strike) Price	New Option Price	Stock Price Change	Option Price Change
$ 26.00	$ 15.00	$ 10.00	$ 16.00	4%	7%
$ 25.50	$ 15.00	$ 10.00	$ 15.50	2%	3%
$ 25.00	$ 15.00	$ 10.00	$ 15.00	0%	0%
$ 24.50	$ 15.00	$ 10.00	$ 14.50	-2%	-3%
$ 24.00	$ 15.00	$ 10.00	$ 14.00	-4%	-7%

Many other options strategies that day traders can use exist, but a discussion of them goes beyond the scope of this book. The Appendix has some resources to help you in your research.

In futures trading

A *futures* contract gives you the obligation to buy or sell an underlying financial or agricultural commodity, assuming you still hold the contract at the expiration date. That underlying product ranges from the value of treasury bonds to barrels of oil and heads of cattle, and you're only putting money down now when you purchase the contract. You don't have to come up with the full amount until the contract comes due — and almost all options and futures traders close out their trades long before the contract expiration date. Futures are discussed in Chapter 3, but here we talk about how leverage works in the futures market.

Although most options and futures contracts settle with cash long before the due date, contract holders have the right to hold them until the due date and, in the case of options on common stock and agricultural derivatives, demand physical delivery. It's rare, but the commodity exchanges have systems in place for determining the transport, specifications, and delivery of grain, cattle, or ethanol. One advantage of day trading is that you close out the same day, without ever even thinking about the fine print of physical delivery.

Because *derivatives* have built-in leverage that allows a trader to have big market exposure for relatively few dollars up front, they've become popular with day traders. Figure 14-4 shows how it works. Here, a trader is buying the Chicago Mercantile Exchange's E-Mini S&P 500 futures contract, which gives traders exposure to the performance of the Standard & Poor's 500 Index, a standard measure of the stock performance of a diversified list of 500 large American companies. The futures contract trades at 50 times the value of the index, rounded to the nearest $0.25. The minimum margin that a trader must put down on the contract is $3,500. Each $0.25 change in the index leads to a $12.50 ($0.25 × 50) change in the value of the contract, and that $12.50 is added to or subtracted from the $3,500 margin.

Figure 14-4: Margin and the derivatives trade with built-in leverage.

A day trader buys a Chicago Mercantile Exchange E-Mini S&P 500 futures contract.
The contract price is $50 x the index level. To buy it, the trader must post margin of $3,500

Initial Index Value	Ending Index Value	Multiplier	Initial Contract Value	Contract Value	Value Change in Dollars	Value Change in Percent	Initial Margin	Ending Margin	Percent Change in Margin
1,457.50	1,458.50	$ 50.00	$ 72,875.00	$ 72,925.00	$ 50.00	0.07%	$ 3,500.00	$ 3,550.00	1.43%
1,457.50	1,458.00	$ 50.00	$ 72,875.00	$ 72,900.00	$ 25.00	0.03%	$ 3,500.00	$ 3,525.00	0.71%
1,457.50	1,457.50	$ 50.00	$ 72,875.00	$ 72,875.00	$ -	0.00%	$ 3,500.00	$ 3,500.00	0.00%
1,457.50	1,457.00	$ 50.00	$ 72,875.00	$ 72,850.00	$ (25.00)	-0.03%	$ 3,500.00	$ 3,475.00	-0.71%
1,457.50	1,456.50	$ 50.00	$ 72,875.00	$ 72,825.00	$ (50.00)	-0.07%	$ 3,500.00	$ 3,450.00	-1.43%

Some exchanges use the term *margin,* and others prefer to use *performance bond.* Either way, it's the same thing: money you put in up front to ensure you can meet the contract terms when it comes due. If you hold the contract overnight, your account is adjusted up or down to reflect the day's profits. If it gets too low, you're asked to add more money.

In foreign exchange

The *foreign exchange,* or *forex,* market is driven by leverage. Exchange rates tend to move slowly, by as little as a tenth or even a hundredth of a penny a day. And the markets are so huge that it's easier to hedge risk. You might have trouble borrowing shares of stock to short them, but you should have no trouble ever borrowing yen. In order to get a big return, forex traders almost always borrow huge amounts of money.

In the stock market, day traders can generally borrow up to three times the amount of cash and securities held in their accounts. Forex trading is also regulated by IIROC. Although some offshore brokers will allow traders to borrow 400 times the amount in their accounts, legitimate Canadian firms will only let people borrow about 20 times (you'll need to put up between 3 percent and 5 percent of a trade).

Forex trading allows for more borrowing than stock trading because the market is open 24/7. This means trading systems can sell a position any time, day or night, before the account goes under margin and the trader loses money. Because there's less risk of squandering big bucks, brokers offer for more leverage. Since stock markets are only open for trading during business hours, there is a chance share prices could decline in the middle of the night. That adds risk; hence a higher margin requirement.

The reason why a forex firm wants to hedge its risks against its day trading customers is that most day traders lose money. The firms know that if they bet against the aggregate trades held by their customers, they'll probably come out ahead. Don't trade in forex or any other market until you've worked out a strategy and practised it, so that you can avoid becoming a statistic. Chapter 11 has information on testing and evaluating trading strategies.

An exchange rate is just the price of money. If the Canadian dollar–American dollar rate is 1.0121, that means one loonie will buy US$1.01.

Borrowing in Your Trading Business

Leverage is only part of the borrowing involved in your day trading business. Like any business owner, sometimes you need more cash than your business generates. Other times, you see expansion opportunities that require more money than you have on hand. In this section, we discuss why and how day traders can borrow money over and above leveraged trading.

Margin loans for cash flow

If day trading is your job, then you face a constant pressure: How do you cover the costs of living while keeping enough money in the market to trade? One way to do this is to have another source of income — from savings, a spouse, or a job that doesn't overlap with market hours. Other day traders take money out of their trading account.

If the market hasn't been cooperative, then there might not be enough to take out of the account while still having enough capital to trade. One option is to arrange a margin loan through a brokerage firm. The firm will let you take out a loan against the securities that you hold. You can spend the money any way you like, but you will be charged interest — and you will have to repay it. Still, it's a good option to have, because day trade earnings tend to be erratic.

Borrowing for trading capital

Some day traders use a double layer of leverage: They borrow the money to set up their trading accounts and then they borrow money for their trading strategies. If the market cooperates this can be a great way to make money, but if not you could end up owing a lot of people money that you don't have.

If you want to take the risk, though, you have a few resources to turn to other than your relatives: You can borrow against your house, use your credit cards, or find a trading firm that will give you some money to work with.

Borrowing against your house

Yes, you can use a mortgage or a home equity line of credit to get the money for your day trading activities. In general, this carries low interest rates because your house is your collateral, plus the loan is tax deductible. This can be a relatively low-cost way to pull value stored in your house for use in trading. The risk? If you can't pay back the loan, you can lose your residence. Just don't borrow against your car, too, as you'll need a place to live when the bank evicts you.

Putting it on the card

The business world is filled with people who started businesses using credit cards. And you can do that. If you have even halfway decent credit, credit card companies are happy to lend you all the money you want.

Naturally, they charge you a mighty high rate of interest, one that even the sharpest traders will have trouble covering from their returns. If the only way you can raise the capital for day trading is through your credit card, consider waiting a few years and saving your money before taking the plunge. Because day trading income can be erratic, you may end up using your credit cards to cover your living expenses some months. You may want to save your credit for that rather than dedicate it directly for your day trading.

Risk capital from an arcade

In Chapters 6 and 7, we discuss *trading arcades,* also called prop firms, office spaces where traders can rent space. These are usually located in major cities. Some trading arcades offer more than just desk space. Some have training programs, whereas others give promising traders some capital to trade in exchange for a cut of the profits. This may be an option for you to consider if you are new to day trading and want to put more money to work than you currently have available.

Assessing Risks and Returns from Short Selling and Leverage

Leverage introduces risk to your day trading, and that can give you greatly increased returns. Most day traders use leverage, at least part of the time, in order to make their trading activities pay off in cold, hard cash. The challenge is to use leverage responsibly. In Chapter 9 we go into money management in detail, but here we cover the two issues most related to leverage: losing your money, and losing your nerve. Understanding those risks can help you determine how much leverage you should take, and how often you can take it.

Losing your money

Losing money is obvious. Leverage magnifies your returns, but it also magnifies your risks. Any borrowings have to be repaid regardless. If you buy or sell a futures or options contract, you are legally obligated to perform, even if you have lost money. That can be really hard. Day trading is risky in large part because of the amount of leverage used. If you don't feel comfortable with that, you may want to use little or no leverage, especially when you are new to day trading or when you are starting to work a new trading strategy.

Losing your nerve

The basic risk and return of your underlying strategy isn't affected by leverage. If you expect that your system will work about 60 percent of the time, then that should hold no matter how much money is at stake or where that money came from. However, it's likely that it does make a difference to you on some subconscious level if you have borrowed the money.

Trading is very much a game of nerves. If you hesitate to make a trade, cut a loss, or otherwise follow your strategy, you're going to run into trouble. (We discuss the mental aspects of day trading in Chapter 8.)

Say you are trading futures and decide that you'll accept three downticks before selling, and will look for five upticks before selling. This means you are willing to accept some loss, cut it if it gets out of hand, and then be disciplined about taking gains when you get them. This strategy keeps a lid on your losses while forcing some discipline on your gains.

Now, suppose you're dealing with lots and lots of leverage. Suddenly, those downticks become too real to you — it's money you don't have. Next thing you know, you accept only two downticks before closing out. But this keeps you from getting winners. Then you decide to ride with your winners, and suddenly you aren't taking profits fast enough, and your positions move against you. Your fear of loss is making you sloppy. That's why many traders find it better to borrow less money and stick to their system, rather than borrow the maximum allowed and let that knowledge cloud their judgment.

Lenders can lose their nerve, too. Your brokerage firm might close your account because of losses, even though waiting just a little longer might turn a losing position into a profit. Check out the sidebar "The dangers of risk: Long-Term Capital Management." That fund was shut by lenders worried about not being repaid. Some evidence exists that if the fund had been allowed to borrow more money, it would have turned a big profit in 1998.

Chapter 15

The World of Arbitrage

In This Chapter

- Finding out about the law of one price
- Making quick profits through scalping
- Considering the costs of your transactions
- Checking out tools used to conduct arbitrage
- Looking at the various types of arbitrage
- Figuring statistical arbitrage, if you dare

Day traders work fast, looking to make lots of little profits during a single day. *Arbitrage* is a trading strategy that looks to make profits from small discrepancies in securities prices. The word *arbitrage* itself comes from the French word for judgment; a person who does arbitrage is an *arbitrageur,* or *arb* for short. The idea is that the arbitrageur arbitrates among the prices in the market to reach one final level.

In theory, arbitrage is riskless. It's illogical for the same asset to trade at different prices, so eventually the two prices must converge. The person who buys at the lower price and sells at the higher one will make money with no risk. The challenge is that everyone is looking for these easy profits, so there may not be many of them out there. Good arbitrageurs have a paradoxical mix of patience, to wait for the right opportunity, and impatience, to place the trade the instant the opportunity appears. If you have the fortitude to watch the market, or if you are willing to have software do it for you (see information on research services in Chapter 7), you'll probably find enough good arbitrage opportunities to keep you busy.

True arbitrage involves buying and selling the same security, and many day traders use arbitrage as their primary investment strategy. They may use high levels of *leverage* (borrowing — see Chapter 14) to boost returns. Other traders follow trading strategies involving similar, but not identical, securities. These fall under the category of *risk arbitrage*. In this chapter, we cover the terms and strategies used by day traders who engage in arbitrage.

We discuss the basics of arbitrage and how it can be put to good use by a patient trader. We outline the tools you can use to profit from price differences among similar securities. Finally, we list the many types of arbitrage you might want to include in your arsenal of trading strategies.

Obeying the Law of One Price

The key to success in any investment is buying low and selling high. But what's low? And what's high? Who knows?

In the financial markets, the general assumption is that, at least in the short run, the market price is the right price. Only investors, those patient, long-suffering accounting nerds willing to hold investments for years, will see deviations between the market price and the true worth of an investment. For everyone else, especially day traders, what you see is what you get.

Under the *law of one price,* the same asset has the same value everywhere. If markets allow for easy trading — and the financial markets certainly do — then any price discrepancies will be short-lived because traders will immediately step in to buy at the low price and sell at the high price.

Punishing violators of the law

But what happens if what you see in Toronto is not what you see in New York? What happens if you notice that futures prices are not tracking movements in the underlying asset? How about if you see that the stock of every company in an industry has reacted to a news event except one?

Well, then, you have an opportunity to make money, but you'd better act fast — other people will probably see it, too. What you do is simple: You sell as much of the high-priced asset in the high-priced market as you can, borrowing shares if you need to, and then you immediately turn around and buy the low-priced asset in the low-priced market.

Think of the markets as a scale, and you, the arbitrageur, must bring fairness to them. When the markets are out of balance, you take from the high-priced market (the heavier side of the scale) and return it to the low-priced market (the lighter side) until both even out at a price in between.

If you start with a high price of $8 and a low price of $6, and then buy at $6 and sell at $8, your maximum profit is $2 — with no risk. Until the point where the two assets balance at $7, you can make a profit on the difference between them.

Of course, most price differences are on the order of pennies, not dollars, but if you can find enough of these little pricing errors and trade them in size, you can make good money.

Understanding arbitrage and market efficiency

The law of one price holds as long as markets are efficient. Market efficiency is a controversial topic in finance. In academic theory, markets are perfectly efficient, and arbitrage simply isn't possible. That makes a lot of sense if you are testing different assumptions about how the markets would work in a perfect world. A long-term investor would say that markets are inefficient in the short run but perfectly efficient in the long run, so they believe that if they do their research now, the rest of the world will eventually come around, allowing them to make good money.

Traders are in between. The market price and volume are pretty much all the information they have to go on. It may be irrational, but that doesn't matter today. The only thing a trader wants to know is whether an opportunity to make money is available given what's going on right now.

In the academic world, market efficiency comes in three flavours, with no form allowing for arbitrage:

- **Strong form:** Everything, even inside information known only to company executives, is reflected in the security's price.
- **Semi-strong form:** Prices include all public information, so it may be possible to profit from insider trading.
- **Weak form:** Prices reflect all historical information, so research that uncovers new trends may be beneficial.

Those efficient-market true believers are convinced that arbitrage is imaginary, because someone would've noticed a price difference between markets already and immediately acted to close it off. But who are those mysterious someones? They are day traders! Even the most devout efficient markets adherent would, if pressed, admit that day traders perform a valuable service in the name of market efficiency.

Those with a less-rigid view of market activity admit that arbitrage opportunities exist, but that they are few and far between. A trader who expects to make money from arbitrage had better pay close attention to the markets to act quickly when a moment happens. And, we'd say this is the case for most arbitrage strategies open to day traders.

Finally, those who don't believe in market efficiency believe that market prices are usually out of sync with asset values. They do research in hopes of learning things that other people don't know. This mindset favours investors more than traders, because it can take time for these price discrepancies to work themselves out.

Because arbitrage requires traders to work fast, it tends to work best for those traders who are willing and able to automate their trading. If you are comfortable with programming and relying on software to do your work, arbitrage might be a great strategy for you.

Scalping for Profits

The law of one price is all well and good, but prices change constantly during the day. They go up a little bit, they go down a little bit, they move every time an order is placed. A way exists for traders to profit from those movements. It's not exactly arbitrage, it's *scalping*. Especially active in commodities markets, scalpers look to take advantage of changes in a security's *bid–ask spread*. That's the difference between the price that a broker will buy a security for from those who want to sell it (the *bid*) and the price that the broker will charge those who want to buy it (the *ask* — also called the *offer* in some markets).

In normal trading, the bid–ask spread tends to be more or less steady over time because the usual flow of supply and demand stays in balance. After all, under market efficiency everyone has the same information, so their trading is consistent and allows the broker-dealers to generate a steady profit.

Sometimes, however, the spread is a little wider or narrower than normal, not because of a change in the information in the market, but because of short-term imbalances in supply and demand.

A basic scalping strategy looks like this:

- If the spread between the bid and the ask is wider than usual, then the ask is higher and the bid is lower than it should be. That's because slightly more people want to buy than sell, so the brokers charge the buyers higher prices. The scalper uses this as a sign to sell.
- If the spread between the bid and the ask is narrower than usual, then the ask is lower and the bid is higher than it would normally be. That happens if there are slightly more sellers than buyers, and the broker wants to find buyers to pick up the slack. The scalper would be in there buying — and hoping that the selling pressure is short lived.

The scalper has to work quickly to make many small trades. He might buy at $20.25, sell at $20.50, and buy again at $20.30. He has to have a low *trade cost structure* in place (discussed later in this chapter) or else he'll pay out all his profits and more to the broker. He also has to be sure that the price changes aren't driven by real information, because that will make market prices too volatile to make scalping profitable. Scalping is "picking up nickels in front of a steamroller," some traders say, because of the risk of focusing on small price changes when bigger changes are underway.

Many day traders rely heavily on scalping, especially on slow market days. Because each trade carries a transaction cost (discussed later in this chapter), it can contribute to more costs than profits. Done right, though, it's a nice way to make some steady profits.

Scalping, as defined here, is perfectly legal. However, the word is also sometimes used to describe some illegal activities, such as promoting a security in public and then selling it in private.

Those Pesky Transaction Costs

Pure arbitrage works best in a world where trading is free. In reality, it costs good money to trade. Sometimes you might notice a price discrepancy that seems to last forever. You can't work it because the profit wouldn't cover your costs. And you know what? That may be true for everyone else out there.

In the real world, trading costs money. Consider all the costs of getting started: buying equipment, paying for Internet access, learning how to trade. Then there are the costs of doing business that vary with each transaction: commissions, fees, interest, the bid–ask spread, and taxes. You don't make a profit on a trade unless it covers those costs.

Even if you work with a broker that charges little or no commission, and even if your broker charges no interest on day trading margin (loans against your securities account), you can bet that your broker is making money off you. That broker's profit is showing up in the spread and the speed of execution, so a cost to arbitrage that must be covered still exists, even on a seemingly free account. Trust us, brokerage firms are in business to make money, whether or not their customers do.

Add up those trading costs, and you can find yourself in a frustrating situation: You can see the opportunity right there staring you in the face, but you can't take it. It either sits there, taunting you, or gets picked off by a trader who has lower costs than you do.

On the other hand, if you know what your costs are, you can avoid unprofitable opportunities. Don't consider your fixed costs, like your office and your equipment. Those expenses don't change with any given trade. (Yes, you have to cover them in the long run to stay in business, but you can ignore them in the short run.) Instead, figure out how much money you give to your broker on any given trade, on an order, per share, or per contract basis. Write that number down on a sticky note, and put it on your monitor so that you remember what you have to clear before you risk a trade. Just don't get so fixated on covering your costs that you avoid exiting trades at the right time.

Risk Arbitrage and Its Tools

In its purest form, arbitrage is riskless because the purchase of an asset in one market and the sale of the asset in another happen simultaneously — you just let those profits flow right into your account. It is possible to do this, but not often. No day trader who pursues only riskless arbitrage stays in business long.

Return is a function of risk. The more risk you take, the greater the return you expect to make.

Because so few opportunities for true arbitrage exist, most day traders looking at arbitrage strategies actually practise *risk arbitrage*. Like true arbitrage, risk arbitrage attempts to generate profits from price discrepancies; but, like the name says, risk arbitrage involves taking some risk. Yes, you buy one security and sell another in risk arbitrage, but it's not always the same security and not always at the same time. For example, a day trader might buy the stock of an acquisition target and sell the stock of an acquirer in the hopes of making a profit as the deal nears the closing date.

Risk arbitrage usually involves strategies that unfold over time — possibly hours, but usually days or weeks. Pursuing these strategies puts you into the world of swing trading (described in Chapter 2), which carries a little more risk than day trading.

In risk arbitrage, a trader is buying and selling similar securities. Much of the risk draws from the fact that the securities are not identical, so the law of one price isn't absolute. Nevertheless, it forms the guiding principle, which is this: If you have two different ways to buy the same thing, then the prices of each purchase should be proportional. If they are not, then an opportunity exists to make money. And what day trader doesn't want to make money?

Arbitrageurs use a mix of different assets and techniques to create these different ways of buying the same thing. In this section we describe some of their favourites.

Derivatives

Derivatives are options, futures, and related financial contracts that draw or derive their value from the value of something else, such as the price of a stock index or the current cost of corn. They offer a lower-cost, lower-obligation method of getting exposure to certain price changes. In the case of agricultural and energy commodities, derivatives are the only practical way for a day trader to own them. Because they are so closely tied to the value of the underlying security, derivatives form a useful "almost, but not quite" asset for traders looking for arbitrage situations. A trader may see a price discrepancy between the derivative and the underlying asset, thus noticing a profitable trading opportunity.

Using a derivative in tandem with its underlying security, traders can construct a range of risk arbitrage trades (and you can read more about them later in this section). For example, a trader looking to set up arbitrage on a merger could trade options on the stocks of the buying and selling companies rather than trading the stocks themselves. More arbitrage opportunities means a greater likelihood of making a low-risk profit.

Levering with leverage

Chapter 14 covers leverage in detail, but I'm bringing it up again here. It's the process of borrowing money to trade in order to increase potential returns. The more money the trader borrows, the greater the return on capital that she can earn. Leverage is commonly used by day traders, because most trades with a one-day time horizon carry low returns unless they are magnified through borrowing.

That magic of magnification becomes especially important in arbitrage, because the price discrepancies between securities tend to be really small. The primary way to get a bigger return is to borrow money to do it.

However, leverage has a downside: Along with improving returns, it increases risk. Because even risk arbitrage strategies tend to have low risk, this may be acceptable. Just remember that you have to repay all borrowed money, no matter what happens to prices. We provide more information on that in Chapter 14.

Short selling

Short selling is another topic from Chapter 14, and it creates another set of alternatives for setting up an arbitrage trade. Short selling allows a day trader to profit when a security's price goes down. Instead of buying low and then selling high, the trader sells high first and then buys back low. The short seller goes to her broker, borrows the security that she thinks will decline in price, sells it, and then buys it back in the market later so that she has the shares to repay the loan. (It all happens electronically, no office visits required!) Assuming she's right and the price does indeed fall, she pockets the difference between the price where she sold the security and the price where she bought it back. Of course, that difference is her loss if the price goes up instead of down.

By adding short selling to the bag of tricks, an arbitrageur can find a lot more ways to profit from a price discrepancy in the market. New combinations of cheap and expensive assets — and more ways to trade them — give a day trader more opportunities to make trades during the day.

The opposite of *short* is *long*. When a trader holds a security, he's said to be long.

Synthetic securities

Feeling creative? Well, then, consider creating *synthetic securities* when looking for arbitrage opportunities. A synthetic security is a combination of assets that have the same profit-and-loss profile as another asset or group of assets. For example, a stock is a combination of a *put option,* which has value if the stock goes down in price, and a *call option,* which has value if the stock goes up in price. By thinking up ways to mimic the behaviour of an asset through a synthetic security, a day trader can find more ways for an asset to be cheaper in one market than in another, leading to more potential arbitrage opportunities.

A typical arbitrage transaction involving a synthetic security involves shorting the real security and then buying a package of derivatives that match its risk and return.

Many of the risk arbitrage techniques covered later in this chapter involve the creation of synthetic securities.

Complex arbitrage trading strategies require more testing and simulation trading (covered in Chapter 11) and may possibly involve losses while you fine-tune your methods. Be sure you feel comfortable with your trading method before you commit big time and big dollars to it.

An Array of Arbitrages

The tools of arbitrage — derivatives, leverage, short selling, synthetic securities — can be used in all sorts of ways to generate potentially profitable trades, and that's what we cover in this section of the chapter. Most day traders who decide to do arbitrage will pick a few strategies to follow. After all, it's hard enough to spot these opportunities; the trader who tries to do too much is the trader who will soon be looking for a new job. Armed with the information here, you can decide whether there's an arbitrage strategy that matches your approach to the market so that you can make it your own.

The varieties of arbitrage transactions are listed here in alphabetical order. It's not exhaustive; plenty of other ways to exploit price differences in the market exist, but some involve more time than a day trader is willing to commit. We've put them in alphabetical order. Some are more complex than others, some generate more opportunities than others, and some work best if you are willing to swing trade (hold for a few days) rather than day trade (close out all positions at the end of the day.)

Many arbitrage strategies work best in combination with other strategies, such as news-driven trading (discussed in Chapter 13). For example, it might take a news announcement to cause people to pay attention to a company's stock so that enough trading activity happens that day to close a price gap. If you know about the pricing problem ahead of time, you can swoop in and make the arbitrage that day.

Other types of arbitrage certainly do exist out there. Wherever people pay close attention to the markets and price changes, they find small price differences to turn into large, low-risk profits. If you think you've found an arbitrage strategy not listed here, by all means, go and test it and see if it will work for you.

Capital structure arbitrage

Companies issue securities in order to finance their business, and investment bankers are in the business of helping them do just that. Some companies are nice and simple. Microsoft, for example, uses only stock for financing and has only one class of stock. Others are far more complicated, using mixtures of different classes of stock and different issues of debt to finance the growth. General Electric, for example, has one class of common stock and seven different debt securities for its parent company and its finance subsidiary.

The way that a company is financed is its *capital structure,* and capital structure arbitrage looks for inappropriate price differences among all the different classes of stock and debt outstanding. Although all securities tied to the same business should trade in a similar fashion, they don't always, and that creates opportunities.

Say, for example, that SuperTech Company has two classes of stock, one on its core business and one that tracks the performance of its nanotechnology subsidiary. (A *tracking stock* is a corporate finance gimmick that goes in and out of style; it's stock on a subsidiary that is controlled by the parent company.) The parent company still has exposure to the nanotechnology subsidiary, but that is not reflected in its stock price. One day, the nanotechnology subsidiary announces great earnings, and the stock goes way up, but SuperTech stock doesn't move even though it benefits. The capital structure arbitrageur immediately shorts the nanotech subsidiary tracking stock and buys the parent company stock (matching the size of the long and short positions so that they move up and down in tandem), waiting for people to realize that the discrepancy is there.

Convertible arbitrage

As part of designing their capital structure, some companies issue *convertible bonds* (sometimes called a *convertible debenture*) or *convertible preferred stock.* These securities are a cross between stocks and bonds. Like an ordinary bond, convertibles pay regular income to those who hold them (interest for convertible bonds and dividends for convertible preferred stock), but they also act a little like stock because the holders have the right to exchange the convertible security for ordinary common stock.

For example: a $1,000 convertible bond pays 7.5 percent interest and is convertible into 25 shares of stock. If the stock is less than $40 per share, the convertible holder will prefer to cash the interest or dividend cheques. If the company's stock trades above $40, the convertible holder would make more money giving up the income in order to get the stock cheap. Because of the benefit of conversion, the interest rate on a convertible security is usually below that on a regular corporate bond.

Because a convertible security carries a built-in option to buy the underlying stock, it generally trades in line with the stock. If the convertible's price gets too high or too low, then an arbitrage opportunity presents itself.

Consider this case: A day trader notices that a convertible bond is selling at a lower price than it should be, given the current level of interest rates and the price of the company's common stock. So, he buys the convertibles and sells the common stock short (see Chapter 14 for more on short selling).

When the stock's price moves back into line, he collects a profit from both sides of the trade.

Fixed income and interest rate arbitrage

Fixed income securities are bonds, notes, and related securities that give their owners a regular interest payment. They are popular with conservative investors, especially retirees, who want to generate a regular income from the quarterly interest payments. They are considered to be safe, predictable, long-run investments, but they can fluctuate wildly in the short term, which makes them attractive to arbitrageurs.

Interest rates are the price of money, and so they affect the value of many kinds of securities. Fixed-income securities have a great deal of interest-rate exposure, because they pay out interest. Some stocks have interest-rate exposure, too. Trading in foreign exchange is an attempt to profit from the changing price of one currency relative to another, and that's usually a function of the difference in interest rates between the two countries. Derivatives have a regular expiration schedule, so they have some time value, and that's measured through interest rates.

With so many different assets affected by changes in interest rates, arbitrageurs pay attention. With *fixed-income arbitrage,* the trader breaks out the following:

- The time value of money
- The level of risk in the economy
- The likelihood of repayment
- The inflation-rate effects on different securities

If one of the numbers is out of whack, the trader constructs and executes an arbitrage trade to profit from it.

It's rarely practical for a day trader to buy bonds outright. Instead, day traders looking at fixed income arbitrage and other interest-rate-sensitive strategies usually rely on interest rate futures, offered by the Montreal Exchange or the Chicago Board of Trade. You can read more about this in Chapter 3.

How would this work? Think of a day trader monitoring interest rates on U.S. government securities. He notices that two-year treasury notes are trading at a higher yield than expected — especially relative to five-year treasury notes. He sells futures on the two-year treasury notes and then buys futures on the five-year treasury notes. When the difference between the two rates falls back where it should be, the futures trade will turn a profit.

Index arbitrage

Market observers talk a lot about the performance of the S&P/TSX Composite Index, or the S&P 500 Index and the Dow Jones Industrial Average, the two main American markets. These are *market indexes,* designed to represent the activity of the market, and are widely published for market observers to follow. The performance of the index is based on the performance of a group of securities, ranging from all of the TSX's large companies, currently about 250 companies, (S&P/TSX Composite Index) to the TSX's 60 largest companies (S&P/TSX 60).

Sure, an arbitrageur could buy all the stocks, and some hedge funds exist to do just that. But very few people can do that. Instead, they get exposure to index performance through the many different securities based on the indexes. Buy-and-hold mutual fund investors can buy funds that hold all the same stocks in the same proportion as the index. Those with shorter-term profits in mind can buy exchange-traded funds, which are baskets of stocks listed on organized exchanges (see Chapter 3), or they can trade futures and options on the indexes.

Arbitrageurs love the idea of an asset — like an index — that has lots of different securities based on its value. That creates lots of opportunities for mispricing. Unless the index, the futures, the options, and the exchange-traded funds are all in line, some canny day trader can step in and make some money.

For example, suppose the S&P/TSX 60 futures contract is looking mighty cheap relative to the price of the S&P/TSX 60 Index. A trader can short an exchange-traded fund on the index and then buy futures contracts to profit from the difference.

Garbitrage

Traders get sloppy when an exciting merger is announced. If one company in an industry gets taken over, the stock in all the companies in the industry will go up, often for no good reason. Some get so carried away that they buy the wrong stock entirely, usually because of confusion over ticker symbols. If GAP Stores, ticker symbol GPS, were to be taken over, chances are good that the stock in Great Atlantic and Pacific Tea Company — operator of the A&P grocery stores, ticker symbol GAP — would also go up. Such bad trading is known as *garbitrage.*

Merger arbitrage

Every day, companies get bought and sold, and that creates arbitrage opportunities. In fact, one of the better-known arbitrage strategies out there is *merger arbitrage,* in which traders try to profit from the change in stock prices after a merger has been announced. It starts by looking at the following details in the merger announcement:

- The name of the acquiring company
- The name of the company being taken over (and no matter what PR people say, no mergers occur between equals)
- The price of the transaction
- The currency (cash, stock, debt)
- The date the merger is expected to close

Until the date that the merger actually closes, which may be different from the date in the merger announcement, any and every one of the announced details can change. The acquiring company may learn new information about the target company and change its mind. A third company might jump in and make an offer for more money. The shareholders may agree to support the deal only if they get cash instead of stock. All that drama creates opportunity, both for traders looking for one-day opportunities and for those willing to hold a position until the merger closing date.

Consider this example. Say that Major Bancorp offers to buy Downtown Bank for $50 per share in cash. Major Bancorp's shares will probably fall in price, because its shareholders will be concerned that the merger will be a lot of trouble. Downtown Bank's shares will go up in price, but not all the way to $50, because its shareholders know that some risk exists the deal won't go through. An arbitrageur would short Major Bancorp and buy Downtown Bank to profit from the concerns. If Overseas Banque decides to step in, then it might be a profitable idea to buy Major Bancorp and short Overseas Banque. (If another bidder steps in and places a higher offer for Downtown Bank, then the whole arbitrage unravels — hence, the risk.)

Option arbitrage

Options form the basis of many arbitrage strategies, especially for those day traders who work the stock market. We discuss them in Chapter 3, but here's a little refresher. First, many types of options are available, even on the same security. The two main categories are *puts,* which bet on the underlying security price falling, and *calls,* which bet on the underlying security price rising. Puts and calls on the same security come in many different strike prices, depending on where you want to bet the price goes. Some options, known as *American options,* can be cashed in at any time between the date of issue and the expiration date, and you can exercise others, known as *European options,* only at the expiration date. (To complicate matters, American and European options can be issued anywhere.) With all those choices, a few price discrepancies are bound to arise for the alert arbitrageur.

Maybe a day trader notices that on a day when a company has a big announcement, the options exchanges seem to be assuming a slightly higher price for the stock than where the stock is actually trading. He decides to buy the underlying stock as well as a put; he also sells a call with the same strike price and expiration date as the put. This creates a synthetic security that has the same payoff as shorting the security, meaning that the trader has pulled off a riskless arbitrage transaction. He effectively bought the security cheap in the stock market and sold it at a higher price in the options market.

Pairs trading

Pairs trading, which involves buying a cheap stock and shorting an expensive stock in the same industry group, is popular with many people who day trade stocks. (It's also the core of traditional hedge-fund investing, although very few hedge funds rely on it nowadays.)

A pairs trader watches an industry group and looks for situations where one company seems to be doing especially well or one is doing especially poorly. That would most likely indicate a problem in the way people are pricing the industry, because in general what's good for one company is good for all of them. A pairs trader would pay particular attention to news events that seem to affect all but one or two companies in the same industry. If one of them appears to be overvalued relative to the others, the pairs trader shorts the pricey stock and buys the cheapest one.

The pairs trader isn't dealing with identical assets, of course, so the simultaneous purchase and sale is a lot riskier than it would be in true arbitrage. Sometimes, one stock is more expensive and one is much cheaper than the rest of the industry for very good reason. Good pairs traders are willing to do a little fundamental research (see Chapter 12) so they can avoid being short the winner and being long the loser in an industry undergoing big changes.

For Propeller-Heads Only: Statistical Arbitrage

Do you love crunching numbers? Are you comfortable with programming? Are you an actuary looking for a career change? If the answers to these questions are yes, then *statistical arbitrage* might be right for you. It involves the use of complex mathematical models to determine where a security should be priced. It's based on the notion that securities prices move randomly along a normal curve. If all results are distributed normally, then *reversion to the mean* holds. So, a security's price will equal the average — the mean — price in the long run. Any huge swings up eventually have to be matched by huge swings down so that the mean does not change.

Think of it like this: A standard die has six sides, and when you roll it you're equally likely to get any one of those six results. The mean of the six sides is 3.5, or (1 + 2 + 3+ 4 + 5 + 6) / 6. If you roll the die 100 times, the average of all those results should be close to the 3.5 mean. If your mean is actually 2.1, then chances are good that your next several rolls will have an average higher than 3.5 so that the total results will begin to close in on that 3.5 mean. If not, you haven't figured out a fabulous new secret to rolling a die; it's more likely that your die is loaded.

In statistical arbitrage, the trader works with huge databases of securities prices to determine where the average should be, especially relative to market conditions such as interest rate levels. If the current price is too high, it's time to short it; if the price is too low, it's time to buy.

How does this work? Well, suppose a day trader has data showing that for the past 20 years, food-processing companies have moved in a fixed percentage relative to unemployment rates. He notices that in the past month, the relationship has diverged, with the stock prices having decreased more than expected relative to the current economy. So, he buys the stocks expecting them to go up in price under the assumption that the normal relationship holds.

You might be a great statistician, but chances are good that the big hedge funds and fancy brand-name brokerage firms have hired statisticians who are even better than you. (And even then, there's no guarantee of success — hedge fund Long-Term Capital Management failed in 1998 and nearly took the world's financial markets down with it despite having two Nobel Prize winners on staff.) Just remember that statistical arbitrage puts you smack against the biggest of the Big Kahunas on Bay and Wall Streets.

Chapter 16

Day Trading for Investors

In This Chapter

- Developing the trader's discipline
- Marking market momentum
- Taking the news into consideration
- Setting targets and limits for your trading and investing
- Discovering how longs can trade for the short term
- Evaluating execution quality

It takes a special person to be a day trader — one who has quick reflexes, a strong stomach, and a short-term perspective on the markets. Not everyone's meant to parcel out their workdays a minute at a time. Most people do better with a long-term perspective on their finances, looking to match their investments with their goals and thinking about their investment performance over months or years rather than right now.

But those patient long-term investors can learn a thing or two from the frenetic day trader, and that's what this chapter is all about. Many day-trading techniques can help swing traders, position traders, and investors — people who hold positions for days, months, or even decades — improve their returns and make smarter decisions when it comes time to buy or sell.

Let's face it: In theory, investors might be willing to wait forever to see great stock picks play out, but in reality, they have only so much time and money. A company's stock may be ridiculously cheap, but can languish a long time before everyone else catches on and bids the price up. The investor who buys and sells well can add a few extra dollars to his investment return, and who doesn't want that?

Not all day traders close out every night, and some long-term investors will take a day trading flyer on a hot idea. In this chapter, we cover some trading and analysis techniques used by day traders to help longer-term investors improve their returns. Then we discuss some ways that long-term investors might want to add day trading to their list of tricks to achieve better total return.

And heck, maybe a few investors want to give day trading a try, especially for those securities that they have followed long enough to know how the market reacts to news and whether those reactions are appropriate. For a long-term investor, given the time to test strategies and set limits, day trading in known markets might result in some nice incremental short-term returns.

The Trader's Discipline

Successful day traders have an innate sense of discipline. They know when to commit more money to a trade and when to cut their losses and close up shop for the day.

Unfortunately, a lot of long-term investors can get sloppy. They have done so much research and committed so much time waiting for a position to work out that they often forget the cardinal rule of the trader: The market doesn't know that you're in it. The stock doesn't know you own it, so it's not going to reward your loyalty. Securities go up and down every day for no good reason, and sometimes you are going to make a mistake and you will have to cut your losses. No shame in that, as long as you learn from it.

Now, how can you get that discipline? Start by developing an investment and trading plan, covered in Chapter 2. Although investing is probably not your primary occupation, you do want to have in writing what your objectives are and how you plan to meet them given other constraints: time, tax considerations, and risk tolerance. Then carefully evaluate your performance (covered in Chapter 11) and keep a trade diary so that you know what you are trading and why. Are there ways to improve? Are you making mistakes that could be avoided?

Traders have to go through these exercises in order to survive. Investors often skip these steps, but they shouldn't.

A quick way for an investor to improve her trading discipline is to set up a sell rule, a rule that tells her when to cut her losses and move on. For example, if a stock is down 20 percent from where it was purchased or where it traded at the beginning of the year, it might be time to sell, regardless of what you hope it will do.

Applying Momentum

Momentum investors look for securities that are going up in price, especially if accompanied by acceleration in underlying growth. In a sense, they are looking for the same thing day traders are — a security that is going to move big — but they have the expectation of making money over a longer period of time. The thought is that if a security is starting to go up in price, it will keep going up unless something dramatic happens to change it. In the meantime, plenty of money is to be made.

The knock on momentum investing is that instead of buying low and selling high, the goal is to buy high and sell even higher.

Like most investors, a momentum investor starts with careful fundamental analysis (described in Chapter 12), analyzing a security to determine what will make it go up. Then the momentum investor looks for certain technical and market indicators, similar to those described in Chapters 12 and 13 and used by day traders. In addition, some momentum investors rely on chart services, especially the Value Line and William O'Neil, to help them identify securities that are likely to have momentum. Canadians can also turn to TMX Money (`www.tmxmoney.com`), a site run by TMX Group, which has charting information and commodity news.

Earnings momentum

Earnings momentum is the province of the investor, not the trader. The investor is looking at the earnings that a company reports every quarter to see if they are going up at a faster rate, say from a steady rate of 10 percent a year to 12, 13, or more. This often happens because of a new technology or product that turns a decent company into a hot property in the stock and options markets. If the earning growth rate is accelerating, then the underlying price should go up at an accelerating rate, too.

Day traders don't look for earnings momentum, but they do look for price momentum. The two are usually related.

Price momentum

When a security goes up in price, especially at a fast clip with strong demand underneath it, it is said to have *price momentum*. Most day traders are looking for price momentum in order to make a swift profit. Many long-term investors should look for momentum in order to avoid being stuck with a position for months before it starts to move.

It pays to be patient, but it pays even better if your money is working for you while you wait.

Many momentum traders don't care why something is going up in price; they only know that it is going up and that they can profit if they're there for even part of the ride. Some of the different indicators that they look at are the following:

- **Relative strength:** There are different ways to calculate this, discussed in Chapter 12, but the basic idea is that if the security is going up faster than the market as a whole, it is showing momentum and might be a buy.
- **Moving average convergence/divergence (MacD):** This indicator looks at how the average price of the security is changing over time. Is it staying relatively level, meaning that the price is moving slowly back and forth, or is the indicator gradually going up, meaning that the price is gradually going up, too? If you plot the moving average against the actual price levels, a wide gap means that the security is moving up or down faster than the average, and if it's moving up, you'd probably want to buy it. (Otherwise, consider shorting the security; you can read about that in Chapter 14.)
- **Stochastics index:** This is the difference between the high and the low price for a security over a given time period. Some analysts look at days, some at weeks. The idea is that if the difference is getting bigger, that may be because the security is moving up or down in price at a faster than normal rate, creating an opportunity for a momentum buyer.

At an extreme, momentum investing leads to *bubbles,* like the infamous dot-com bubble in the late 1990s. People were buying the stocks because they were going up, not because they necessarily thought that the businesses were worth much. It was fun while it lasted, but a lot of people lost a lot of money when reality set in during March and April of 2000.

For investors only: Momentum research systems

Many day traders rely on different research systems to help them identify buy and sell opportunities in the course of a trading day. These systems usually don't work for an investor, simply because investors are less concerned about short-term movements. They wouldn't see the value in systems that scan the market and identify short-term price discrepancies, for example.

However, many investors use their own research services to help identify good buy and sell opportunities. Some of the more popular ones are Value Line, the William O'Neil charts, and TMX Money.

Value Line

`www.valueline.com`

Value Line is one of the oldest investment research services. The company's analysts combine price and trading volume information on stocks with financial data. The numbers are crunched through a proprietary model to generate two rankings: a stock's timeliness and its safety. The higher the stock is on the timeliness ranking, the better it is to buy or hold it now. Historically, Value Line's most timely stocks have outperformed the Dow Jones Industrial Average and the S&P 500, so people are willing to pay for access to the company's data. In addition, many libraries subscribe to Value Line's print service or online database, so you may be able to get access that way. (Hey, one of the advantages of being an investor is that you have the time to go to the library to look something up, a marvel to a day trader who's afraid to go and get a cup of coffee.)

William O'Neil

`www.williamoneil.com`

William O'Neil started a company to distribute his technical analysis system on stocks and the stock market, started a newspaper called *Investor's Business Daily,* and wrote a book called *How to Make Money in Stocks* (see the Appendix for more information about it). The company's data services are available only to large institutional investors, such as mutual fund and insurance companies, but between the book and the newspaper, individual investors can learn a lot about identifying momentum in order to pick good times to buy or sell a stock.

Many traders — in all securities, not just stocks — find *Investor's Business Daily* to be at least as useful as *The Wall Street Journal,* because it looks at the markets from a short-term trading perspective more than from a long-term, business management angle.

The company's ranking system is based on what it calls CAN SLIM, which is a mnemonic for a list of criteria that a good stock should meet. Note that it combines both fundamental and technical indicators:

- **Current quarterly earnings** should be up 25 percent from a year ago.
- **Annual earnings** should be up 25 percent from a year ago.
- **New products or services** should be driving earnings growth, not acquisitions or changes in accounting.
- **Supply and demand**, meaning that the number of shares being purchased each day is going up.

- **Leading company in leading industry** is the stock in the best position to do well.
- **Institutional sponsorship** means that the stock is becoming more popular with mutual funds, pension funds, and other large shareowners.
- **Market indexes**, such as the Dow, the NASDAQ, and the S&P 500, should all be up.

Of course, there aren't too many stocks out there that meet all the CAN SLIM criteria, but the indicators can give an investor a way of thinking about better times to buy (when more criteria are met) or sell (when fewer are being met).

The most serious momentum investors tend to be swing traders, who hold positions for a few weeks or months. Longer-term investors often rely on some momentum signals, though, to help them identify when it's a good time to buy a stock that has been languishing.

TMX Money

`www.tmxmoney.com`

TMX Money was launched by TMX Group, the company that runs the TSX and MX, in 2008. It's got a whole host of features, including detailed quotes and company information on U.S. stocks listed on the NYSE, NASDAQ, AEX, and OTCBB. The portfolio tracking tool includes interactive charting, technical indicators, and fundamental data, while its financial calculators can even help you figure out how much you need to save for retirement. (And don't forget to put some of your profits away for the long term!) The TMX Group enlisted the help of Dow Jones Client Solutions to create much of this site, including the quotes.

Breaking News and Breaking Markets

One reason why the markets are so volatile is that they are responding to news events. Prices reflect information. That's why prices change when any little bit of information comes into the market — even if it is just that someone wants to buy and someone wants to sell right now. The problem is that sometimes the market participants don't react in proportion to the news they receive. Good traders have an almost innate ability to discern news that creates a buy from news that creates a sell. (You can read more about that in Chapter 13.) Sometimes traders want to go with the market and sometimes they want to go against it.

When it's your investment idea that's been affected by a news announcement, you need to consider how your position — and you — will react. After all, no matter how long your time horizon and how careful your research, things happen to companies: CEOs have heart attacks, major products are found to be defective, financial statements turn out to be fraudulent. How are you going to respond?

The first point is that you have to respond. The market doesn't know your position, and the market doesn't care. (Have we mentioned that already?) You need to assess the situation and decide what to do. Given the information, is it time to buy, sell, or stay put? It's often okay to hold your long-term position in the face of long-term news, but that should be an active decision, not a fallback. The trick is to be objective, and that's not easy when real dollars are at stake.

Successful day traders are able to keep their emotions under control and keep the market separate from the rest of their lives. Good investors should be able to do the same. Chapter 8 has some ideas that might help.

When evaluating news, day traders look at how the news is different from expectations. Investors can also consider how the news is different relative to the known facts about the company to date.

For example, let's suppose that the Timely Timer Company is expected to report earnings of $0.10 per share. Instead, the news hits the tape saying that earnings will be only $0.05 because of accounting charges. The trader might see that the earnings are below expectations and sell all his shares to minimize his losses for the day, moving on to another position. The investor might know that the accounting charges were expected and go in and buy more shares while the price is depressed.

The fact that a way exists for a buyer and a seller to match their differing needs is the whole reason why we have financial markets!

To a day trader, perception is reality. To a keen-eyed investor, the difference between perception and reality might be an opportunity to make money.

Day traders have to think about the psychology of the market, because everything moves so quickly. Investors sometimes forget about psychology because they can wait for logic to prevail. When it comes time to place a buy or sell order, however, understanding the psychological climate that day can give the investor a price advantage, and every bit of profit improvement goes straight to the bottom line.

Day traders keep their sanity by closing out positions at the end of the day, so that they get on with their lives until the next market open. Investors, on the other hand, might want to know what's happening to their positions at other times. Many brokerage firms offer mobile phone alert services and now smartphone apps — which are terrible ideas for the day trader but not bad tools for an investor.

Setting Targets and Limits

Good day traders set limits. They often place stop and limit orders to automatically close out their positions when they reach a certain price level. They have profit targets in mind and know how much they are willing to risk in the pursuit of those gains.

Good investors should set similar limits. It can be harder for them, because they have often done so much research that they feel almost clairvoyant. Why worry about the downside when the research shows that the stock has to go up?

Well, the research might overlook certain realities. And even if the analysis was thorough, things change. That's why even the most ardent fundamentalist needs to have a downside risk limit. In most cases, stop and limit orders are bad ideas for a long-term investor because they'll force the sale of a security during a short-term market fluctuation and they'll force the sale when it's really a good time to buy more. Investors have a different risk profile than day traders, so they need to manage risk differently. They still need to manage risk, though.

With a *stop* order, the broker buys or sells the security as soon as a predetermined price is met, even if the price quickly moves back to where it was before the order took effect. A *limit* order is executed only if the security hits the predetermined level, and it stays in effect only if the price is at that level or lower (for a buy limit order) or at that level or higher (for a sell limit order).

Martha Stewart's defence in her insider trading case was that she sold her ImClone stock because she had a pre-arranged sell order in place with her broker, but it was not actually a stop order. The phone call with possible inside information had nothing to do with it, she said, and in fact the prosecutors could not disprove her. She was found guilty of obstruction of justice, not insider trading.

Day traders close out their positions at the end of each day, so they rarely review their limits. A swing trader or an investor, holding for a longer period of time, needs to review those limits frequently. How much should a position move each month, quarter, or year before it's time to cover losses or cash out with a profit? How has the security changed over time, and do the limits need to change with it?

When the position is working out, an investor will think of letting it ride forever. But, alas, few investments work that long into the future, so the investor also needs to think in terms of relative performance. Is it time to sell and put the money into something else with greater potential?

When managing money, day traders usually think about maximizing return while minimizing the risk of ruin. For an investor, the goal is maximizing return relative to a list of long-term objectives, including a target for risk. But because long-term objectives change, the portfolio will have to as well. A position that has been working out fine might have to be changed in order to meet the new portfolio goals. The discussion is starting to get beyond the scope of this book, but the point remains: Like successful day traders, successful investors have a plan for how they will allocate their money among different investments, and they adjust it as necessary.

Although investing is a long-term proposition and lacks the frenzy of trading, it is still an active endeavour. Instead of putting energy into buying and selling, the investor puts it into monitoring.

When an Investor Should Go Short Term

Many day traders are also long-term investors. Sure, they trade for the short term, but they regularly take some of their profits and put them toward investments that have a longer time frame. It's smart risk management for a business that has a high wash-out rate. After all, even a short-term trader has long-term goals.

But does it ever make sense for a long-term investor to take up short-term trading? It might, for three reasons: the idea proves itself to be short-term, the research shows short-term trading patterns that might be profitable, and fundamental analysis supports short selling.

Don't try riskier trading strategies unless your portfolio can handle the risk. As with full-time day trading, part-time and occasional trading strategies should be done only with risk capital, which is money that the trader can afford to lose. Money needed to pay the mortgage this month or pay for retirement in 30 years is not risk capital.

The idea proves to have a short shelf life

It happens to every long-term investor once or twice: He buys a security intending to hold it forever, and within a few days or weeks, some really bad news comes out. Or he buys only to see two days later that the company is being sold. That great long-term buy-and-hold idea no long fits the original parameters, so it's time to sell. Despite the goal of holding forever, it's time to get out and move on, even if it's only a day later.

Your research shows you some trading opportunities

Good investors monitor their holdings, and some become intimate with the nuances of a security's short-term price movements even though the objective is to hold the position for the long term. An investor who gets a feel for the trading patterns of a specific holding might want to turn that into swing trading and day trading opportunities. Yes, it adds risk to the portfolio (and the risks of day trading are covered extensively throughout this book), but it can also increase return.

For example, suppose that an investor who is fascinated with technology stocks notices that the stocks always rise in price right before big industry conferences and then fall when the conference is over. She might not want to change any of her portfolio holdings based on this, but she might also want a way to profit. So, she buys call options on big technology companies before the conference and then sells them on the meeting's first day. That short-term trade allows her to capture benefits of the price run-up without affecting her portfolio position.

You see some great short opportunities

Short selling allows a trader to profit from a decline in the price of a security. The trader borrows a security from the broker, sells it in the market, and then waits in hopes that the price goes down. When it does, the trader buys the security back at the lower price and repays the loan, keeping the difference between the purchase price and the sale price.

Because the broker charges interest on the loaned securities, short selling can get expensive. Traders who sell short are usually looking for a relatively short-term profit, not necessarily over a single day, but over months rather than years.

In addition to the interest, short selling faces another risk, which is that the security can go up in price while the trader is waiting for it to go down. In order to reduce that risk, most short sellers do careful research to make sure that they're right about the security being all wrong. And who else does careful research? Many long-term investors.

For the investor who loves to do research and who has some appetite for risk, short selling is a way to make money from those securities that would make terrible long-term holdings because it seems obvious that they aren't going to do well. When these investors come across securities that are headed for trouble, they can short them in the hope of making a nice short-term profit.

Judging Execution Quality

Day traders rely on outstanding trade execution from their brokers. They need to keep costs as low as possible in order to clear a profit from their trading, especially because their profits are relatively small.

Investors may have a greater likelihood of making a profit, given that they are waiting for a position to work out rather than closing it out every night. Even then, better execution will lead to better profits. The magnitude of the few extra cents might be smaller relative to the entire profit, but it still counts.

Your broker makes buy charging a commission to make the trade. Some charge a flat fee on 1,000 shares while others charge a few pennies per share. Prices change depending on the type of security you trade, and costs vary per broker, so make sure to shop around and decide which commission structure will have the least impact on your rate of return.

When choosing a broker, consider *total execution costs,* not just commission. Some brokers offering deep commission discounts make money from high levels of trading volume, but others make their money from execution.

The broker has a few tricks for improving execution. The first trick is to invest heavily in information systems that can route and match orders, as even one second can make a difference if the markets are moving. The second is to have a large enough customer base to be able to match customer orders quickly. Finally, and most importantly, the firm has to decide that execution is a strategic advantage it can use to keep customers happy. Many brokerage firms would rather concentrate on research, financial planning, customer service, or other offerings to keep customers happy instead of offering excellent execution.

In general, a firm that offers low commissions and emphasizes its services to active traders will have better execution than a firm that emphasizes its full-service research and advisory expertise. But there are exceptions, and in some cases the exceptions vary with account size.

Certainly, your results will vary based on what types of securities you are trading, what market conditions are like when you are trading, and how big of an account you have with the firm. But investigating the averages for a brokerage firm can help long-term investors decide whether it makes sense to change firms in order to improve profits.

So what can you do to improve your execution? Here are three suggestions:

- **Ask the brokerage firm for its policies.** The firm should be willing to provide this, as well as to give you some of its recent data, so that you can decide whether the total value of the firm's services matches the total cost.
- **Check *The Globe and Mail*'s annual online broker survey.** It looks at commission costs, trading speed, customer satisfaction, tools, and more.
- **Update your own hardware and Internet connection so that it's as fast as possible.** If you're a day trader, it's imperative to have good data (see Chapter 6 for more information). If you're not a day trader but actively manage your investment account, you too might want to consider an upgrade. A few seconds can make a difference.

Part IV
The Part of Tens

"Oh Martin, you scared me half to death! Next time let me know when you're picking a new stock."

In this part . . .

In this *. . .For Dummies*–only part, you get to enjoy some top-ten lists. We present ten reasons to day trade, ten reasons to *not* day trade, ten common mistakes that day traders make, and ten alternative careers for people who love the excitement of trading but who don't want to work for themselves as day traders. We also include an appendix full of references so that you can get more information to help you build your trading business.

Chapter 17

Ten Good Reasons to Day Trade

In This Chapter

- Getting ready to be your own boss
- Loving the investing business
- Figuring out what to expect from the markets
- Understanding the importance of financial and personal support systems

Day trading is a great career option for the right person in the right circumstances. It requires a strong, decisive personality who wants to be running the show every step of the way, from backing up the computers to collecting all the profits. And good day traders have some financial cushion and good personal support systems to get them through the tough times.

In this chapter, we list ten really good reasons to take up day trading. (For balance, we cover ten bad reasons in Chapter 18.) Think you have what it takes? Are you ready to go into business for yourself as a day trader? See how many of these characteristics fit your life right now.

You Love Being Independent

Day trading is like owning any small business. You're the boss and you call the shots. Each day's successes — and failures — are due to you and you alone. Most likely, you're working by yourself all day, so you're responsible for everything from the temperature in the office, to the functioning of the computers, to the accounting for trades.

Good day traders are independent. They don't want someone to tell them what to do; they want to figure it out for themselves. They love that challenge, whether it's finding a good bargain on office supplies or developing a profitable way to arbitrage currency prices.

If you would like to work for yourself and control your own destiny, keep reading. Day trading might be for you. And if not, go to Chapter 20 to see some alternative careers that involve the markets but do not put all of the onus on you for success.

You Want to Work Anywhere You Like

All you need to day trade is a computer, an account with an online brokerage firm, and high-speed Internet access. Nowadays you can find these tools almost anywhere: at home, at the library, in a bar; in a big city, in a small town, in the mountains, or in another country. Day trading offers a lot of geographic flexibility, which few other businesses do. You can trade while travelling as easily as you would trade at home. You have the luxury of setting up shop wherever you please, and if you decide to move, you can pack up your laptop and move your trading activities to your new destination.

You Are Comfortable with Technology

Long before everyone and her grandmother were online, securities traders were using complex electronic communications networks to buy and sell securities. The financial services industry was one of the first to embrace computer technology in a big way in the 1960s, and it is still a technology-intensive industry. For all the images of people in coloured cotton jackets running around the exchange floor, waving their hands and yelling at each other, most trading takes place over computer networks via machines.

Day traders use software to develop and refine their trading strategies. They trade online, using software to monitor and automate their trades. They track their trades in spreadsheets and other software. They spend their days in front of a screen, communicating online with other traders all over the world. They don't interact much with human beings during the trading day. It's all about the hardware boxes and the software interface between the trader and the market data.

Day traders are also self-employed, and many work from home. When their software crashes, they have to fix it. They have to handle the upgrades, install the firewalls, back up the data. Sure, it may be possible to pay someone to do it, but that cost is probably prohibitive — and the tech consultant probably won't be able to drop everything to get you up and trading again immediately.

Does this sound familiar? You're about to make *the* trade of the day. If you sell right now you could make a killing. In all that excitement you knock a pop can over, it spills directly on your laptop and out goes the power. Before you throw it across the room in a fit of rage, take a deep breath and go to your kitchen. No, you're not getting a bottle of vodka out of the freezer. Grab a bag, fill it with rice and put the laptop in with the Uncle Ben's. Whatever you do, do not turn on the computer. Leave it for a day (don't worry, another great trade will come up soon) and it should work. If it doesn't then you'll have to shell out for a new one, or, if you have a Mac, you can take it to an Apple Store and hope the nice lady at the Genius Bar will fix it for free. (Trust us, that can happen!)

Good day traders are comfortable with technology. If you like to mess around with programs, don't mind maintaining your computer, and understand how to set up your hardware for maximum efficiency, you're in good shape for day trading. (Chapter 6 has some more on this, too.)

Day trading is like any other entrepreneurial business. You, the entrepreneur, are responsible for everything! Some days, it's wonderful, but some days, it's a real drag.

You Want to Eat What You Kill

You don't have to be a self-employed day trader to trade securities. Brokerage firms, hedge funds, and exchange traders employ people to trade for them, and in fact most securities trading takes place through such larger organizations. But maybe you don't want to share your profits with someone else. Maybe you don't want someone dictating your strategy, placing limits on your trades, or determining your bonus based as much on factors such as teamwork and firm profitability as on what you brought in. You want to eat what you kill, as they say, and day trading is one way you can do that.

When you day trade, you're responsible for your profits and your losses. That means you reap the rewards and you don't have to share them with anyone else — a powerful incentive for independent people!

You Love the Markets

Good day traders have always been fascinated with the markets and how they move. If you watch BNN for fun and have been following the securities business for years, no matter what your day jobs have been, then you might be a good candidate for day trading. Of course, we hope you've picked up more than "some people make a lot of money doing this!" A lengthy immersion in the cycles and systems that drive securities prices will give you a good foundation for developing your own trading strategies and knowing what you are up against.

And the markets are amazing, aren't they? All these buyers and sellers, with all their different needs, come together and find the price that gets the deal done. The prices assimilate all kinds of information about the state of the world, the desires of the people trading, and the future expectations for the economy. It's capitalism in its purest form, and it's almost magical to watch how it works. If you love how the markets work and want to learn first-hand what they tell you about making money, then by all means keep reading.

The market isn't your opponent, because the market doesn't know that you are out there. The market is simply a playing field for your trading strategies and execution style.

You Have Investing Experience

If you have never opened an account with a brokerage firm, purchased a stock, or invested in a mutual fund, you might not be suited for day trading. It's not that those activities are adequate preparation for day trading — they aren't — but they can help you understand what all can happen that can cause you to make or lose money. If you've made some trades in the past, you know some of the language and some of the limitations of the markets. And that will give you a base to work from.

If you have not made any trades before, don't quit your day job to day trade. Instead, head to Chapter 16 for some ideas on how you can use short-term trading in an investment portfolio. That way, you can learn more and build up your savings before taking the plunge.

You Have Studied Trading Systems and Know What Works for You

Much of the work of day trading takes place long before entering the buy or sell order. You have to define your trading system, see how it would have worked in the past, and tested it to see how it works now. It's not as exciting as actually doing the day trading, because you won't be making real money — but you won't be losing money, either.

Short-term trading has a huge potential for loss, and many traders are chasing the exact same ideas. The more you know about how your strategy works in different market conditions, the better prepared you will be to act appropriately and profitably.

Backtesting a strategy, which means checking it against historical securities prices to see what would have happened if you had used the strategy in the past, can give you a sense of how realistic and effective your strategy is. Maybe you find that it's profitable, but the conditions to make it work don't happen enough for you to make good money. Maybe you find that it's too complex to remember. Maybe you find that it worked when most of the security's trading took place in open-outcry pits on the exchange floor, but now that more of the trading is electronic, it no longer works well. Such information is power, because it can help you be a better trader.

It can take a long time to find a strategy that works enough of the time to make it worth your while. Many day traders spend months developing, testing, and refining their day trading strategy. You can read more about the process of strategy testing in Chapter 11.

If you've taken the time to create and test a good strategy, then you're ready to go.

Because backtesting uses historical prices, you can do much of the work on the side, at night and on weekends, before you start day trading full time. It's a good way to get prepared for your trading business while you save your money and make other preparations for your new day trading venture.

You Are Decisive and Persistent

Can you make a decision and act on it? Can you assimilate information quickly into a good strategy? If you screw up, do you figure out what you did wrong so that it doesn't happen again and then move on? If so, you have the basic personality of a good day trader. Traders see a lot of information come at them quickly, and they have to be able to discern what the market is saying so that they can find their entry points and then exit at a good time.

Short-term traders don't have the luxury of thinking too much about what they are doing. Trading has to become intuitive. They have to be able to act on what they see when they see it — no room for second guessing, hesitation, choking, or panic attacks.

Good day traders are also persistent. After they find a strategy that they trust, they stick with it no matter how things are going. That's how they're able to buy low and sell high.

Even great traders go through bad periods, but if they trust their system and continue to stick with it, they usually pull out of it, often with money ahead. If you've been able to stick things out other times in your life when things went wrong, you know what to expect when day trading.

You Can Afford to Lose Money

Obviously, you want to be a day trader to make money. That's the whole idea. But day trading is difficult. Most traders quit in the first year. Some can't take the stress, some lose all their money, and some simply don't make enough money to make it worth their time.

Like any small business, you're taking a risk when you set up shop as a day trader. That risk is easier if you can afford to lose money. We're not saying you need to have so much money that you won't miss it when it's gone, but you shouldn't be day trading with money you need to live on, any more than you would open a store or start a law practice with money you need to buy groceries and pay the mortgage.

If your household does not have a second source of income, be sure to set aside enough money to cover your living expenses while you get started. And keep a second pot of money, your *walk-away* fund (see Chapter 8), so that you're free to quit day trading and move on to your next adventure if you decide it's not for you.

It's especially important to have a financial cushion when you are day trading so that you can ride your winners, stay in the market when things get bad, and better handle the stress.

You can afford to commit to your trading

Having your living expenses covered, at least at first, isn't just about dealing with losses. It's also about being able to stick with your trading. If you have a constant need for cash to pay your bills, you may be tempted to take money out of the market whenever you're doing well. This may keep you from reinvesting your profits. You won't be sticking to your strategy, and your trading capital will not grow as fast. Think of this as building a long-term asset, not as generating a steady stream of current income.

You can stay in the market through the rough times

You know the old saw that the best way to make money is to buy low and sell high, right? Well, this means that the best time to buy is usually when securities prices have been beaten up and you've lost a lot of money (hello global financial crisis!). If you can afford to lose some money, it will be easier for you to stay in the game and stick to your strategy so that you can profit big when the market finally turns.

You can handle the stress of losses

Not all your trades are going to work out. You are going to lose money. That's a given. If you have enough money that you do not fear loss, you'll be able to make better decisions. You're less likely to panic if you know that you'll still be able to eat, that your lights are still going to turn on when you flip the switch, and that you'll have a roof to sleep under at night. You'll be better able to view the markets clearly and follow a winning strategy. Trading is very much a game of psychology. Give yourself an edge by waiting until you can afford to do it.

You Have a Support System

Trading is stressful. The markets gyrate with news events that no one can foresee. Things just happen, and no one else who's trading that day cares how these events affect you. It's enough to make you crazy some days — and unfortunately, some traders do get crazy. Alcoholism, depression, divorce, and suicide seem to be occupational hazards, often because day traders have trouble separating what's happening to them in the market with who they are as people.

The securities markets are wonderful mechanisms for bringing together diverse buyers and sellers. They are not wonderful for propping up your ego, helping you through a rough time in your life, or slipping you a little extra money when you most need it. The markets are not human. They are ruthless machines designed to generate the best price for the aggregate of the buyers and sellers participating that day, and some days, you're going to suffer.

Good day traders are psychologically strong. They understand how their weaknesses come out when they are stressed. They have people and activities in their lives who help give their brains a break from trading, ranging from regular exercise routines to good friends to hobbies.

If you are going to be a day trader, you need to have some support in your life for when things go wrong. Because some days, they will go wrong, and real money will be lost, and it will feel terrible.

Chapter 8 talks about managing the stress of day trading, and in many ways, it's the most important chapter in this book.

Chapter 18

Ten Good Reasons to Avoid Day Trading

In This Chapter

- Considering other ways to invest that suit you better
- Finding out day trading is your own small business
- Deciding whether your personality is right for day trading
- Putting a damper on unrealistic expectations

Day trading isn't right for everyone. In fact, it's a bad idea for most people. It requires a strong personality, someone who can face the gyrations of the markets day in and day out. And it also requires someone with enough attention to detail to run a business. It's a great career option for the right person in the right circumstances. But for people who have trouble keeping cool, who don't have the patience to learn how to trade, and for anyone who has a gambling problem, day trading can be a quick road to ruin.

In this chapter, we list eleven signs that maybe day trading isn't right for you right now. Take them seriously. Most day traders lose money, in part because a lot of people who aren't cut out for day trading try it anyway. Don't fret if it turns out that you aren't day trader material. Most people aren't. That's why Chapter 16 and Chapter 20 offer alternatives that might be better for your money and your career.

You Want to Learn Investing by Day Trading

Many people want to manage their own investments, and it's certainly possible. It requires taking the time to learn about the basics of finance, such as the relationship between risk and return, proper diversification, and figuring out your time horizon. In fact, we know of a great book called *Investing For Canadians For Dummies* by Eric Tyson and Tony Martin (Wiley) that can help.

Some people confuse investing with day trading, though, and they are not the same. We list tons of information on the differences in Chapter 4, but here's the condensed version: Day trading involves rapid buying and selling of securities to take advantage of small movements in prices. This can be a successful strategy for part of your investment account, but it is not a good idea to day trade with all your money.

It is entirely possible to buy and sell securities on your own without being a day trader. And if you don't know another good term for "self-employed person managing her own money," just tell people you run your own hedge fund. You'll get better tables at restaurants that way.

You Love Fundamental Research

Fundamental research, discussed in Chapter 12, is the process of analyzing a company to see how good its business is and what the company's securities are worth. Fundamental analysts crunch numbers, build forecasts, check out products, and look for stocks that are going to do well over the long term. They dream of uncovering the next Research In Motion or the next Walmart and holding the stock all the way up.

Fundamental research is antithetical to day trading. Day traders look for profit opportunities in short-term price movements. They often do not know what industry a company is in, nor do they care. If you love the fundamentals, you're probably too analytical to be a good day trader.

You're Short on Time and Capital

Getting started in day trading is a lot like buying a small business. It takes commitment of both time and money. If you don't have enough time, it is difficult to learn technical patterns. If you don't have the money, you won't be able to work through rough cycles.

And there will be rough cycles. That's day trading's only sure thing.

Some day traders are able to trade part time. If you are disciplined, you can be successful at it. The key is to close out your positions at the end of your designated trading period as though the market day were ending. If your plan is to trade for two hours a day, then trade for two hours a day and no more. Use an alarm clock as your personal trading bell.

You Like Working as Part of a Group

A decade ago, most large cities had day trading offices, called *trading arcades,* where traders could go each day to buy and sell securities. The big advantage these firms offered was high-speed Internet access. Now almost everyone can get high-speed Internet access at home, so little need exists for day traders to go elsewhere, and most of these offices are closed.

Working at home is great for some people. If you prefer camaraderie during the day, like the support of a team, and want friendly faces around you, you're likely to be miserable day trading. It's just you and the market, and the market doesn't have a great sense of humour.

You Can't Be Bothered with the Details of Running a Business

Day traders are small-businesspeople, and their entrepreneurial flair goes beyond making their own buy and sell decisions. They also buy equipment, shop for supplies, and maintain careful income tax records. To some, this is exhilarating: no more mean office manager who decides how many and what kind of pens must be used. No more going through hoops and bringing in letters from a doctor to get a fancy ergonomic chair. You're the boss, and if you want it, you can have it.

But to others, all this responsibility is overwhelming. Picking out pens? Creating backup procedures? Worrying about accounting software? It's too much. If the mere thought of standing at the office supply store gives you the heebie-jeebies, you might want to consider trading as an employee rather than trading for your own account.

You Crave Excitement

Trading *seems* so exciting. You've seen the stereotypical picture of the people on the floor at American stock exchanges, wearing bright-coloured jackets and loud ties, screaming and waving their arms. It gets Ann's blood running to just think about it. Of course, they may be shouting out coffee orders and waving their arms in a debate over the Cubs versus the Sox. With so many people together, they can make their own excitement on days when the market isn't doing anything interesting.

For that matter, the number of people trading on exchange floors is small and getting smaller. The Toronto Stock Exchange closed its trading floor and went virtual in 1997. The Chicago Board of Trade merged with the Chicago Mercantile Exchange, partly because of changes in how people trade. Nowadays, most traders sit in offices in front of computer screens. They have to stay focused on the little blips in front of them, and it can be deathly dull. Some days few, if any, opportunities come up to trade using your system.

If you crave excitement and have trouble staying focused, you might find that day trading is too boring for you. It can involve intense stress with few opportunities to work it off during the day.

You're Impulsive

With the frenzy of trades and the rapid-fire decisions involved, day trading might seem like a perfect career for an impulsive person. It's all about instinct, about acting on your hunches, about pulling the trigger and seeing what happens. Right? Uh, no. To be a good day trader, you have to trust your trading system more than your hunches. Sometimes you'll make trades when it doesn't seem right and you'll sit out periods even though you are itching to get in. Good day traders are quick thinkers, but they do think. If you like to act now and deal with the consequences later, day trading isn't a good idea for you.

You Love Going to the Casino

Do you get a big rush out of gambling? Do you love trying to beat the odds? Does day trading seem like a visit to Vegas without the airfare? Then you know what? You shouldn't be day trading. Unlike at a casino, no one is even going to give you free drinks in exchange for your massive losses.

A lot of traders like to gamble. Every trader has some crazy story about playing liar's poker with the serial numbers on dollar bills instead of with cards, or about a friend of a friend who bet on whether the person walking in front of him would turn right or left. And that's fine if they keep their gambling in perspective and bet no more than they can afford to lose.

Trading isn't necessarily gambling, but it can be, especially if you get carried away with the market and don't stick to your trading and money management systems. But remember this: in gambling, the odds always favour the house. When you cross the line, you hand your profit potential over to someone else.

The line between day trading and gambling is thin. Check the questions at `www.gamblersanonymous.org/20questions.html` to see whether you might have a gambling problem. Substitute *day trading* for *gambling* and see what you come up with. And by all means, get help if you have a problem. Don't take up day trading.

You Have Trouble Setting Boundaries

Successful day traders are disciplined. They have set trading hours, which they stick to, and set systems for planning trades and managing their money. They took the time to carefully test their trading strategy (see Chapter 11 for more on how you can do that). They understand that if they don't have a system and manage their risk, they are more likely to become one of those numerous day traders who lose everything early on.

The whole idea behind day trading is that you limit risk by closing out your positions at the end of the day. The financial markets are global, though, so in theory the trading day never ends. If you have a hard time turning off the lights at the end of the day, you might not be the best day trader. If you resent rules, you might rebel against the rules that you've set for yourself.

Good day traders know that they are cut out for day trading before they even begin. They've taken the time to assess how their personality and psychological makeup mix with the demands of the job. And one key trait is discipline.

You Want to Get Rich Quick

Day traders look for short-term profit opportunities, so it follows that day trading leads to big, fast profits, right? Wrong. Day traders make money by collecting a large number of small profits. Those who make money usually do it through patience and persistence. Yeah, there may be one or two out there who managed to make a killing in a week, but they are the exception.

Research shows that 80 percent of day traders lose their capital and are gone from the business within one year. Instead of getting rich, you are more likely to go broke quick from day trading. If you don't like those odds, try something else with your money.

You Trust the Guy on the Infomercial Who Said It Would Work

A lot of money can be made in day trading, but sometimes it seems like more money is made selling day trading training systems. Some of these are heavily marketed, even through television infomercials. The sales pitch makes day trading seem like an easy, safe, fun way to make money using your own smarts. It leaves out pesky details about researching and testing systems, high levels of risk, and the pressure trading can place on a person.

Day trading is great for some people. But like anything, if it sounds too good to be true, it probably is. Don't let a strong-arm sales pitch cost you your hard-earned money.

Chapter 19

Ten Common Day Trading Mistakes

In This Chapter

- Planning your business and your strategy
- Evaluating and controlling risks
- Trading not too much, not too little, but just right
- Developing confidence in your trading system
- Keeping your emotions in check

Day trading is tough. Many popular markets are *zero-sum games,* meaning that for every winner, there's a loser. Other markets, such as the stock market, have a *positive bias,* meaning they have a tendency to increase in value over time, but you may rarely see big moves in any one day. And the whole point of day trading is to close your positions each night. Most day traders lose money, in part because they make obvious, avoidable mistakes.

This list of ten mistakes will help you avoid the most serious ones so that you can be more successful from the get-go. Following them is no guarantee that you will make money trading, but it will certainly reduce your risk and improve your odds. And that's half the battle.

Starting with Unrealistic Expectations

Most day traders lose money. Some research shows that 80 percent of day traders wash out in the first year. Brokerage firms that deal with day traders are constantly figuring out ways to attract new customers, because it is so hard to retain the ones they have for the long term.

Yes, some traders make money. A few make a lot of money. But they are the exception. It is tough to make money day trading, and even tougher to make enough money to cover the value of your time. If you go into trading knowing that it's hard, that you should risk only money that you can afford to lose, and that you need to think about it as a business, you'll have a leg up on those who think they've found an easy way to make millions from the comfort of their own home — and who are then stunned to discover they are broke.

Starting without a Business Plan

Trading is a business. When you decide to day trade, you are committing capital to an entrepreneurial business with a high risk of failure. You are no different from your brother-in-law who decides to open a sandwich shop franchise; your neighbour who joined a startup company for little salary and lots of equity; or your university buddy who has been trying to make a go of it as a full-commissioned life insurance salesman. You are all out on your own, risking your capital in the hope of great success but knowing that many others doing the same thing fail.

Successful businesses have business plans, and your trading business is no different. You need to specify what you are going to trade, and when, and how, and with how much money, before you get started. You need to determine what equipment you need, what services and training you want, and how you will measure your success. Chapter 2 can help you with a business plan, and the rest of the book can help you fill in the appropriate sections of it. Having the plan will keep your expectations in line and create a professional starting point for your new trading venture.

Failing to plan is planning to fail, as the cliché goes. You are risking too much of your hard-earned money to skip careful upfront planning. Take responsibility for your trading.

Starting without a Trading Plan

A business plan sets the framework for your trading business, but you need to fill in the details. How are you going to trade? What signals will you watch for? Why will you enter a position, and why will you close it? That's your trading plan. Good traders have trading plans, so that they know exactly what they will do as they see opportunities in the market. This reduces the fear and doubt that can unsettle most traders and it heads off the panic that destroys more than a few. Read Part III for ideas on how to trade.

Good trading plans have to be tested and evaluated. Chapter 11 has good information on testing and evaluation so that you have enough confidence in your system to follow it, even when the market gets squirrelly on you.

Failing to Manage Risk

Day trading is risky business, and most day traders quit because of losses. (Have we mentioned that already?) Even traders who stick with it have many losing trades. That's why they have risk management systems in place. Their trading plans include *stops,* which automatically execute buy or sell orders when securities reach predetermined levels. (Stops are discussed in Chapter 2.) They also have a money management system (discussed in Chapter 9) so that they risk their capital appropriately.

The day trader looking for trouble places orders without thinking about how much of a security to buy or sell at any one time, and she thinks that she'll just know when to sell. And then she second-guesses herself and finds herself with bigger losses than she intended.

If you're going to day trade, be safe. You know what the risks are (that's why you picked up this book), so use the protection offered by stops and sound money management.

Most day traders lose money. Don't risk money you can't afford to lose, and plan for the risks that you take.

Not Committing the Time and Money to Do It Right

Day trading is a job. It's a small business endeavour that requires research and training well in advance of the first trade. It's not something you can squeeze into an hour a day as a hobby. To do well, you need to set regular hours and have enough money to generate reasonable returns without unreasonable risks.

Many people think day trading is something that's easy to get into, and that they can generate profits while their kids are napping. That's a mistake. If you can't dedicate the time to studying the markets and understanding how you react to them, you will have trouble staying in the trading business.

Successful traders start out with enough money to last through periods of drawdown and are still able to generate meaningful dollar returns. Day trading is a business of frequent trades with small percentage gains and a high potential for loss. If you have days of losses, a small account will quickly end up with too little money to meet minimum order sizes. On the upside, a 1 percent return on $1,000 is equal to $10, and a 1 percent return on $100,000 is $1,000. If you have more money to begin with, the dollars you make from day trading will seem more real to you.

Canada doesn't have rules on how much money you need to day trade, but brokers often require a trader have a minimum amount of dough in their account to get started. It depends on what you plan to trade, but it can range between $1,000 for stocks and $25,000 for options. Some Canadian brokers follow the U.S. Securities and Exchange Commission rules that define "pattern day traders" based on their trading activity and as customers with $25,000 in their accounts. In any case, if you have $25,000 you can afford to lose you're more likely to be a successful day trader than if you have only $2,500.

You are going to lose money. All day traders have bad days, and they are more likely to lose money early in their trading career before they get a feel for the markets and their own reactions to them. If you have enough money when you begin, you can consider these losses to be part of your apprenticeship.

Chasing the Herd

Everyone in the market is looking at the same data and the same technical indicators (like those we discuss in Chapter 12). Good day traders follow market trends, but with the goal of being early or on time. Those who get in late get crushed — they buy too high, they sell too low. It's an easy temptation, because it's so hard to watch the market moving away from you.

Day trading requires quick reactions. It's video games and psychology, some people joke, because the trader who can figure out what others in the market are doing and then click on the mouse button fastest has a huge advantage. The trader who hesitates or goes along for the ride is likely to be ruined.

No easy solution for this exists. It helps if you know that you are psychologically cut out for day trading (covered in Chapter 8) and have confidence in the long-term performance of your trading system (covered in Chapter 11). But to a big extent, you just have to have some experience in the markets to know how your trading system matches what's in your head.

Switching among Research Systems

Day traders lose money, at least part of the time. That can cause a day trader to lose trust in his trading system. And many day traders do what seems logical, which is move to a trading system that seems to be working. The problem is that no system works all the time — if one did, everyone would use it. And sometimes things look worst before they turn. A school of thought suggests that by switching systems whenever things look bad, the trader never learns the nuances of how a given system works for him. And he's likely to get stuck on another down trend, picking up the new system right when the old one starts to work again. But each system has its pros and cons. If you can master more than one — and it is possible — you can get the best that every broker has to offer. Also, nothing is more upsetting than being minutes from making a trade and having a system go down. It's rare, but it can happen. Ensuring another system up and running as backup is a good idea. Of course, you don't want an exorbitant number of charts, graphs and trading platforms getting in your way, but using a couple can make sense.

Markets go in cycles. No system will work for you all the time, but if you panic and start trying new things without doing a lot of upfront work you're likely to make things worse. Chapter 11 covers performance evaluation and system testing in great detail. The more you understand your system and how it works, the less likely you are to be brought down by floundering around for new systems all the time.

Anyone who has a magic trading system that works in all markets is retired and living on a beach in Maui. Everyone else has to live through a few rough stretches.

Overtrading

Because day traders don't hold positions for long periods of time, they rarely enjoy big and profitable price moves. Instead, they make money from lots of transactions with small profits. They are crazy people, moving in and out for short periods. But believe it or not, the day trader who trades too much will lose out. She won't be in the market for large intra-day moves, and she'll get killed on commissions and other transaction costs.

As paradoxical as it seems, many day traders do better by making fewer trades each day. That way, commissions and fees take a smaller bite of the profit. One way to profit from fewer trades is with better money management, discussed in Chapter 9. A trader who puts money to work appropriately can often make more money than one who trades frenetically.

Sticking Too Long with Losing Trades

This a corollary to the overtrading mistake. Day traders are often overcome with fear, doubt, greed, and hope. They are afraid to recognize a loss. They wonder if they are good traders. They don't want to pay the commission to get out of the loser. And if the security was a good buy at the higher price, it's surely a better buy now that it's gone down in price. These traders think that if they just keep a positive mental attitude, everything will work out all right in the end.

Good traders have systems in place to limit their losses. They use stop orders (Chapter 2) to force themselves out of bad trades. They would rather put the money to work on a good trade than stick out a bad one.

The market doesn't know your position. Therefore, no amount of wishing and hoping will cause it to reward you for your patience. If a trade isn't working, get out. Tomorrow is another day.

Getting Too Emotionally Involved

Trading is a stressful business. You're up against an impersonal market that moves seemingly at random (and many academics would say that it moves truly at random.) It involves money, which to some people is a way to keep score in life and to others is their primary source of security. Losing trades mean a loss of status and a loss of safety. It's easy to think that the entire market is conspiring against you — yes, you, specifically. It's no wonder so many traders are head cases.

The best traders are almost Zen-like in their lack of attachment to the market. They are able to remove themselves from the frenzy of the trading day so that they are not susceptible to fear, doubt, greed, and hope. Chapter 8 has some advice that can help you approach the trading day in a calmer manner. Only you know whether you are capable of that.

Chapter 20

Almost Ten Alternatives to Day Trading

In This Chapter

- Considering career options for traders
- Finding other ways to manage your money
- Getting the excitement without the risk of ruin

Maybe you like the idea of trading, but after reading this book you've decided that working for yourself making large numbers of short-term trades isn't exactly what you want to do. But then what options are there? In this chapter, I put forward several ideas for alternative activities that might match your interests better than day trading. These include other career options, different ways to invest your money, and entertainment that gives you the excitement of trading without the same amount of risk.

Proprietary Trading for an Investment Company or Hedge Fund

Day trading is a solitary pursuit, and not everyone who wants to trade also wants to run his own business and work by himself all day. Good thing many companies need people to trade for them. Investment companies, brokerage firms, and hedge funds hire traders. These people are often known as *prop traders,* short for *proprietary,* and their job is to trade money for the firm's account. These traders may have to follow a set style, or they may be free to trade as they see fit. Prop traders don't keep all their profits, but they get a small salary, benefits, and a bonus that represents a generous cut of the money they make.

Proprietary trading lets you combine the safety net and camaraderie of a job with the excitement and potential huge returns of trading. It's a good option for those who want to spend their days with other people.

Many firms have training programs that pay entry-level employees low salaries, no matter how much money they may have made at other jobs. These junior staffers often do a lot of clerical work and run errands for the senior traders. If they show an aptitude for the business, they'll be promoted quickly. The market is a meritocracy.

Trading for an Agricultural, Energy, or Commodities Company

The options and futures markets (discussed in Chapter 3) were developed to help commodity companies manage their income and expenses better. That's why the traditional products on those exchanges almost seem funny in the era of modern finance: pork bellies, soybeans, and orange juice.

But you know what? Those traditional customers for those traditional products are still active, and they need people to help them. Energy companies, growers, food processors, and metals companies need someone to trade barrels of oil, bushels of corn, live cattle, and silver futures. They are often more interested in *hedging* — using trading to reduce risk rather than increase return — than in trading to maximize return, but depending on market conditions and firm philosophies, they may be open to traders who want to take on risk.

Joining a Market Making Firm

In the olden days, day trading was impossible because individuals could not afford to get a data feed, let alone execute orders. People who wanted to trade for themselves had to move to a city with an exchange, submit their membership application, pay their fees, and go to work on the floor.

Times have changed, though, at least in Canada where the exchanges are virtual. You won't be able to join the TSX and buy and sell on the floor, but you can be part of a market maker firm that trades stocks in order to keep the markets liquid. Market makers maintain activity in the markets, service odd lots, help keep the markets two sided, and also do a whole lot more.

Becoming a trader at a firm requires experience and hard work. First you have to get hired by one of the 20 TSX market maker companies, then work junior jobs and prove to your boss that you have the chops to trade. It's a good idea to have an MBA or another financial degree, experience in the industry, and — most importantly — a strong knack for numbers and markets.

Traditional Investing for Your Own Account

Some people who buy this book probably don't want to day trade. Instead, they want to manage their own investment accounts during the day rather than having a regular job. You can manage your money yourself without making a high volume of short-term trades, and given the huge numbers of day traders who wash out (80 percent, according to some studies) you might be better off. True, you won't have the drama of day trading, and you won't need to focus your attention for hours on end. Instead, you'll be researching stocks and mutual funds, allocating your portfolio among several different assets, and tracking your tax liabilities. If you aren't sure where to start, consider picking up a copy of *Investing For Canadians For Dummies* by Eric Tyson and Tony Martin (Wiley).

In addition, Chapter 16 has some ideas for ways that you can use day trading techniques for long-term accounts.

Taking a Swing at Swing Trading

Swing trading is a cross between day trading and longer-term investing. Instead of closing out their positions at the end of each day, swing traders may hold their positions for a few days or even weeks. It's a way to change the risk and return profile. Price changes can happen overnight when you're away from your computer monitors, but the luxury of time means more opportunities for your position to work out.

Swing trading favours traders who have a little bit of patience, who can handle the risk of holding open positions overnight, and who have some interest in industry news and fundamental information. We discuss it a little bit in Chapter 2.

Gambling for the Fun of It

Sloppy day traders are often gamblers: they aren't following a strategy; they just like the rush and the expectation of the positive return. This means that they aren't always paying attention to the market, nor are they ready to commit to the discipline of spending days in front of a screen and evenings reviewing market activities. If you are more of a gambler than a trader, why not just admit it?

Assuming you're not a problem gambler (see `www.gamblersanonymous.org/20questions.html`), keep your day job, contribute to your retirement plan, and set aside a portion of your spending money to take to the casino. And don't gamble more money than you bring.

When you gamble, the odds always favour the house, so you'll probably lose money. When you day trade, the odds on each particular trade are even or slightly in your favour, at least before considering commissions, but not so much that you're guaranteed an easy return. So if it's the rush and not the return you want, admit it and book a flight to Las Vegas.

In a casino, you get some of your losses returned to you in the form of drinks, show tickets, and other comps. Of course, it's cheaper to hold on to your money and pay cash for your drinks. That's a good strategy. We hate to lose, so we don't gamble in the first place.

Play Day Trading Video Games

Want the excitement of day trading without the risk of losing your money, either to the markets or to the casino owner? Think you can figure out the markets, but don't want to put real money or your job on the line to find out? Then why not play a day trading video game?

Well, okay, it's not exactly a game; it's a simulator designed to teach you to day trade. The RapidSP Day Trading Simulator, available at `www.tradingsimulatorsoftware.com`, gives you all the excitement of day trading without risk to your capital and without the sales pitch. It's a low-cost, low-risk way to enjoy the day trading experience.

A simulation doesn't involve real money. Many traders find that when their own money is on the line, they don't trade as well as when they trade for fake money or for someone else. That's part of the psychology of facing the markets; you can get some tips for managing that in Chapter 8.

Trade in Demo Accounts

Simulators are a good way to learn day trading, but they cost money. If you're looking for a free way to try day trading in general, or if you're a day trader thinking of adding new securities to your repertoire, you can trade in demo accounts. Many brokerage firms (see Chapter 6 for a list of some that deal with day traders) allow prospective customers to start with a demonstration account, both to check out the broker's capabilities and to see whether day trading is right for you. Some brokers even run contests where prospective traders trade paper accounts (that is, not real money) and the winners receive money for a real trading account.

These demo accounts will let you try out everything the broker offers, but they do come with trial periods. Your free account may be locked out after 30 days; you'll have to open a real one if you want to continue trading at that particular broker. If you've got the day trading bug, but aren't yet ready to trade real dollars, open a demo account at another brokerage firm. It's a good idea to test more than one out anyway, just to see what each company has to offer. In any case, you owe it to yourself to do some simulation to work through your trading system. And if you just like the idea of playing around with trading, paper trading in a demonstration account can help you have fun without risking your hard-earned money.

Brokerage firms offer demo accounts to entice you to buy, and you can expect that someone will call or e-mail you to see how things went. You can cut down on clutter in your e-mail inbox by opening a free Web mail account just for your demo trading. Google Mail (www.gmail.com), Hotmail (www.hotmail.com), and Yahoo! (www.yahoo.com) are companies that offer free e-mail accounts.

Sign Up for a Trading Contest

Each year, some prominent financial media companies offer trading contests. People can sign up for them, manage a paper portfolio (investing or day trading, as they please), and the participant with the greatest return wins a cash prize.

Two popular ones are

- Financial Post Stock Market Challenge: http://stockstar.financialpost.com
- CNBC's Million Dollar Portfolio Challenge: www.cnbc.com

These offer all the fun of trading with none of the risk — although past cheating scandals have scuttled many of the more popular contests. Consider also that they offer all the fun of trading with none of the oversight of the provincial securities commissions or the SEC.

Appendix

Resources for Day Traders

As much as we hate to admit it, *Day Trading For Canadians For Dummies* doesn't tell you all you need to know to get started in day trading. This appendix lists books, Web sites, periodicals, and other resources offering trading strategies and techniques and ideas on managing risk, taxes, and stress.

Great Books for Great Trading

Have a shelf that looks a little bare? Fill it up with a few of these beauties.

Basic trading guides

The following books offer nuts-and-bolts information on day trading.

Barron's Dictionary of Finance and Investment Terms, by John Downes and Jordan Elliott Goodman (Barron's Educational Series)

This is not the same *Barron's* as the weekly newspaper, but it's about as indispensable to investors. This dictionary is a handy guide to the technical terms and jargon you'll come across when trading. It's especially good when you are almost, but not quite, sure of what a word means.

Day Trading the Currency Market: Technical and Fundamental Strategies to Profit from Market Swings, by Kathy Lien (Wiley)

The foreign exchange (forex) market is becoming popular with day traders, but it's a little different from the stock and futures markets. It relies heavily on leverage, and market participants have more motivations than simply hedging or speculating. If you're interested in trading currencies, this book can help you get started.

The Electronic Day Trader: Successful Strategies for On-line Trading, by Marc Friedfertig and George West (McGraw-Hill)

This book is mostly about day trading in the stock market. It covers technical analysis, trading strategies, and some of the market psychology that affects buy and sell decisions.

Mastering the Trade, by John F. Carter (McGraw-Hill)

The author, an experienced trader, walks day traders and swing traders through the ins and outs of the markets, including specific advice on different trading opportunities. He includes charts and data that explain when to place a trade and when to close it out. It's practical, useful, and detailed.

The New Money Management: A Framework for Asset Allocation, by Ralph Vince (Wiley)

Money management can keep traders in the game longer while maximizing potential returns. It's a key discipline that can mean the difference between long-run success and failure. Unfortunately, many day traders completely overlook money management. (We cover this topic in Chapter 2.)

Trading Rules That Work: The 28 Lessons Every Trader Must Master, by Jason Jankovsky (Wiley)

If it were possible to get rich by knowing a handful of specific trading indicators, every trader would retire and run huge charitable foundations. But it's not that easy. Instead, a disciplined, professional approach to the market makes a difference over the long run. This book is a useful overview of different trading rules, why they work, and how traders should apply them.

Trading For Canadians For Dummies, by Michael Griffis, Lita Epstein, and Christopher Cottier (Wiley)

A number of ...*For Dummies* guides can help you find out a few more things about various aspects of day trading, including this one. Although *Trading For Canadians For Dummies* covers stock trading, it also offers some useful information on technical analysis, money management techniques, and position trading.

Technical analysis guides

Technical analysis is a system of looking at price and volume trends to determine supply and demand levels in the market. Supply and demand, of course, drive price changes, so it's pretty darn useful. In this section we list a few books that cover technical analysis in depth.

Candlestick Charting Explained, by Gregory Morris (McGraw-Hill)

Candlestick charts were developed in Japan and are the basis of a system of technical analysis that's popular with short-term traders, including day traders. This book explains how to identify and use candlestick patterns.

Mind Over Markets: Power Trading with Market Generated Information, by James Dalton, Eric Jones, and Robert Bevan Dalton (Traders Press)

Don't let the title fool you. This book is not about trading psychology. Instead, it covers a price charting and technical analysis system in great depth, especially the relationships between price changes and volume changes. The system, called *market profile,* is especially useful for day traders working in futures markets.

Tape Reading and Market Tactics, by B. Neill Humphrey (Marketplace Books)

In the early part of the 20th century, traders looked at price and volume information that came across ticker tapes. Traders still rely on an analysis of price and volume information, just with different tools. This book was originally written in 1931, but many day traders find Humphrey's advice on what to look for and what to avoid when looking at price data still holds true.

Technical Analysis for Dummies, by Barbara Rockefeller (Wiley)

Day traders use technical analysis to help gauge market activity, and this book is a detailed guide on reading charts and applying the information to trading in an intelligent way. What else would a . . . *For Dummies* book offer?

Schools of price theory

Most day traders take an eclectic approach to the markets. They find a few indicators that help them and apply them to the situation in the market. Over time, they refine their system, but some traders rely on specific theories for how prices should move. We've created a list of some basic texts to check out.

Dow Theory Today, by Richard Russell (Fraser Publishing)

The Dow Theory, developed by Charles Dow, publisher of *The Wall Street Journal,* predicts overall market performance based on the performance of different industry sectors. These essays from the 1950s and 1960s explain the theory and how market analysts can use it to figure out where prices are going.

Elliott Wave Principle: Key to Market Behavior, by A.J. Frost and Robert R. Prechter, Jr. (Wiley)

The Elliott Wave theory is a strange animal. It looks for really long-term patterns in the markets — over decades and even centuries — based on the *Fibonacci series*, a number series found in nature. It's not widely used, but some traders swear by it.

How to Make Profits in Commodities, by W.D. Gann (Lambert Gann)

It's not exactly an easy read, but many analysts believe that Gann's system can help them figure out how prices change over time. Reissued in 1976, the text dates from the 1940s. Some find it dated, others think it's timeless.

How to Make Money in Stocks: A Winning System in Good Times or Bad, by William J. O'Neill (McGraw-Hill)

William O'Neill's system will be of most interest to people who are swing trading or investing in common stock, but it might help day traders understand what other participants in the market are looking at when they place orders. The book explains *momentum* investing, which looks for stocks of companies with improving business trends and performance.

Trading psychology

Good traders are mentally tough. They need the confidence to face the market, the decisiveness to place orders, and the fortitude to take losses — and do it against a faceless mix of everyone else trading that day. Several books address trading psychology specifically; others on mental strength are also popular with traders because their lessons can be applied to the markets.

The Art of War, by Sun Tzu

It seems like every trader has a copy of *The Art of War*. It's a Chinese text describing military strategy, including the importance of mental toughness and strict discipline. First translated into a European language in 1782, several different versions and translations are in print.

Awaken the Giant Within, by Anthony Robbins (Pocket Books)

This is a basic self-help book that's popular with all sorts of folks. Many traders find that Robbins' methods give them confidence and help them control their minds when they are trading.

The Crowd: A Study of the Popular Mind, by Gustave LeBon (Dover Books)

In the 19th century, Gustave LeBon wrote this treatise on crowd psychology. He didn't think much of his fellow human being, but many traders have found that his insights explain some short-term irrational behaviour in the markets. Understanding why traders make mistakes can help you make profits.

The Disciplined Trader: Developing Winning Attitudes, by Mark Douglas (Prentice Hall)

Mark Douglas is a trader who lost a lot of money and tried to figure out why. As he did that, he developed a great deal of insight into the psychological aspects of trading. Namely, the market doesn't care about who is trading in it, so every trader is responsible for his or her own results. Many experienced day traders swear by the information in this book.

The Inner Game of Trading, by Robert Koppel (McGraw-Hill)

Day trading requires a lot of mental discipline. A trader has a short time to make a profit, and some panic at the idea. Others succumb to doubt, fear, greed, and hope, using emotion to avoid making good trading decisions. This is a classic guide to managing the emotional aspects of trading. The author has written other books on different aspects of trading psychology as well.

History and memoir

We're not willing to accept the Elliott Wave and say that all market movements are part of overarching trends, but market history — like all history — tends to repeat. Why? Because people are people, and no matter how commerce and the economy change, people do the same things over and over again.

Double Down: Reflections on Gambling and Loss, by Frederick and Stephen Barthelme (Harvest Books)

Want to see what a gambling addiction looks like? The Barthelme brothers are writers and English professors who inherited $250,000 from their father's estate and then lost it all playing casino blackjack. It's a story of how complicated relationships with money cause people to make bad decisions. For a day trader, this book tells what happens when people cannot place limits for emotional reasons, a route to ruin in the casino or during the trading day.

Fortune's Formula: The Untold Story of the Scientific Betting System That Beat the Casinos and Wall Street, by William Poundstone (Hill and Wang)

Claude Shannon and John Kelly were Bell Labs scientists working on queuing theories for long-distance calls when they stumbled on what is known as the Kelly criterion: the ideal proportion of money to bet can be found by the ratio of your edge in the market divided by the odds of winning. The "edge/odds" formula can be used by day traders to figure out how much money to allocate to a trade. This book explains how the system works, though it never quite proves that it works when applied to legitimate casinos or to trading.

Reminiscences of a Stock Operator, by Edwin LeFevre (Wiley)

This classic, written before the 1929 market crash, tells of the adventures of Jesse Livermore, one of the most successful traders of his time. It's a disguised memoir of speculation, with a character named Larry Livingston standing in for Livermore. Some traders like it for the lessons they can learn from Livermore, others are just amused by how unchanged the art of day trading is despite dramatic changes in technology.

Organizations for Day Traders

Day traders are an independent lot, with a corresponding lack of organizations, trade associations, and lobbying groups. Still, if you're trying to find other day traders out there, in this section we provide a few ideas.

Canadian Society of Technical Analysts

As its name suggests, the CSTA (`www.csta.org`) is all about technical analysis. The group holds conferences and events and promotes educational training for investors. Ten chapters operate across the country, where local traders gather for meetings or to hear speakers. If a guest is talking in a specific city, the CSTA will webcast the session to its members around Canada. The CSTA is affiliated with U.S.-based Market Technicians Association.

Meetups

Meetup.com is a Web site that lets people with similar interests find each other and get together wherever they live. Many Meetup groups are designed for day traders. Go to `http://daytraders.meetup.com` to find day traders, or type *forex, commodities, investing,* and other trading-related terms into the search bar to find other meetups nearby. It's possible you'll find a number of Canadian day trader groups of various sizes and experience levels.

The Trader's Internet

Day trading was made possible by the Internet. When high-speed connectivity to market data became affordable, almost anyone could trade with the same speed as folks working on the exchange floor or a brokerage trading desk. And yet, the Internet can be a terrible distraction to a day trader or to anyone else working alone. Here are some good Web sites for day traders, but you might want to limit your use of them to before and after trading hours.

Bill Cara

Bill Cara isn't a day trader, but he is a full-time investor who pays careful attention to the markets. Each day on his blog (`http://caracommunity.com`) he records his observations about what's happening. It's good reading.

Zen Trader

Vancouver's Jeff Pierce has been trading for 11 years. He's a momentum trader, focusing on market timing. He updates his blog (`www.zentrader.ca`) daily and has a plethora of interesting charts, economic commentary, and tips on how to trade stocks.

IndexArb.com

Interested in trading futures on the market indexes? This site, `http://indexarb.com`, has useful information. It lists the premiums on different contracts, offers strategies for different market conditions, and gives you some good background information to help you make your own decisions.

MyPivots.com

This site, `www.mypivots.com`, runs through key price and economic data every morning, with trading calculators and a forum. It's of most interest to people working with eMini index futures.

TraderInterviews.com

Looking for something educational and inspirational for your MP3 player? TraderInterviews.com (www.traderinterviews.com) features discussions with different traders.

Trader Mike

Michael Seneadza, a day trader, frequently updates his thought-provoking blog at www.tradermike.net. It includes his trading journal, thoughts on the markets, and his own advice on day trading, which he admits is not definitive.

Traders Laboratory

If you're interested in meeting other day traders online, finding Web-based seminars, reading traders' blogs, or checking out economic release calendars, then Traders Laboratory, www.traderslaboratory.com, is the site for you.

Facebook Pages and Groups

Facebook is useful for more than just reconnecting long-lost friends; it has also brought together like-minded individuals who share their thoughts and ideas on different topics, including day trading. Type "day trader" into the Facebook search bar to see the groups that are available; we'll get you started with a couple of the good ones.

Day Trading–Options Trading

It's not the catchiest name for a Facebook page, but Day Trading–Options Trading's 3,500 members are a vocal bunch. They share ideas and strategies, not to mention several options-related videos on their YouTube tab. The group is run by OptionAlpha, an options strategy and education blog that allows paid members to sign up for alerts and advice.

Investing, Speculation, Trading: Forex, Commodity, Index, Stocks

Clearly, day traders are too busy to come up with clever names, but a clunky moniker hasn't deterred nearly 6,000 people from "liking" this Facebook page. Not much discussion takes place among members, but the site has many insightful trading-related notes. It's almost more of a blog than a typical page.

Twitter

It's hard to learn about day trading in 140 characters or less, but Twitter is home to many interesting traders and investment professionals who are worth following. The best Tweeters post links to news sources, share their opinions on the markets, and engage with others; we think the following day traders are worth checking out.

- Jeff Pierce, @zentrader — We talk about his blog in this chapter; he's also got an entertaining Twitter feed with links back to his Web site.
- Mike Jackson, @bondscoop — This Canadian bond trader tweets about bonds and other economic insights.
- Jeremy Korpela, @docjck — Korpela is a Calgary-based swing trader who posts his thoughts on the markets.
- Brian Shannon, @alphatrends — Shannon, a trader for 11 years, is author of *Technical Analysis Using Multiple Timeframes*.
- Timothy Sykes, @timothysykes — This penny stock trader turned $12,415 of his bar mitzvah money into $2 million.
- Ashraf Laidi, @alaidi — CMC Markets' chief market strategist has more than 8,000 followers who play close attention to his advice on the forex market.

Other Mainstream Media

The mainstream media offer plenty of trading-related insights — both on the internet and in their physical copies. Here are a few brand names worth looking at.

Barron's

Barron's (www.barrons.com) is a weekly financial newspaper published by Dow Jones & Company. The primary emphasis is on long-term investing, but it carries in-depth market analysis and often interviews outstanding traders.

Financial Post

The *Financial Post* (www.financialpost.com) is a good place to park your eyeballs when you need a break from trading. It contains plenty of personal finance and long-term investor-focused tips, and traders may want to look at the site's slick stock and currency market charts and graphs.

GlobeinvestorGold

You can get some insightful commentary from the Globe Investor Web site, but pay a little extra for GlobeInvestorGold (gold.globeinvestor.com) and you have access to a treasure trove of information. Get updates on options, commodities, stocks, and more.

Investor's Business Daily

This newspaper, www.investors.com, is published by the William O'Neill Company, which also publishes charts and technical analysis systems used by stock investors. (See Chapter 16.) Every morning, *IBD* has new trade ideas and market analysis for active traders, especially those in the stock market.

Index

• A •

• B •

• C •

• E •

• F •

• G •

• H •

• I •

• J •

• K •

• L •

• M •

• N •

• O •

• Q •

• R •

• T •

• U •

• V •

• W •

• Z •

Notes

Notes

Notes

Notes

PERSONAL FINANCE & BUSINESS

978-0470-96402-6

978-0-470-67988-3

Also available:

- 78 Tax Tips For Canadians For Dummies 978-0-470-67658-5
- Accounting For Canadians For Dummies 978-0-470-83878-5
- Bookkeeping For Canadians For Dummies 978-0-470-73762-0
- Canadian Small Business Kit For Dummies 978-0-470-93652-8
- Investing For Canadians For Dummies 978-0-470-16029-9
- Trading For Canadians For Dummies 978-0-470-67744-5

EDUCATION, HISTORY & REFERENCE

978-0-7645-2498-1

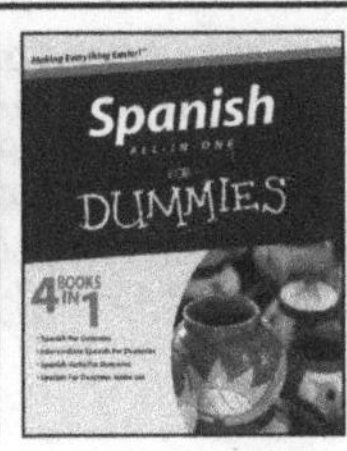

978-0-470-46244-7

Also available:

- Algebra For Dummies 978-0-470-55964-2
- Art History For Dummies 978-0-470-09910-0
- Chemistry For Dummies 978-0-7645-5430-8
- English Grammar For Dummies 978-0-470-54664-2
- French For Dummies 978-0-7645-5193-2
- Statistics For Dummies 978-0-7645-5423-0
- World History For Dummies 978-0-470-44654-6

SPORTS & FITNESS

978-0-470-67659-2

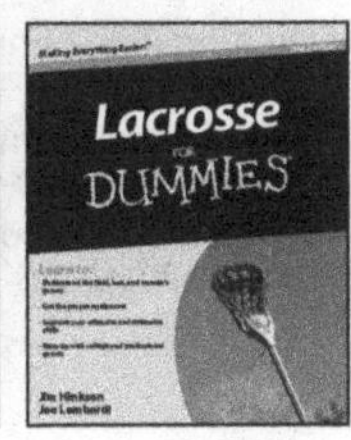

978-0-470-73855-9

Also available:

- Exercise Balls For Dummies 978-0-7645-5623-4
- Coaching Volleyball For Dummies 978-0-470-46469-4
- Curling For Dummies 978-0-470-83828-0
- Fitness For Dummies 978-0-470-76759-7
- Golf For Dummies 978-0-470-88279-5
- Mixed Martial Arts For Dummies 978-0-470-39071-9
- Wilderness Survival For Dummies 978-0-470-45306-3
- Yoga with Weights For Dummies 978-0-471-74937-0

FOOD, HOME, & MUSIC

978-0-7645-9904-0 978-0-470-43111-5

Also available:

- 30-Minute Meals For Dummies 978-0-7645-2589-6
- Bartending For Dummies 978-0-470-63312-0
- Brain Games For Dummies 978-0-470-37378-1
- Gluten-Free Cooking For Dummies 978-0-470-17810-2
- Home Winemaking For Dummies 978-0-470-67895-4
- Home Improvement All-in-One Desk Reference For Dummies 978-0-7645-5680-7
- Violin For Dummies 978-0-470-83838-9
- Wine For Dummies 978-0-470-04579-4

HEALTH & SELF-HELP

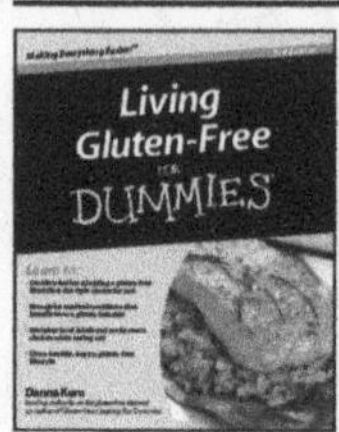

978-0-470-58589-4 978-0-470-16036-7

Also available:

- Borderline Personality Disorder For Dummies 978-0-470-46653-7
- Breast Cancer For Dummies 978-0-7645-2482-0
- Cognitive Behavioural Therapy For Dummies 978-0-470-66541-1
- Emotional Intelligence For Dummies 978-0-470-15732-9
- Healthy Aging For Dummies 978-0-470-14975-1
- Neuro-linguistic Programming For Dummies 978-0-470-66543-5
- Understanding Autism For Dummies 978-0-7645-2547-6

HOBBIES & CRAFTS

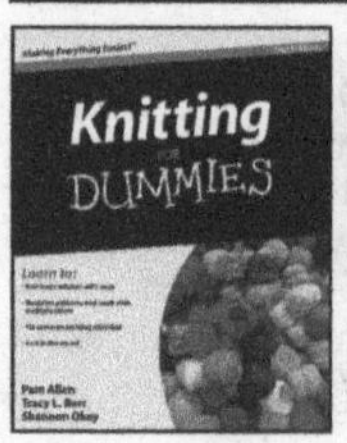

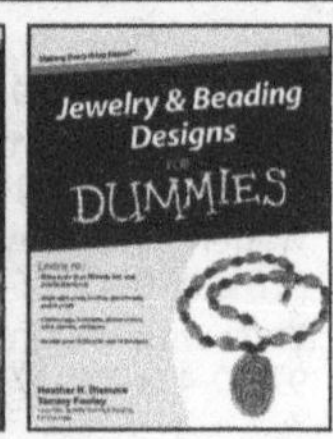

978-0-470-28747-7 978-0-470-29112-2

Also available:

- Crochet Patterns For Dummies 97-0-470-04555-8
- Digital Scrapbooking For Dummies 978-0-7645-8419-0
- Knitting Patterns For Dummies 978-0-470-04556-5
- Oil Painting For Dummies 978-0-470-18230-7
- Quilting For Dummies 978-0-7645-9799-2
- Sewing For Dummies 978-0-470-62320-6
- Word Searches For Dummies 978-0-470-45366-7

HOME & BUSINESS COMPUTER BASICS

978-0-470-49743-2 978-0-470-48953-6

Also available:

- Office 2010 All-in-One Desk Reference For Dummies 978-0-470-49748-7
- Pay Per Click Search Engine Marketing For Dummies 978-0-471-75494-7
- Search Engine Optimization For Dummies 978-0-470-88104-0
- Web Analytics For Dummies 978-0-470-09824-0
- Word 2010 For Dummies 978-0-470-48772-3

INTERNET & DIGITAL MEDIA

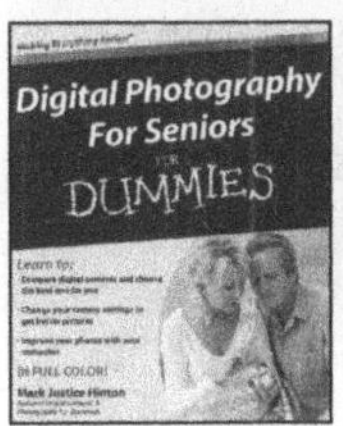

978-0-470-44417-7

978-0-470-87871-2

Also available:

- Blogging For Dummies
  978-0-470-56556-8
- MySpace For Dummies
  978-0-470-27555-9
- The Internet For Dummies
  978-0-470-56095-2
- Twitter For Dummies
  978-0-470-76879-2
- YouTube For Dummies
  978-0-470-14925-6

MACINTOSH

978-0-470-87868-2

978-0-470-58027-1

Also available:

- iMac For Dummies
  978-0-470-60737-4
- iPod Touch For Dummies
  978-0-470-88001-2
- iPod & iTunes For Dummies
  978-0-470-39062-7
- MacBook For Dummies
  978-0-470-76918-8
- Macs For Seniors For Dummies
  978-0-470-43779-7
- Mac OS X Snow Leopard All-in-One Desk Reference For Dummies
  978-0-470-43541-0

NETWORKING & SECURITY

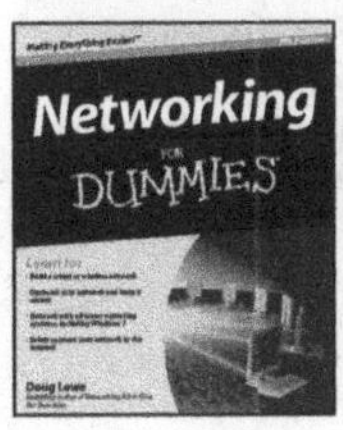

978-0-470-53405-2

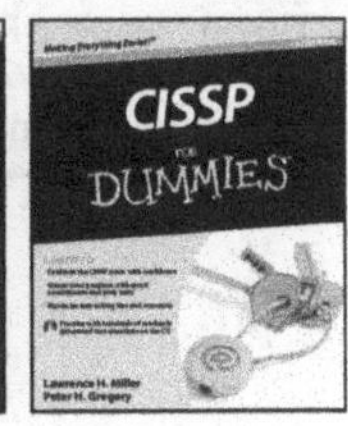

978-0-470-53791-6

Also available:

- Active Directory For Dummies
  978-0-470-28720-0
- Firewalls For Dummies
  978-0-7645-4048-6
- Identity Theft For Dummies
  978-0-470-56521-6
- TCP/IP For Dummies
  978-0-470-45060-4
- Wireless All-in-One For Dummies
  978-0-470-49013-6

WEB DEVELOPMENT

978-0-470-38541-8

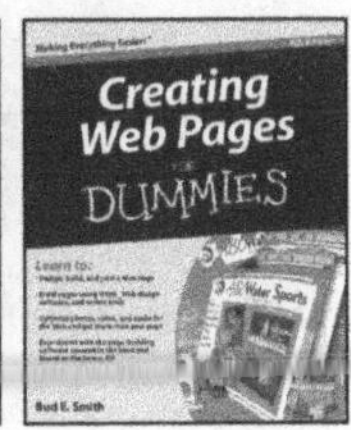

978-0-470-38535-7

Also available:

- Adobe Creative Suite 4 Web Premium All-in-One For Dummies
  978-0-470-41407-1
- CSS Web Design For Dummies
  978-0-7645-8425-1
- HTML, XHTML & CSS For Dummies
  978-0-470-91659-9
- Joomla! For Dummies
  978-0-470-59902-0
- Web Design For Dummies
  978-0-471-78117-2
- Wikis For Dummies
  978-0-470-04399-8

GARDENING

978-0-470-58161-2 978-0-470-57705-9

Also available:

- Gardening Basics For Dummies 978-0-470-03749-2
- Organic Gardening For Dummies 978-0-470-43067-5
- Sustainable Landscaping For Dummies 978-0-470-41149-0
- Vegetable Gardening For Dummies 978-0-470-49870-5

PETS

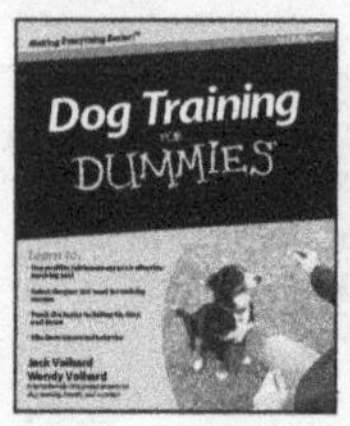

978-0-470-60029-0 978-0-7645-5267-0

Also available:

- Cats For Dummies 978-0-7645-5275-5
- Ferrets For Dummies 978-0-470-13943-1
- Horses For Dummies 978-0-7645-9797-8
- Kittens For Dummies 978-0-7645-4150-6
- Puppies For Dummies 978-0-470-03717-1

GREEN/SUSTAINABLE

978-0-470-84098-6 978-0-470-17569-9

Also available:

- Alternative Energy For Dummies 978-0-470-43062-0
- Energy Efficient Homes For Dummies 978-0-470-37602-7
- Green Building & Remodelling For Dummies 978-0-470-17559-0
- Green Cleaning For Dummies 978-0-470-39106-8
- Green Your Home All-in-One For Dummies 978-0-470-59678-4